A DEEPER LOOK AT THE CHINESE ECONOMY

From Mao to Xi Jinping and Donald Trump

Dr. Antonio Graceffo

A Deeper Look at the Chinese Economy by Antonio Graceffo

Published by Mary Labita Press, Long Island, New York
© 2018 Antonio Graceffo

ISBN: 978-0-9998305-4-3

CONTENTS

CHAPTER 1:

SOCIALIST MARKET ECONOMY WITH CHINESE CHARACTERISTICS

China has been called the first developing country to become a world power.[1] Over the past fifty years, China has moved from being one of the world's poorest countries in per capita terms to having the world's second largest economy. The country's GDP has increased 45-fold since 1949, lifting 800 million people out of poverty.[2] China is the world's largest exporter; the largest recipient of foreign direct investment (FDI) in the world; and the second largest source of FDI. The central bank holds over US$3 trillion, making China the world's largest holder of foreign currency reserves.[3]

Centralized authoritarian power has allowed China to implement social and economic plans on a national scale, while also being able to react instantly to major economic shocks, such as the global financial crisis of 2007–2008. It was this ability to plan and control the economy that has led to consistent GDP growth exceeding 10% per year for most of the past two decades. In the first quarter of 2018, China was already on pace for total annual GDP growth of 6.8%.[4] With a top down authoritarian system, China has been able to implement radical social programs such as the one-child policy, which kept population growth at a manageable level. They have also achieved mass urbanization, the proportion of

1

the population living in cities going from just 35% in 2000 to over 57% in 2016.[5] During the same period, the average Chinese person saw their annual personal income increase from just over US$3,000 to over US$11,000.[6] To increase citizens' faith in the system, the government has embarked on an anti-corruption campaign which has resulted in more than one million arrests.[7] What is more, the recent abolition of presidential term limits has given President Xi Jinping the ability to create and steer long-term plans for China's future.[8]

How China's economy works

By a simple measure of GDP, China is now the world's second largest economy, overtaking the stagnating Japanese economy. In 2017, US GDP stood at US$19.362 trillion, China's at US$11.937 trillion, and Japan's at US$4.884 trillion.[9] Many factors have contributed to China's ascension. However, it has mainly been the result of rapid industrialization and high, often double-digit, GDP growth over a period of three decades.[10] Through its tremendous foreign exchange reserves, as well as its importance as a consumer of commodities such as oil, coal, and iron ore, China is asserting its global economic dominance.

The Chinese Communist Party exercises significant control over the economy and has used economic growth to reshape the global economic landscape. One strategy the government uses to build GDP is to order state-owned banks to make favorable loans to state-owned enterprises (SOEs) making purchases and investments abroad. The central government also controls the currency, and is able to keep the exchange rate low. This keeps China's exports cheap and competitive in international markets. Domestically, economic growth has been driven by government spending and investment in infrastructure projects funded by state-owned banks.[11]

An alternative short answer for how China became the world's no. 2 economy and why it will most likely pass the US is this: Size. China's population is four times that of the US, so China's GDP per capita only has to reach 25% of US per capita GDP to make its national GDP as large as that of the US.

China's rapid economic development has taken the country through a number of important milestones, among them membership of the WTO from 2001. In 2013, President Xi Jinping proposed the Chinese-led One Belt One Road, now called the Belt and Road Initiative (BRI), a multi-trillion US$ infrastructure project which will include more than 60 countries across Asia, the Middle East, Europe, and Africa.[12] In 2015, the IMF approved the inclusion of the Chinese yuan as a Special Drawing Rights currency (SDR). Chinese nationals are some of the largest purchasers of overseas homes[13]; in 2016, Chinese were the single largest overseas buyers of US residential real estate. In 2016, Chinese were the single largest foreign buyers of US residential property, investing US$22 billion in US real estate alone.[14] Also in 2016, China had 172 companies on the Forbes Global 2000 list.[15] Among them were the world's three largest companies: Industrial and Commercial Bank of China (ICBC), China Construction Bank (CCB), and Agricultural Bank of China (ABC).[16] Other large-scale Chinese companies, including those in the technology and energy industry, have a growing global presence. As China seeks to become the dominant world player in key sectors, the promotion of key large-scale companies will continue and could ultimately change market competition domestically and globally.

The political economy of China has been instrumental in positioning China as the second largest economy in the world. In 1949, when the People's Republic of China was founded, the country was extremely poor. Over a period of less than 20 years, China moved from a fully planned communist economy to one which has been called Socialism with Chinese characteristics, or Market Socialism. It is a hybrid system which allows for private ownership and profit-driven private enterprise within the context of government-led initiatives and five-year plans. To understand how China achieved its transformation to a position of world economic leadership, it is important to first understand China's political economy.

The political economy of China

The term "political economy" could be used to describe any country's economy. In China, however, this phrase is especially appropriate. Although the country began to move from a planned economy to a market economy nearly forty years ago, the government still has a great deal of influence over the direction and pace of development. In recent times, presidential terms of office in China have been ten years, and each successive decade has brought a new wave of economic reforms. These reforms, while tremendously impactful, are not synonymous with political reform or a movement toward democracy. This is a unique characteristic of China's political economy.

Many Westerners equate economic liberalization with political liberalization. China, however, has shown that the two need not go hand-in-hand. Deng Xiaoping, the man credited with reforming China's economy, is reported to have told US President George H.W. Bush in a 1989 meeting: "If all one billion of us undertake multiparty elections, we will certainly run into a full-scale civil war."[17] This single statement by China's former leader and economic reformer encapsulates the very essence of China's political economy.

"For Mr. Deng, China's economic reform could only occur under the authoritarian rule of the Communist Party."[18]

Today, while Chinese citizens are allowed to own private property, form companies, earn profits, make investments, seek private employment, and are even encouraged to expand their companies overseas, the government still controls significant sectors of the economy, such as banking and telecommunications. The central government makes plans for GDP growth, and while these plans include the private sector, the growth and many of the fundamental elements of China's economy are controlled, directly or indirectly, by Beijing.

Economic reform through successive administrations

Prior to the reform era, the government had a near monopoly on deciding how goods and services were allocated. Agriculture was collectivized, and the country suffered periods of famine, as well as general shortages of goods. This started to change in 1978 with Deng Xiaoping (paramount leader from 1978 to 1989), the architect of China's economic reforms.[19] The concept of Socialism with Chinese characteristics, basically a largely planned but somewhat market-driven economy, was embodied in the 1978 article "Putting into Effect the Socialist Principle of Distribution According to Work" which was written on Deng's orders. The very concept of "distribution according to work" sounds as if people who worked more would earn more, which is a basic component of a market economy.

An early reform was the granting of land-use rights to citizens in 1978.[20] By 1981–83, the previously-collectivized farmland had been redivided and distributed among rural families who were now free to choose what crops to grow and to earn profits on surplus produce. Deng also began to open parts of the country to foreign investment.[21] Under Deng, Chinese citizens saw their personal wealth hugely increase.

Jiang Zemin (China's president 1993–2003) was credited with having invented the term "socialist market economy" as he moved the centrally-planned socialist economy into a government-regulated capitalist market economy. He established special economic zones (SEZs) where commerce and international trade were encouraged with government oversight. Twelve companies were authorized by the government to enjoy a monopoly on foreign trade.[22]

It was Jiang Zemin who first legitimized China's private sector economy by including entrepreneurs in his theory of "Three Represents" which was ratified by the 16th National Congress of the Communist Party of China in 2002.[23] At the previous congress, in 1997, Jiang announced a plan to begin privatizing state-owned enterprises (SOEs). Privatizations led to managerial buyouts, economic growth, unemployment, and the growth of the private sector.[24] Privatization and the sale of government assets also sparked an underlying culture of rent-seeking behavior as individuals took financial advantage of the disposal of government assets. Even this rent-seeking added to the size of the private sector as it encouraged the sale of government assets. However, these assets could only be sold with government permission, so even this marginal economy functioned within government control.

Zhu Rongji, who became premier in 1998, devised a strategy for overhauling China's bloated SOEs called "grasping the big and letting go of the small." This meant the government would retain control of major SOEs, helping them to grow even larger, while selling off or merging smaller ones. Next, some SOEs listed on the stock exchange, and sold off minority stakes to the public. In 1997, there were 262,000

SOEs; however, a regimen of restructuring, mergers, and closures reduced the number to 174,000 in 2001.[25] The majority of the 83 SOEs that were liquidated over the past 13 years were merged with other state-run businesses, while a few were conglomerated into new SOEs.[26]

Land reform and improved technology enabled farmers to move to the cities and seek employment in the newly privatized factories. However, this labor migration, which was fundamental to the continued development of the private sector, was controlled by the government through the hukou system (a birth registration law explained in greater detail below). Government approval had to be obtained if laborers were to move from one location to another and receive access to public services.

President Hu Jintao and Premier Wen Jiabao (both held office 2003–13) saw annual GDP growth averaging 10%. The average Chinese citizen experienced personal income growth from US$2,800 to US$9,100 between 2002 and 2012. Hu's reforms went so far as to take the unprecedented step of allowing state-owned banks to list on the stock exchange. This economic growth was subject to government regulation. To reign in the dramatically overpriced real-estate sector, Hu even strengthened SOE dominance over certain sectors. In 2012, SOE output still accounted for roughly 26% of GDP.[27]

In 2003, the State-Owned Assets Supervision and Administration Commission was established to oversee the management of China's SOEs.[28] Its purpose is to enact industrial policies which can transform the top 40 SOEs into national champions, meaning that these selected SOEs will become the largest companies in their industry in China, and then challenge for global dominance in the same sector.[29] Examples of national champions would be China's largest banks; they have become the largest banks in the world. In

7

2016, China sent a clear message to the world that foreign companies would be facing bigger competitors from China, as the country's continued SOE reform concentrates on making SOEs larger, not smaller.[30] This was further evidenced when Beijing announced that it would merge two state-owned nuclear energy companies.[31]

Recognizing that technological innovation plays a significant role in economic growth, the Chinese government introduced policies promoting domestic innovation in 2006. Beijing encouraged government departments to give preference to domestic firms when selecting bids for government contracts.[32] Having more government contracts meant that companies had more money to support research and development. One clear example of this is Huawei Technologies Co., Ltd., whose first big break came when it was awarded government contracts to build domestic telecommunications networks.[33] This gave Huawei much needed capital which the company used to establish research and development centers in China, India and the US. Today, Huawei is the largest telecommunications company in the world.

Xi Jinping, China's current president, has announced a program of "supply-side structural reform" which aims to decrease the number of SOEs, make them more efficient, and increase their economies of scale. This should reduce taxes and increase investment in the private sector. These reforms are meant to foster a private economy; the size of the cuts and where those cuts are made will determine where and by how much the private sector economy grows. "Several economists said Mr. Xi's supply-side initiative may turn out to be cosmetic, promising market liberalization yet magnifying state control."[34]

A partly planned economy

After forty years of economic reforms, Beijing still plays a guiding role in the allocation of goods and services in SOEs which include nearly all of the banks, and by far the greater part of the health care, financial services, and telecommunications sectors. With so many fundamental industries being controlled by the government, it could be said that this control touches every citizen, every day. The privileged status of SOEs means they generally have easier access to favorable financing from state-owned banks. SOEs are also given preference when bidding on government contracts.[35] The government also appoints the CEOs and top management of SOEs, which still made up 20% of the economy in 2010.[36] This means the government has direct control over a significant percentage of the economy while exuding indirect control over much of the rest.

The government promotes the development of the private sector by including the private sector in its overall economic plans. Beijing sets very ambitious GDP growth targets in support of the country's overall economic development and the private sector has becomes one of the components used to meet those goals. Privately-owned enterprises (POEs) drive the economy, so the government supports them with legislation. However, the government still has the power to set interest rates, banking regulations, reserve requirements, and set certain limits and restrictions on the stock market, as well as on capital outflow and inflation. The government can also limit access to and investment in certain restricted and strategic sectors. Therefore, while the economy is clearly opening up and moving to a more market-driven economy, the government still remains at the helm steering the country's development in a way that conforms to Beijing's vision.

Some factions within the government prefer the public sector over the private sector for ideological and historical reasons, or because the former is easier to control. Some in government prefer the public sector because it creates a lot of employment. For decades, state-run enterprises have supported millions of employees and their families. As the state divests itself of SOEs, it needs to create programs to replace these employees' incomes. As a result, rent-seeking behavior is commonplace.

The central government has passed a lot of economic power to local governments. The latter make decisions at township- and village-level about production and allocation of resources. These decisions are often made for reasons other than profit maximization, and are a facet of larger rent-seeking behavior. As a consequence, local governments control an estimated 33% of China's GDP.[37]

China's government and the global economy

During the Mao era, foreign investment played almost no role in the economy. Today, foreign trade, particularly the "going out" strategy, plays a significant role in the government's long-term financial plans. And this foreign trade and development occurs under government supervision.

China's investment laws define the country's engagement with the rest of the world. By regulating inbound foreign-direct investment (FDI), the government can determine the size and number of foreign companies in China. FDI can come in the form of a joint venture (JV) or wholly foreign owned enterprise (WFOE). Further, the law can restrict foreign entities from competing in or even investing in certain sectors. These rules, combined with market forces, determine what type of economic growth the country will experience, and whether international trade or domestic consumption will drive GDP growth. Even in cases of Chinese investment going to other countries, the government favors SOEs over POEs. This allows the SOEs to increase in both size and geographic scope, making them more competitive in world markets.

Economic policy under President Xi Jinping

Since coming to power in 2012, President Xi Jinping has enacted a number of economic policies with the apparent intent of further liberalizing China's economy and achieving the GDP growth rates set out in the country's five-year plans (see Chapter 4). Some of his policies are modifications of policies enacted by previous administrations; others completely repeal earlier policies.

Some experts believe Xi's focus is on governmental reform rather than economic reform, and that his programs – such as the anti-corruption campaign which between 2013 and late 2017 resulted in 1.3 million government officials being investigated and punished – have been initiated to improve governance.[38] Regardless of the focus on political matters, Xi's programs are furthering China's economic development.[39] Xi's new policies will need to differ from those of past administrations. Through the 1990s and into the early 2000s, when China was still a low-income country, the ancillary benefits of the programs put in place twenty years ago helped catapult the country to an upper-middle income country with a per capita national income of US$6,560. For China to take the next step in economic development, the country needs to build a more reliable legal system and further reduce corruption.[40] Reforms in both directions are part of Xi's plan to build a stronger financial and economic platform for the country. To accomplish this, China is currently completing a major taxation and governmental spending system overhaul.[41] Other ongoing reforms include relaxing monetary policy and removing restrictions on home purchases in order to prevent the real-estate market from crashing.[42]

Several of Xi's programs are significant economic reforms, yet have not been properly reported in foreign media.[43] These include: eliminating registered-capital requirements for new firms; taxing coal based on value, rather than volume; deregulating pharmaceutical prices; "mixed-ownership" reform of state enterprises in each province; the Shanghai-Hong Kong Stock Connect program linking the Shanghai and Hong Kong stock exchanges; draft rules on deposit insurance; and liberalization of deposit interest rates.[44]

Further reforms

The National People's Congress (NPC) held in March 2015, called for SOE reform, legal reform, and expanding the number of industries open to foreign and private investment. Public debt (now equal to 230% of GDP[45]) has the potential to be a huge problem for China, and the central government plans to work more closely with local governments on financial reforms.[46] A large proportion of the debt is the result of land-based local government financing, whereby local governments borrow money from state-owned banks using inflated real-estate holdings as collateral. Local government debt has been capped at US$2.5 trillion,[47] and the land-based lending system will be replaced by financing through bond issues. The tax system will also be restructured to reduce local government shortfalls, and the role of local governments will shift from promoting economic growth to providing public services.[48]

Premier Li Keqiang intends to convert the large, frequently unprofitable SOEs into globally competitive firms. Part of this plan is to encourage mixed ownership by transferring equity to state-owned holding companies. In keeping with President Xi's anti-corruption campaign, Premier Li has frequently spoken out against corruption and rent-seeking opportunities which are rampant in the large SOEs.[49]

The NPC supported the State Council's proposal for increased foreign investment by reducing restrictions within certain industries. Previously there were 79 restricted industries in which foreign firms were not permitted to invest; the NPC reduced this to 39.[50] Further steps taken to promote foreign investment include removing the requirement that every foreign business has a local partner. In the past, foreign companies could only open in China as part of a joint venture, with a local Chinese partner controlling. Now, under the new rules, foreign companies are allowed to establish wholly foreign owned entities (WFOE). In 2014, the minimum capital requirements for WFOE were reduced.[51]

In line with economic reform agendas, the People's Bank of China (PBoC, the PRC's central bank) liberalized interest rates and called for the development of credit reporting systems. PBoC announced a plan to establish a deposit insurance system similar to the US FDIC insurance.Creating a national credit system is on PBoC's agenda. China currently does not have a unified agency, instead, the eight leading credit agencies are affiliated with e-commerce giants Alibaba and Tencent, who maintain tremendous databases of customer information. PBoC has asked these companies to cooperate in a national credit agency which will use data analytic technology to formulate credit scores.[52]

Private investment, innovation and entrepreneurship was

also on the 2016 agenda as part of the government's "Made in China 2025" strategy, which they hope will transform the country into a global technology producer. This program includes the "Internet Plus" action plan which will integrate big data and cloud computing into modern manufacturing. Tax deductions and incentives will be used to encourage R&D for the further development of technology.[53]

Banking reforms

Bank of Communications, an SOE with minority private ownership, will now be allowed to release more of its stock to private citizens. In addition to being an act of straightforward privatization, it is hoped this move will introduce strategic management and enhance the bank's performance through employee incentives and stock ownership plans.[54]

The government can use monetary policy, enacted through state-owned banks, to counter a slowing economy by increasing the money supply. The government can also reduce banks' reserve requirements and decrease interest rates.[55] In 2015, the government cut interest rates and implemented a 1.5% reduction in the required reserve ratio.[56] Over the years, the government has used these tools, as well as fiscal policy, to keep the Chinese economy growing. In August 2015, in order to buoy the falling yuan and bail out the stock market, Beijing dipped into its US$1.3 trillion of foreign reserves and liquidated US$94 billion in US treasury notes.[57] An example of fiscal policies enacted through state-owned banks is PBoC granting US$25 billion in subsidized loans to China Development Bank to support the construction of affordable housing.[58]

Repeal of the one-child policy

One of the most dramatic changes made by the Xi government was the repeal of the one-child policy. According to a BBC report, the policy (which since 1979 had restricted most couples to having only one baby) had prevented 400 million births. However, the working-age population (defined as those aged 15–59 years old) peaked in 2011, when the total workforce was 925 million. Since then, the size of China's workforce has declined each year. Not only has the number of workers decreased each year, but with each successive year, it is falling at a faster rate. In 2014, the workforce shrank by 3.71 million, and 2015 saw a drop of 4.87 million.[59] With a fall of roughly 3.5 million in 2016, this means China's total workforce decreased by more than 12 million in three short years. China's population is rapidly aging, and will eventually be made up of many elderly retired people, with too few young people working to support them.

The economic impact of the one-child policy is already being felt. Recently, China's rapid economic growth has slowed. To promote growth, the government is encouraging consumption to help build service industries and internal GDP. Because older people tend to consume less than young people, the problem of weak consumption will become more serious as the population ages.[60]

To combat this issue, there was a loosening in late 2013 of the one-child which allowed couples who were both only children to have two children. Eleven million couples were then entitled to have a second child; however, this only resulted in 1.45 million extra births.[61] In 2015, the one-child policy was replaced with a two-child policy.[62] Many experts feel the change in policy may have come too late to save the economy, and the cost of having a second child may prevent most eligible couples from doing so. A drop in the birthrate is common with economic development, making a baby boom in China highly unlikely. Even if China were to experience a baby boom, it would be decades before the economic effects would be felt.[63]

Difficulties reforming the hukou system

Some of the policies from previous administrations are proving more difficult to reform, specifically the hukou system.

Implemented in 1958, the hukou system categorized citizens as urban or rural.[64] Hukou is basically a birth registration system modeled after the Soviet Propiska (internal passport) system, whereby a baby is registered in a certain geographic location at birth. This location is generally the same birth registration location as the parents regardless of where the baby is actually born. The rights of Chinese citizens to move from one city to another – or to visit or live in Hong Kong or Macao – are dependent on that citizen's hukou registration.[65] One's hukou also determines what kind of services a citizen is entitled to, and where he/she can receive them.

On one level, the system was extremely successful. The hukou system was implemented to prevent unchecked urban migration, and it has effectively prevented the emergence of huge migrant slums like those common in Latin American and parts of Asia. A farmer toiling in the fields in some western province for less than 1,000 yuan a month would probably rather move to a city, earn more money, send his children to better schools, have more to eat, live in air-conditioning, and have access to better government services.[66] Without a hukou from the province or city, migrants may be denied government services, and blocked from owning a home, as home purchases are restricted to those residents who can prove that they have paid social security and taxes in their current city for the previous five years.

A reason often given for not repealing the hukou system is that doing so would create a flood of migrants. However, many experts say that nearly everyone who wants to or can move to a city already has, and that rural populations are now comprised largely of old people and small children who will not be moving. In fact, the very villages these migrants came from are disappearing. "900,000 villages were abandoned or destroyed in the first decade of this century."[67]

More compelling reasons for not repealing the system are strictly economic. A repeal of the system may cause the loss of a large pool of cheap labor for China's manufacturing and construction sectors which are dominated by migrant workers.[68] The salaries paid to migrants are much lower than those paid to local residents. In 2012, the average monthly wage for a migrant worker was just 2,290 yuan, compared to 3,897 yuan for permanent urban residents.[69]

Another reason for not repealing the hukou system is that it would cause a sudden surge in the demand for public services in cities. Currently, hundreds of millions of Chinese migrants live in cities and contribute to the economies of those cities. However, they are not entitled to draw on the government services and benefits provided by the municipal governments.[70] If these people were suddenly allowed access to public education, medical care, and housing subsidies, this would put a tremendous burden on those cities. Local governments have expressed their opposition to a repeal of the system for this reason.[71]

Consequences of the global financial crisis

After the financial crisis of 2007–08, the former CEO of the investment firm PIMCO Mohamed El-Erain, coined the phrase, "The New Normal," meaning that the GFC would result in a semi-permanent reset of the world economy.[72] President Xi has used this same term to mean a new kind of growth for China, one which would be slower, more balanced, and of higher quality.[73]

For more than thirty years, China's economy has been growing at an incredible pace, often at more than 10% per year. This growth, driven by the manufacturing sector and an export-oriented economy, has come with a number of costs. Among them are: income inequality; a growing rural-urban divide; and heavy pollution. More recently, the growth rate has slowed as the country reaches a peak of its current productive capacity. The economy and society as a whole are maturing in terms of skills, technology, and demographics. As a result, the country is entering an era of "New Normal" where growth will be slower, but paired with government policies promoting energy efficiency and clean energy.

Prior to 2008, the government was investing at a rate of 50% of GDP and accumulating debt at a rate of 15% of GDP per annum. The economy depended on this "debt-fueled investment in infrastructure, housing and heavy industry."[74] Beijing realized that the high pace of debt-fueled growth leading up to the 2008 peak was setting the country up for a Japan-style crash and that growth had to slow down.

Over the last forty years, China's economy has moved from fully-planned to partly planned. With each successive presidential administration, the economy has been consistently opened up more to external market forces. As a result, China has moved from being one of the poorest countries in the world to one of the wealthiest. However, this remarkable growth does not mean that Beijing has relinquished control of the economy to free market forces. On the contrary, the government maintains direct control over SOEs and restricted sectors such as telecommunications, energy, and banking. The government exudes indirect control over other sectors of the economy by determining the disposition of government construction contracts, raw materials, and financing. In the history of the world, never has so controlled an economy grown to be so large and important. China's political economy is truly a socialist-market economy with Chinese characteristics.

CHAPTER 2:

ECONOMIC REFORM
AND TRANSITION

The People's Republic of China was founded in 1949, and for decades it operated a strictly planned economy directly modeled on that of the Soviet Union during Joseph Stalin's rule. It has been called the largest economic experiment ever undertaken in human history.[1] This rigid system continued until 1978 when, under Deng Xiaoping, the economy began to move toward what has been dubbed "Socialism with Chinese Characteristics." Any analysis of the pre-1978 economy should consider a two-sector model: agriculture and non-agricultural industry. Before 1978, there was almost no service sector, and no private sector as nearly all companies were state-owned enterprises (SOEs).

After the economic reforms of 1978, the country has gone through successive transitions and liberalizations. The first was to allow SOE managers and farmers to sell some of what they produced for profit. After this cautious initial step came the corporatization and then privatization of SOEs. The 1980s and 1990s saw the beginnings of foreign direct investment (FDI) and joint venture partnerships with foreign firms. During the 1990s, the formation of privately-owned enterprises (POEs) was not only allowed, but even encouraged. In the 21st century, SOEs and POEs began outbound investment, pouring money into companies and projects in Africa, Europe, Latin America, other parts of Asia, and even the United States.

The Chinese economic transition has been considered a major success: China has been transformed from one of the poorest countries in the world to one of the richest; doubled its GDP each decade; and lifted 400 million people out of poverty during the first thirty years of reforms.[2]

Russia is the other large communist country to have made the transition from communism to a more market-based economy. However, Russia has experienced an extremely difficult transformation, undergoing periods of high inflation, high unemployment, and serious crime. After more than 25 years of economic reforms, Russia's GDP (US$1.283 trillion in 2016) was less than one ninth of China's, according to World Bank data. Whereas China now has the second largest GDP in the world, Russia only places ninth, and falls behind countries with much smaller populations such as the UK, and has a smaller economy than Brazil.[3] Russia has experienced double-digit inflation nearly every year since the 1991 breakup of the Soviet Union, with a high of 92% inflation in 1999. China, with the exception of 25% inflation in 1994 and 10% in 1995, has kept inflation to single digits during the entire transition period.[4] Today, Russia's crime index is higher than that of China (45.20 as opposed to China's 39.44 as of 2018) and the murder rate is nine times higher than in China.[5]

China's transition has not been without its bumps. However, there are reasons why China has transitioned more successfully than Russia. Both China and Russia experienced corruption immediately after their transitions began, but the Communist Party maintained full control in China. In Russia, by contrast, there was a breakdown of governmental control, resulting in a free-for-all of rent seeking and the rampant

21

selling off of government assets for personal gain.[6] Additionally, the Russian transition was attempted overnight, whereas the Chinese transition was gradual. Furthermore, the Russian transition began with political upheaval whereas the political system remained more or less unchanged in China. The primary change in China was that the economic system became more liberalized. Yet these differences are not the only reasons why China's transition has been so much more successful than Russia's.

This chapter will analyze the features of China's reforms which have led to China becoming a global economic superpower.

A history of China's economic reforms

China's early economic reforms liberated a significant number of farmers from agricultural work. This allowed them to move to cities and to the industrial sector where their labor provided more added value and had a greater impact on GDP growth.[7] Meanwhile, in township and village enterprises as well as SOEs, managers were permitted to keep a portion of the profits. This made them think and behave in a more entrepreneurial, profit-driven manner, which added to efficiency and productivity. In 1986, the government's Seventh Five-Year Plan called for coastal regions to focus on manufacturing work for foreign firms. These reforms were a clear success with China's annual GDP growth rate between 1978 and 2003 averaging 9.4%. The benefit to the population was that between 1978 and 2005, per capita income rose from US$150 to US$1,700 per year.[8]

During these early reforms, the state sector was left intact, with SOEs providing both lifetime employment and welfare benefits to employees. The SOEs were also favored with "soft" loans from state banks to keep them afloat; however, private-sector firms began to increase in number. Without the burden of social welfare programs and without easy access to bank loans, the private firms were forced to think entrepreneurially and operate on leaner budgets. As a result, the efficiency and profitability of private-sector firms were higher than that of SOEs. Higher profitability allowed private-sector firms to offer better salaries and incentives, and to recruit more productive workers. This resulted in a shift in employment away from SOEs toward POEs. The percentage of the workforce employed in SOEs dropped from 80% in 1978 to 29% in 2000. In 1994, the gradual privatization of some of the smaller SOEs began first with corporatization and hybridization, the government maintaining at least partial ownership while allowing managers to participate in profits.[9] Many SOEs, particularly township and village enterprises, had local or familial allegiance which encouraged greater accountability.

When the economic reforms began, China accounted for a mere 0.8% of world trade. By 2005, this figure had risen to 7.7%.[10] This stands as proof of the success of the reforms, and heralds China's emergence as an economic world power.

Why China's economy boomed

Prior to the economic reforms, China's GDP grew at an average of 4% per year.[11] In the post-reform period, from 1978 to 2004, China's real GDP per capita grew at an annual average rate of 8.16%.[12] Reasons why China's economy grew include: structural reforms; agricultural reforms; increased labor productivity; a general increase in efficiency; the rise of the private sector, the development of financial markets; and foreign investment.

Structural reforms

The important structural transformations of moving from a fully planned economy to a more market-driven economy included decreasing employment in agriculture as a percentage of the total labor force. Between the start of the reform period and 2012, farm employment dropped from 69% of the workforce to 33% by 2012, and many of these workers moved to the manufacturing sector. Another extremely important transformation was the corporatization and privatization of SOEs, both of which resulted in a smaller percentage of the population working for SOEs. Consequently, SOE employment dropped from 52% to 13%. Not only were more people than ever employed in the manufacturing sector, but worker productivity also increased by an aggregate 6.96% annually. In manufacturing, worker productivity increased by 4.65% per year.[13]

Agricultural reforms

Before 1978, the Chinese agricultural sector was extremely inefficient and required a huge amount of labor. As workers were reallocated to other sectors, the impact on farm output was minimal, whereas the workers' contribution to GDP increased dramatically.[14] As a result of the reforms, agriculture became more efficient; agricultural worker productivity increased by 6.75% per year.[15] This benefited the GDP in two ways. Firstly, agricultural output contributes directly to GDP; therefore, increased agricultural output results in an increased GDP. Secondly, greater efficiency in agriculture liberates farm workers who can then enter the manufacturing sector, which has an even greater impact on GDP.

Labor productivity

Labor productivity is a measure which economists use to determine the amount by which one hour of labor increases the GDP of a country. As societies develop and use better technology, labor productivity increases, meaning each worker contributes more to GDP by working the same hours. For example, US workers rank fifth among OECD countries in terms of worker productivity. For each hour worked, a US worker contributes US$68 to GDP. Mexico, on the other hand has much lower worker productivity. For each hour worked, a Mexican worker contributes only US$38 to GDP.[17] As a result of the economic reforms, labor productivity in China doubled.[18]

Labor productivity increased in part because of a relaxation of the hukou (birth registration) system. This allowed workers to move from agricultural jobs in the countryside to factory jobs in the cities. The relaxation of the hukou system also allowed workers to move from the less efficient SOEs to more efficient POEs. Having the right workers in the right sectors, and offering them economic incentives, increased overall worker productivity.[19]

Another factor which led to increased worker productivity was the increased rate of urbanization during the two decades leading up to the economic reforms of 1978. The government's focus on developing China's cities created a 6:1 gap in output between industrial workers and those engaged in agriculture. POEs are concentrated in the urban areas; therefore, as the urban population increased, private-sector employment also increased. Despite the private sector initially being a small component of the economy, POEs were significantly times more efficient than SOEs.[20]

Increased efficiency driven by the private sector

Total factor production (TFP) is a measure that economists use to determine how efficiently resources such as labor and materials are used. As TFP increases, GDP increases even if the amounts of labor and materials employed remain the same.

Research has shown that TFP grew by an average 4.33% per year between 1978 and 2004. In addition, TFP growth added 2.83% to GDP growth, meaning 40% of China's total GDP growth during this period can be attributed to increases in TFP.[21] At the same time, non-state sector employment increased exponentially from 48.9 million in 1978 to 446 million in 2004. While the state sector did improve its TFP, it only grew by one third of that seen in the private sector.[22]

The modest increase in TFP of SOEs was not enough to compete with POEs. During the 1980s, when private companies first came into existence and began to grow steadily, the performance of SOEs gradually declined.[23] One reason for the abysmal performance of SOEs during this period was that "government subsidies covering operating losses of SOEs and collectively-owned enterprises increased from 2% of total budget in 1979 to 7.7% 1985, and [were still] 2.2% in 1991."[24] SOEs were inefficient and incapable of competing with profit-driven private enterprises. Consequently, the government was forced to support them with soft loans. One reason why overall productivity increased across the economy is that workers left the less productive state sector and moved into the private sector, where they had a greater impact on both GDP growth and productivity growth.

It seems the Chinese economy could possibly have grown even faster had the state sector been even further downsized.[25]

When comparing the different rates of development in different parts of China, it has been determined that provinces where state-sector employment was greater experienced slower economic development. A larger percentage of bank financing ended up going to SOEs,[26] and overall labor productivity growth rates were lower in these provinces.

Rise of the Private Sector

As the production of consumer goods became privatized, prices increased. An increase in prices then attracted other producers to make similar product, but to do so more efficiently, and more cheaply. Another phenomenon which encouraged competition in the domestic market was the demonopolization of production. When the state was the only producer, there was no impetus to improve the goods, develop new ones, or extend product lines. Furthermore, there was no motivation to improve productivity or efficiency, or to reduce prices. However, once the production of goods moved to the private sector, a desire to win market share and earn profits drove firms to produce newer and better products at lower prices.

Development of financial markets

The development of financial markets is another factor that has allowed China's economy to grow. Markets for securities, stocks, and bonds, as well as lending and merchant banking services provided capital to the private sector.[27] Other business services such as real estate, labor, information and technology markets have made it possible for private-sector firms to do business and expand. Price reforms and the establishment of a taxation system separating the micro- and macroeconomic roles of government facilitated private-sector growth. The government was then able to establish regulatory and support institutions such as business law, courts, social security, health insurance, and labor administration. These developments attracted foreign capital investment and technology exchange, both of which have contributed to the country's growth.

Influx of foreign investment

In 2015, China received US$135.61 billion in FDI. The following year, another US$133.70 billion of foreign capital was invested in China,[28] making China the world's largest recipient of FDI.[29] The benefits that China derives from foreign investment include capital availability to finance the development of Chinese joint venture (JV) companies, and competitiveness through access to know-how and technology from JV partners.[30] FDI also gives China a competitive advantage in world export markets.[31] A large percentage of FDI went into JVs and foreign-invested enterprises (FIE). This FDI fueled China's exports, which in 2015 represented 22.1% of GDP, according to World Bank data.[32]

Approximately 30% of China's exports come from foreign companies or JVs.[33] This suggests that FDI is instrumental in helping China maintain its legendary trade surplus. A closer examination of product content origin reveals that before China joined the WTO in 2001, domestic content in exports was around 50%. Since then, the figure has risen to 60%. However, this varies by sector; in some sectors, it is as low as 30%.[34] This clearly demonstrates that JVs have been crucial for export sector.

The future growth of China's economy

Over the last twenty years, China's economy has been growing at an astounding rate, often exceeding 10% per annum. However, over the last three years, there has been a constant decrease in GDP growth rate, with 2016 seeing only 6.7% growth.[35] If economic growth is to continue at present levels, several systemic changes will have to be made: the shrinking labor force will have to addressed; SOEs will need to be further reformed; and non-performing loans at state-owned banks will have to be resolved.

As mentioned in Chapter 1, because the one-child policy limited most families in the past thirty-five years to having only a single child, China's working age population is now shrinking.[36] This is driving up labor costs, and reducing China's competitive advantage in world markets. This problem is further exacerbated by the fact that Chinese people are living longer. Over the past thirty years, average life expectancy has risen from 67 to 75,[37] so a growing number of elderly people are drawing pensions and utilizing health services, with fewer active workers to support them.

To deal with an aging population and declining workforce, China will need to either increase immigration, as the US and Singapore have done, build robots, as the Japanese are doing, and/or move up the production chain and shift its economic backbone from low-end labor-intensive manufacturing to higher value-added industries and the service sector.

If China's economy is to continue to expand, POEs will need support to grow in both size and number. POEs are extremely important to GDP growth because they are more efficient than SOEs, meaning that investment for each unit of labor or material input yields a greater return. Even with a declining workforce, China could generate an equal or perhaps even greater GDP by increasing efficiency. Because the marketplace is competitive, POEs generally lead the way in invention, innovation, and new product development. This again adds to efficiency, as POEs develop labor-saving devices and processes. POEs frequently offer higher salaries, enabling them to attract top talent, and this perpetuates the culture of invention and innovation. The presence of entrepreneurs in a society is obviously very important for the economy.

Over the past decade and a half, the entrepreneurial class in China has grown rapidly, attracting people from: SOEs; former SOEs converted into stock companies; private companies; and foreign-funded companies or joint ventures.[38] Between 2000 and 2013, total revenues of China's SOEs rose 600%, yet total revenues of the country's POEs increased 18-fold.

If the economy is to continue to develop, further reforming the SOEs seems essential. State-run companies still account for more than 30% of the country's economic output, and more than 35% of fixed-asset investment. During economic downturns, such as 2015–16, POEs have been hit particularly hard; SOEs, by contrast, can simply obtain more loans from the government. In the long run, this exacerbates the negative influence SOEs have on the economy,[39] and is why SOEs account for a significant percentage of China's non-performing loans.[40]

The obvious solution would be to dismantle the SOEs, but the problem is not that simple. SOE managers have close ties to the government, and would oppose dismantling the SOEs as this would greatly reduce their income, status, and political power. Rather than simply doing away with SOEs, another policy option for the government would be to say that state-run businesses must face open competition from POEs without access to soft loans from the government. This would force SOEs to become more productive or face bankruptcy.

China's government had been pushing SOEs to behave more like POEs in order to make them more efficient. However, in 2016, when it appeared that Chinese economy would slow down, the government reverted to its old policy of supporting SOEs. Rather than ask state-run companies to cut spending, the government actually encouraged them to spend money in an effort to stimulate the economy. Apart from creating employment, SOEs are the government's vehicle for fiscal spending in the form of infrastructure investment. In fact, 72% of China's infrastructure investment comes via SOEs.[41]

Government support for SOEs has led to a potential debt crisis in China. China's public debt in 2016 was 250% of GDP.[42] Some economists see this debt as a ticking time bomb which could eventually take down the Chinese economy.

Many observers have pointed out similarities between the rise of Japan and the rise of China, predicting that China's economy will continue to grow and eventually overtake the US. However, when Japan was the world's no. 2 economic power, they had very little public debt. In Japan in the late 1980s, the stock market dropped significantly, largely because of corporate debt.[43] The real-estate bubble burst and Japan's economy has never fully recovered. There are other differences, too. In 1970, for example, before Japan's economic rise, per capita GDP in that country was one fifth that in the US. This is where China stands today. This suggests that China could continue to experience "catch up growth" as its economy continues to mature. Once again, it seems the best strategy for the Chinese government to implement would be to close down or privatize unprofitable SOEs. Economists believe that China's state sector should be cut by as much as half. To encourage the growth of POEs, the government should open currently-protected industry sectors, liberalize the financial system, and restrict lending to only the most productive enterprises.[44]

China's economic transformation between 1978 and the present day has been nothing short of miraculous, with China moving from one of the poorest countries in the world to one of the wealthiest. This growth was achieved through a combination of labor reform, which allowed for greater labor migration, the promotion of POEs, and embracing foreign investment. In recent years, China's economic growth has slowed. In order to resume its robust growth, China will need to address the challenge presented by its aging problem, reform its massive SOEs, clean up its public debt, and continue to attract foreign investment.

CHAPTER 3:

STATE-OWNED ENTERPRISES: A MAJOR FORCE IN CHINA'S ECONOMY AND ABROAD

Many people, when they hear the term "state-owned enterprise" (SOE), picture large concrete buildings with thick black smoke pouring out of them. But most of China's SOEs are not oil or steel companies. They operate in many different sectors of the economy, and include restaurants, construction firms, and shopping malls.[1]

Under the pre-1978 communist economic system, nearly all companies were SOEs. Since 1978, the private sector has grown steadily, both in size and importance, but it would be a mistake to believe that China's SOEs have all been privatized, or that the remaining SOEs do not dominate the Chinese economy. Most banks are still state-owned, and SOEs can obtain preferential financing, often making it difficult for the private sector to obtain business loans. SOEs are leading China's outbound investments, including massive projects such as the Belt and Road Initiative (see Chapter 10). SOEs investing abroad are often tasked with obtaining minerals and fuel which is then repatriated to China. There, SOEs are given privileged access to these raw materials. SOEs remain a significant employer in China, and as a result of partial privatizations, some of the largest Chinese firms trading on stock markets around the world are still largely owned by the Chinese government.

A history of state-owned enterprises

In 2014, there were around 150,000 SOEs, and they accounted for 17% of urban employment.[2] Prior to reforms began in 1978, SOEs directly employed a much higher proportion of the population, and directly impacted the lives of other Chinese citizens. During the "iron rice-bowl" era, SOEs provided lifetime employment, services such as clinics and schools, and pensions for employees and their families. These benefits were certainly welcomed by employees, yet they detracted from the profitability of the SOEs.[3]

When the planned economy reigned supreme from 1950 to 1984, the only legal form of ownership was state ownership. The state could hire and fire SOE executives at any time.[4] In the communist model, SOE assets belonged to the people. Local governments were the stewards of those assets, protecting the interests of the people. Managers were entrusted with the day-to-day operation of those assets, and had an ongoing duty to generate a return on assets. However, they had no discretion regarding asset transfer. Local governments tended to be highly involved in the operation of SOEs and gave managers very little real authority.[5]

At that time, SOEs accounted for nearly 100% of non-agricultural employment.[6] As the reforms of the 1980s and 1990s took effect, the proportion of the population employed by SOEs steadily fell.[7] Economic reforms led not only to a great increase in the number of private companies, but also to changes in the laws that regulated SOEs. The 1993 Corporation Law divided SOEs into two categories: that of closely-held corporations, including wholly state-owned corporations and foreign-invested corporations; and publicly-held corporations, which includes listed and non-listed corporations. There are four organizational forms in the second category: limited liability companies, limited liability stock companies, employee shareholding cooperatives, and private enterprises.[8]

The constitution of the PRC was amended in 2004 to give legal status to the non-public sector for the first time.[9] As the private sector developed, the SOE sector also became more market-oriented; SOEs began to function as for-profit businesses. SOE productivity improved with the introduction of incentive contract systems in the mid-1980s. These new systems gave the management of SOEs more autonomy in decision making, and allowed the organization to keep some of the profits. Workers' salaries increased because they now had a chance to earn bonuses for increased production.[10] These bonuses also stimulated productivity increases.

Corporatization of SOEs

One of the ways in which China's government has reformed SOEs is by corporatizing some of them. Corporatization allows the government to retain ownership and control of the SOE, but is intended to allow the CEO, CFO and other executives to run the enterprise more efficiently. Having these managers in place results in a more efficient flow of information; combined with incentives, this results in greater profitability.[11] Since the 1980s, the system of managing SOEs has become more streamlined in order to increase efficiency. Changes have been made to reduce bureaucracy within SOEs, making them more nimble and competitive.[12]

In 1983, the government implemented the Contract Management Responsibility System, followed in 1993 by the

Modern Enterprise System. Both granted greater autonomy to SOE managers without the state giving up ownership; state intervention on the micro level was thereby reduced.[13] SOE managers now have autonomy over pricing, investments, accounting, human resources, material supply and acquisition, and other decisions relating to enterprise operations. Under the old system, they did not enjoy these powers. Additionally, SOEs no longer report directly to the central government; instead, they are controlled by provincial and local governments.[14] Although it looks as if the party has taken a step back from managing day-to-day operations of SOEs, many have adopted a "one-man responsibility system" whereby the management team includes party secretaries.[15]

Reformed corporate SOEs remain a significant force in the economy. They dominate numerous sectors, including: automobiles, information technology, petrochemicals, aviation, insurance, energy, banking, railways, media, shipping, construction, metals, telecommunications, industrial chemicals, alternative and new energy technologies, new generation IT, biotechnology, new generation automobile technology, high-end equipment manufacturing, new energy sectors, and new and advanced material sectors.[16] In 2013, there were 155,000 SOEs valued at approximately US$17.4 trillion.[17] These SOEs employ tens of millions of people, making them a source of steady employment.[18]

The size of SOEs today

Several of the new-style corporate SOEs have grown through mergers and foreign investment into some of the largest companies in China or even the world. The Industrial and Commercial Bank of China (ICBC), for example, is the world's largest bank in terms of assets.[19]

Among 2018's Fortune Global 500 there are 128 US-based companies, making the US the world leader among global companies. China places second with 98. The top 12 Chinese companies on the list are SOEs, including banks and oil companies, and SOEs account for 22 of the 98 companies.[20]

In 2015, SOEs were prominent among the top 500 Chinese enterprises.[21] The largest SOEs are in the petroleum and energy sectors, with SinoPec at the top, followed by China National Petroleum Corporation, and then by State Grid, China's largest electricity utility.[22] China Mobile, another SOE, is the world's biggest phone company.[23] One of the world's biggest hotel groups, with both five-star and budget hotels, is Jin Jiang, controlled by the Shanghai Municipal People's Government.

For all of their impressive growth and immense size, China's SOEs are still fraught with profitability issues. Underscoring the problems inherent to SOE performance, of the Fortune Global 500, the 16 companies with greatest losses last year were Chinese,[24] and most of them were SOEs.

SOE performance

Because of pricing regulations and SOEs' non-financial functions, evaluating the financial performance of these enterprises is problematic. The government determines the prices of both inputs and outputs; this pricing, as well as the allocating of raw materials to SOEs rather than POEs, occurs independently of market forces. What is more, SOEs' social functions include providing jobs for workers they do not need.[25] They underperform, it is often said, because decision-making is not solely based on profit maximization, but also aims to meet certain political goals.[26] From 1980 to 1995, the proportion of SOEs making losses rose from 19.2% to 33.5%.[27] Despite losing money, many of these SOEs continue to operate because they serve non-financial purposes.

Even if mismanaged, SOEs generally do not face the threat of bankruptcy, because they enjoy easy access to state credit. Government subsidies help them stay in business.[28] The history of certain Chinese SOEs confirms this.[29] However, SOEs are not without their advantages. World-famous investor Warren Buffet, for example, likes certain Chinese SOEs. In 2003, Berkshire Hathaway bought a US$500 million stake in PetroChina, selling it four years later for more than US$3 billion.[30] SOEs can be very profitable, sometimes because they enjoy preferential treatment in their home country.[31]

However, not all SOEs are profitable. Many, in fact, are fundamentally flawed in a way that prevents them from being profitable. By maintaining surplus employees, or making decisions which are contrary to market demands, SOEs rack up losses.[32] SOE return-on-assets have consistently fallen short of privately-owned enterprises' returns. The average return-on-assets for a POE is 9.1%, whereas the average for an SOE is only 4.6%.[33] Nicholas Lardy, a senior fellow at the Peterson Institute for International Economics estimates that the return on assets of SOEs is between a third and half that of private companies.[34]

One reason why SOEs have such low returns is there is sometimes a conflict between their business role and their political role. SOE managers are faced with two sets of obligations: turning a profit, and following government mandates. It seems that when these two goals conflict, SOE managers favor the government mandate, even though the authorities have repeatedly said they would not meddle in the affairs of the SOEs. The government has said it now requires the SOEs to be profit driven, functioning according to market forces, rather than government management.[35] The reality, however, seems to be different. It seems that when state interests diverge from business interests, state interests win out.[36]

One of the many political roles that SOEs play in the economy is as a vehicle to transmit to the wider economy government stimuli. These come in the form of loans from state banks.[37] This role can cause conflict between chasing profit and following the party line.

Privately-owned enterprises (POE)

POEs generally perform better than SOEs, a considerable achievement considering the advantages SOEs enjoy, such as easy credit and cheap raw materials. One reason why the POEs outperform SOEs is because they have superior managerial systems. Not only are POE managers real entrepreneurs, but when POEs obtain financing from banks, those lenders fulfill an oversight function and monitor management decisions.[38]

Mixed ownership firms

In the early days of foreign-controlled businesses (FCB), the government offered a number of incentives to convince foreign companies to invest in China. FCBs are generally large multinational corporations (MNC) which tend to operate according to the norms of Western corporate culture.[39] Many FCBs function as joint ventures: The foreign partner provides technology, experience and access to foreign markets, while the local partner contributes land, plus government and local connections. FCBs tend to adhere to international accounting standards and follow Western management practices.[40]

Tian and Estrin found that in mixed ownership companies, if the state holds just a small stake, state ownership has very little impact on the firm's performance. However, in firms where the state owns a large percentage of the shares, the influence of state part-ownership on performance is slightly positive. A firm with large state and private shareholders has to provide incentives to motivate both sides, and this seems to produce positive results.[41]

State-owned Assets Supervision and Administration Commission of the State Council (SASAC)

In 2003, the State-owned Assets Supervision and Administration Commission of the State Council (SASAC) was established to reduce the conflict between political goals and profit making, and to remove the government from the daily operations of SOEs. SASAC oversees state-owned assets belonging to the enterprises, to "enhance the management of state-owned assets, increasing the value of state-owned assets, promote the government's financial reform measures and the modern enterprise system, improves corporate governance, appoint and remove corporate officers, and evaluate the performance of companies under its supervision."[42] SASAC functions like a holding company which owns the shares of the SOEs on behalf of the state and is responsible for SOE reform. To improve asset management, SASAC is meant to guide the transition of loss-producing SOEs into productive POEs or corporate-style SOEs.

In fact, multiple SASACs exist across various levels of government, overseeing SOEs from central down to the provincial and local levels. China has approximately 300 central government SASACs, as well as about 30 provincial SASACs. In addition, numerous municipal SASACs supervise local SOEs.[43]

Before the creation of these SASACs, industries were managed by various government ministries. The financial sector was handled separately from other industries, and the Ministry of Finance set up Central Huijin Investment Ltd. to manage the state's shares in financial institutions including China's four largest banks. In 2007, Huijin became a wholly state-owned subsidiary of China Investment Corporation, the Chinese sovereign wealth fund.[44] SASACs function as owners; they exercise voting rights, select management, and have a right to profits that are distributed. SASACs can also evaluate, appoint, and remove managers and executives within SOEs.[45]

The SASAC was established with two primary aims in mind. One was reform and unify the management of state assets. The other was to clearly demarcate the jurisdictions of central and local governments, to ensure they do not overlap or conflict. The new Company Law makes clear SASACs' ultimate power over SOEs.[46]

However, creating SASACs has failed to resolve the conflict between profit and politics. Because SASACs function as both regulator and owner, this can cause obvious conflicts of interest, often ending in failure. As part of a crackdown on asset stripping and corruption, SASACs have restricted ownership transfers, which seemed like a good strategy. However, SASACs have been known to randomly reshuffle SOE management with chaotic results. While it seems logical that the government would want SASACs to oversee the reinvestment of profits, it also seems unlikely that government employees in SASACs could be any better at this than state-appointed SOE managers and directors.[47]

Under the administration of SASACs, some SOEs have thrived, even becoming Fortune 500 companies. However, the conflicting roles of SASACs, as regulators and owners, are seen as impeding the further development of SOEs. As a result, the 2014 government work report on SOE reform called for less government interference in the day-today operations of SOEs. The report stated the government's goal of granting the SOE boards of directors the authority to hire, evaluate and determine the remuneration of managers.[48] To create a fairer competitive environment for SOEs and POEs, the government said they would allow the markets to determine the allocation of resources, and that SOEs would step away from certain sectors to give POEs a chance.[49]

Employment in modern SOEs

SOEs tend to be important employers inland and in the north, less so in prosperous coastal regions like Jiangsu, Zhejiang, Fujian, Shandong, Guangdong, and Guangxi.[50]

In the pre-reform era, SOE salaries were extremely low, but employees were given health and welfare benefits.[51] Their jobs were extremely secure, generally guaranteeing lifetime employment and benefits. Social welfare expenses, such as pensions, were born by the larger SOEs. These benefit and pension programs, combined with over-employment, decreased the profitability of SOEs.[52]

After the economy was reformed and private companies emerged, lifetime employment was no longer a given. Employment contracts were introduced in 1986.[53] In 1993, SOEs began following the Modern Enterprise System, whereby SOE employment was no longer guaranteed for life. A large number of white-collar staff, formerly employed for life, were reassigned to lower positions to reduce bureaucracy.[54] Bonuses and other incentives were introduced. The change from lifetime state-employment to contract SOE or POE employment was a slow but steady progression. In 1990, only 10% of workers were on contracts.[55] By 2009, the percentage of workers in the Pearl River Delta region covered by contract had reached 62%.[56] By 2005, 70% of all employment contracts, across the entire country including SOEs and POEs, were fixed term. Even in SOEs, the percentage of lifetime or open-ended contracts had by then dropped to 20%.[57]

Fixed-term contracts cause the majority of China's employment disputes. They are also the cause of friction and dynamism in the China job market. Because employees do not enjoy secure employment, they are more likely to change jobs if they perceive a better opportunity arising elsewhere.[58]

To attract the best managers and employees, SOEs need to be able to pay market salaries, something they were unable to do in the past. When politicians see SOE managers earning a lot of money, they react negatively.[59] Furthermore, offering more money to successful SOE managers does not guarantee they will stay at that enterprise. SOEs can offer financial incentives and perhapst lifetime employment to employees who are essential to the enterprise's performance due to their training and experience. However, these valuable employees are also much coveted by POEs. If POEs can offer them sufficient financial incentives, they will leave the state sector and move to the private sector.[60]

In spite of the corporatization of SOEs, the Chinese Communist Party still remains influential in many of them. The state closely controls labor relations through the party, which oversees a system of policies, regulations, and "party controls personnel." The party may get involved in decision making, as well as hiring, firing, and promoting managers.[61] Party representatives with direct control over hiring and firing may make those decisions based on politics, rather than profit maximization. This reduces the benefits of delegating authority to competent managers.[62] A survey found that 92% of directors were CCP members, suggesting the party has a

43

great deal of influence over who these directors appointed and what decisions they took.[63] Therefore it is questionable whether the directors can be called independent.[64] Their allegiance may not be to the enterprise, but to a political agenda.

Over the years, SOEs have slowly changed their internal culture, approaching international norms, in order to be more competitive globally.[65] Some of these changes include reducing staff, giving incentives and bonuses, increasing responsibility, and increasing pressure to turn a profit. Combined, these factors make China's job market extremely dynamic, with employees frequently leaving one company and joining another. Turnover is an issue in both the state and the private sector. That said, SOEs see less turnover than POEs. In 2010, average employee turnover in SOEs was 10%, while turnover at POEs was 18.5%.

Changes in corporate governance

In many privatized firms, the government remains the majority shareholder, which defeats the purpose of privatization. The reason the firms were privatized in the first place was that the state recognized that it was not good at company management. Unfortunately, even after privatization the state maintains a large stake and still controls the company's operations, negating the advantage of private management and ownership. The Bureau of State Asset Management (BSAM) monitors listed SOEs, but BSAM officials are government employees paid standard civil servants' wages. Their compensation is in no way tied to the performance of the firms they oversee, so there is no incentive for them to ensure that the SOEs maximize their profits.[66]

Good corporate governance is still not prevalent in China's

stock market. Publicly traded SOEs are often debt-ridden enterprises which were made to look temporarily appealing just before their IPOs.[67] Although they will be publicly traded, they are still controlled by parent companies which stand to earn money on the IPO. This statement demonstrates two very serious concerns. First is the concept of "window dressing" – making the company look as if its financial health is better than it really is, in order to help the sell off. Next is the obvious conflict of interest that exists in any partial privatization of an SOE. The goal of a publicly traded company is to earn money and maximize returns to shareholders, yet SOEs may have goals apart from earning profits.

SOE managers are often motivated by goals apart from boosting profits. Often, management appointments are given to high ranking party officials. Similarly, high-profile SOE managers are sometimes appointed to government positions, further blurring the lines between the state and private sectors.[68] Their goals will often be a mix of economic and political.[69] The companies do not fear bankruptcy and the politically-minded managers may lack entrepreneurial skills.[70] Separating the SOEs from the government and installing private-sector managers would solve many of these problems. Privatizing some SOEs while corporatizing others creates two conflicting systems in a single economy. The Chinese government refers to their hybrid system as "socialism with Chinese characteristics."[71]

China's culture, political system, and business management system are all pyramid-shaped. The pyramid structure of a Chinese SOE creates inefficiencies and inaccuracies in information transfer. Information has to pass through several layers of management before reaching the top. Along the way, it may be in someone's self-interest, either financial or political, to misreport the information or fail to forward the message all together.[72] The system of having SASACs – rather than local governments – manage SOEs creates one more layer of management through which information has to pass, adding to the inefficiency.[73]

To improve accounting, disclosure and corporate governance in general, the government passed the PRC Company Law of 1994, which combined with the Securities Law of 1999 were instrumental in the early stages of securities regulation. Since then, the China Securities Regulatory Commission (CSRC) has published Code of Corporate Governance for Listed Companies to evaluate corporate governance. Furthermore, the CSRC and other agencies have created laws and regulations governing "disclosure, mergers and acquisition, accounting, related party transactions, independent directors and securities litigation."[74]

In this new free-market system, the accounting practices and management style of many SOEs are outdated. Western-style accounting systems have been slowly introduced. Those which adopted Western standards most rapidly were those most exposed to market forces.[75] However, not all companies follow disclosure laws or corporate governance laws. PRC laws are increasingly becoming like Western laws, yet Chinese companies still suffer from a lack of transparency and disclosure.[76]

Currently, the purpose of financial reporting and disclosure in China seems to be to serve the needs of the tax authorities as opposed to the shareholders. Add to this that the financial data is often falsified to attract investors, and the system of disclosure and transmission of information becomes very unreliable, even prosecutable. This was the case with Yinguangxia, China's first blue-chip stock.[77]

From 1999 to 2000, Yinguangxia's share price nearly tripled, making it the highest ranking stock on the Shenzhen Stock Exchange. When news leaked that Yinguangxia had forged their financial data, the share price plunged. This caused a trading frenzy across China's entire stock market, with many individuals and institutions losing large sums of money. This was China's first major case of violations of the Securities Law. The law clearly states that firms must make clear, accurate, and timely disclosure of financial data. Such blatant fraud shook the confidence of Chinese investors who were new to the whole concept of having a stock exchange in their country. The case called into question the accounting standards of the company and how best to calculate and record corporate value, losses, and gains.[78] Since the Yinguangxia case, corporate governance has become the primary concern of China's regulatory agencies.[79]

Another "window dressing" scandal involved the firm Baiwen, which was found to be faking its financial data.[80] Zhengzhou Baiwen was converted from an underperforming SOE to a shareholding company which was listed in 1996. In 1999, after three years of losses, Baiwen faced bankruptcy. But rather than being allowed to fail, the company was rescued through a deal brokered with a local government. Details of the case are widely published, but the final outcome was that the court supported a buyout of the company by Sanlian and the restructuring of the company in such a fashion that the majority shareholders were not held accountable but the minority shareholders, the A-shareholders, suffered losses when they were forced to sell their shares to Sanlian.[81]

Corruption in SOEs

In accordance with President Xi Jinping's anti-corruption campaign, nearly 80 senior SOE executives were investigated by the Disciplinary Commission of the Central Party Committee in the ten months that followed the 18th Party Congress.[82] Xi's anti-corruption campaign is considered to be the most impactful such campaign in PRC history; in total, more than 100 top SOE executives have been detained, including some who worked at PetroChina, China Southern Airlines, China Resources, FAW, and Sinopec.[83] Many private-sector firms have retired senior government officials serving on their boards, and this creates opportunities for bribery and other forms of misconduct. Over 40,700 officials have resigned, or have been removed from SOEs, in order to avoid being implicated.[84]

In a large organization such as an SOE, a government agency, acting as owner, may sit atop a pyramid-shaped hierarchy. Below the owner is a manager who may have some decision-making authority in order to carry out daily operations. According to agency theory, an owner can allow a manager more authority to allow the business to run efficiently, until the manager has so much authority that he begins acting in his own, and not the owner's best interest. At that point, the owner would step in and take control away from the manager. One fundamental problem facing an SOE is that there is no physical owner.[85] This departure from the standard agency model may help explain why there is so much corruption in SOEs, and why they often fail to perform financially.

This is not to suggest the government has no control over SOEs. In the case of traditional SOEs, they can fire managers. In the case of corporatized SOEs, they can exercise their voting rights and restructure the management.[86] It is more a question of motivation and volition. A faceless state-owner is less likely to step in and protect its owner's rights compared to a private individual or a board.

Outbound investment by SOEs

One reason for Chinese SOEs to expand overseas is to make them larger and less of a target for liquidation under China's policy of cutting the smallest SOEs.[87]

To compete in the global economy, the government has adopted a "going out" strategy investing in foreign countries.[88] Much of China's overseas investment is carried out by SOEs. "By the end of 2009, China's 108 central government-owned SOEs had invested in 5,901 foreign firms,"[89] accounting for nearly 38% of total profits for SOEs.[90] Many of these acquisitions are in the fields of minerals and energy to guarantee access to raw materials.[91] Chinese SOEs dominate certain global sectors. In fact, the international raw-material sector is dominated by China because China purchases commodities used for production which fuels China's economy. SOEs are in a better position to invest abroad than privately-owned firms, as the SOEs have better access to bank loans.[92]

Through mergers and acquisitions, some Chinese SOEs have become the largest companies in their sector, and in the world. However, their names remain little known outside of China. The Chinese companies with global recognition are all POEs, like Alibaba, Tencent, Baidu and Xiaomi, all of which are too small to make the Fortune Global 500 list.[93] Some Chinese SOEs have grown so large that they are now purchasing companies in foreign countries. For example, state-owned oil company CNOOC Ltd., the world's largest energy explorer, took over the Canadian firm Nexen. In 2012, China was rated by UN Conference on Trade and Development as one of the top twelve outbound investors in the world.[94]

Chinese outbound investment includes construction projects in the United States. "China Construction America,

49

Inc. (CCA) is a wholly-owned US subsidiary of China State Construction Engineering Corporation Limited (CSCEC)…listed on the Shanghai Stock Exchange."[95] SASAC is the primary owner of CSCEC. In 2009, when the company went publicly, it was the largest IPO in the world.[96]

China's SOEs are involved in both the developing and developed world. For example, 400 Canadian businesses currently operate in China, making China Canada's no. 2 export market. Some Canadian companies have entered into joint ventures with Chinese SOEs, for example Bombardier, the Quebec-based aerospace and rail transportation firm.[97] Chinese outbound investment can be found everywhere and in every sector. Chinese SOEs have invested in energy projects in Africa,[98] among them the Gibe III dam in Ethiopia, the Kajbar dam in Sudan, and the US$729 million Bui project in Ghana.[99]

The PRC government is considering investing in renewable energy, geothermal energy, and infrastructure in West Sumatra, Indonesia, where other Chinese firms are already working on hydropower plants, road building, and agribusiness. In addition to investing in energy, PRC companies are investing in agriculture and tourism.[100] In 2015, after the US-Iran nuclear deal lifted sanctions, Sinopec Group – parent of Sinopec Corp. and China National Petroleum Corp. – started producing at the Yadavaran oilfield.[101]

The PRC's aggressive outbound investment strategy has been met with some resistance. China has been repeatedly criticized for "buying up the world." Developed countries which are receiving large amounts of Chinese SOE investment often raise security concerns related to having a foreign government controlling domestic assets.[102]

Historically, SOEs were large, inefficient enterprises, operated in a domestic market where they often had a monopoly. Therefore, risk analysis was not a consideration. The lack of competition meant they did not have to concern themselves with advertising or marketing. They were given preferential access to raw materials and when all else failed – and it frequently did – they simply obtained direct aid from the government or preferential loans, which they were not expected to pay back. Since expanding into foreign markets, the road has bumpy for Chinese SOEs because the same conditions which allowed them to thrive domestically are not present internationally.

Once the SOEs left the comfort and privilege of their home market, they faced challenges and obstacles they were ill prepared for. This resulted in a number of their overseas' investments failing. For example, 12 of the highest-profile overseas investments by Chinese Investment Corporation (CIC), China's largest sovereign wealth fund, reported losses.[103] It is clear that Chinese outbound firms are facing a steep learning curve when it comes to complying with international trade rules and regulations.[104] Disclosure and due diligence seem to be two areas where Chinese companies have opinions which differ from Western industry norms.

State secrecy laws sometimes prevent disclosure and due diligence, and impede fair competition for foreign companies against SOEs. One example would be the Rio Tinto case where executives of an Australian company were charged with espionage, bribery, and stealing state secrets. The steel industry is a key industry closely guarded by the Chinese government, and they felt that stealing secret information in that sector undermined national security.[105] In the Rio Tinto case, charges of bribery were eventually accepted by the company, and the employees were fired. It remains unclear whether bribery or simple due diligence was the actual reason for the case being brought in the first place. Either way, Rio

Tinto stands as a cautionary tale about how difficult it can be in China to obtain or to disclose company data.

China maintains a strict battery of laws against unfair competition, secrecy, and bribery, but in the case of SOEs, many outsiders feel enforcement is selective. The basis of the government's anti-corruption campaign is China's Criminal Law and Anti-Unfair Competition Law.[106] These laws involve state secrets and make it illegal to seek an "improper benefit". A company which holds classified commercial data would be considered to have an "improper benefit." The normal disclosure and due diligence related to listing can result in data from SOEs, considered to be state secrets, being leaked. PRC companies listing abroad, for example in the US, may be forced to violate state secrets laws in order to comply with US listing requirements. This may hamper the ability of a PRC firm to expand into the US.[107]

Despite bumps in the road, failings, and setbacks, China SOEs are some of the top outbound investors in the world. SOEs account for 69% of China's outbound stock investments. In 2013, ICBC and China Construction Bank were numbers one and two on the Forbes Global 2000. In 2012 alone, according to the China Entrepreneur Research Institute, Chinese companies expanded into 117 countries.[108]

SOEs as of 2018

Xi mentioned SOE reform in his address to the 19th Party Congress, but it was only a vague mention with no clear steps outlined. Rather than reforming the SOEs, it seems that the new plan is to create a hybrid corporate governance structure through the cross-appointment system, established in 2015. Li Rongrong, former chairman of the State Council's SASAC spoke in favor of this system, saying it was an "effective measure to combine corporate governance with the party, which is the political core of the company."[109] It seems the party will remain in control of SOEs managed by SASAC; these happen to be some of China's largest SOEs, among them most of those listed on the Fortune Global 500. The leaders of these SOEs are appointed by the party's Organization Department, and are ranked as vice ministers.[110]

In some cases, the government seems to be making a show of SOE reform, with no appreciable diminution of governmental control. China Unicom, one of the country's largest telecommunications companies, is a good example. Officially, the government decreased its stake from 62.7% to 36.7%. On closer examination, however, 35% of the company's shares were purchased by 14 investors, the largest of which is an SOE, China Life, which purchased 10.2%.[111] These 14 new investors were given three of the nine seats on the board. The six remaining seats will be appointed by "institutions controlled by the state, including Unicom's holding company; the 25.4% of shares owned by the public will not be given any representation on the board.[112]

Political agendas aside, there are solid economic reasons why SOE reform has been difficult.

One issue is that private investors fear their investment could be nationalized and they would lose their money. Another issue is that SOE revenue underperforms the private sector in most industries, including steel and construction.[113] The tremendous debt-to-asset ratio of SOEs is another legitimate concern. China Railway Corp. (CRC) has been attempting to restructure and privatize, but the corporation was formed carrying US$428 billion in debt from the Railway Ministry in 2013, and it has continued to borrow; as of September 2017, it had total debt of US$760 billion, a debt-to-assets ratio of 64.76%.[114] CRC's debt-to-asset ratio is high even by SOE standards which tend run about 60%.[115] Debt servicing cost so much of CRC's revenue that they depend on government subsidies each year to turn a profit.[116] These are not the types of financials that attract private investors.

Whether for political reasons or purely economic ones, the percentage of SOE total revenue remains quite high in many sectors. As of 2017, state-run companies' share of total revenue was 81.25% in key industries such as oil and gas, shipping, aviation, coal, and rail. In pillar industries, it was 46.41%. Pillar industries include, auto making, chemical, construction, electronics, equipment manufacturing, nonferrous metals, prospecting, steel, and technology. In normal industries, SOEs only accounted for 16.24% of total revenue. Normal industries include agriculture, pharmaceutical, real-estate, tourism, investment professional services, general, trade, and general manufacturing.[117]

In many industries where SOE share of total revenue has decreased in the last few years, such as auto making, the decrease occurred because private companies entered the field or were listed on the bourse, rather than the government divesting itself of SOEs.[118]

This chapter has given a brief history and overview of the SOEs, including their problems and their strengths. State-run businesses, on average, have lower employee turnover, but also lower return-on-assets compared to POEs. Problems inherent in SOEs include corruption, overemployment, non-performing loans, political constraints, and unprofitability. While the number of SOEs in China has decreased, as have their employee numbers, they remain a driving force, accounting for a significant percentage of China's GDP and making up the bulk of China's stock exchange. SOEs are also an incredibly powerful vehicle which China can employ to expand into foreign countries, and secure raw materials, energy, and foreign markets. For all of their problems of low return-on-assets and high government intervention, the modern, corporatized SOEs are some of the largest firms in the world. The increase in size and importance of Chinese SOEs seems to be a trend domestically and globally. Government pledges to privatize or reform the enterprises they own seem to be in name only, as the government retains its tight control on the appointment of the boards of directors.

CHAPTER 4:

EXPLORING CHINA'S FIVE-YEAR PLANS

China's government operates on five-year plans, and incoming presidents inherit a five-year plan that is already in progress. When that plan ends, he authors his own five-year plan which he then sees through to completion. Both President Jiang Zemin and President Hu Jintao also oversaw the writing of another five-year plan which they handed over to their successors.

The current five-year plan, the Thirteenth, will run from 2016–20. It was both authored, and will be seen to completion, by incumbent PRC President Xi Jinping.[1] Now that China has become the world's second-largest economy, its five-year plans may have a tremendous impact on economies around the world. For this reason, it seems appropriate to explore and understand the concept of the five-year plan, as these have played a significant role in China's economic development since the earliest days of the People's Republic.

The First Five-Year Plan

After establishing the People's Republic of China in 1949, Mao Zedong transformed the country into a single, cohesive party state under the Chinese Communist Party.[2] At that time, China was far behind much of the rest of the world in terms of technological and economic development.[3] After returning from a visit to Russia in 1949–50, Mao was convinced that the only way for China to develop was to transform itself into a modern industrial power.[4]

Inspired by Stalin's five-year plans, China's First Five-Year Plan, begun in 1953, had the intention of lifting China's industrial capacity and catching up with the West.[5] Russia was one of China's few allies and the new nation's main supporter; Moscow provided money and engineers to help China modernize.[6] The First Five-Year Plan focused on heavy industry, fuels, electric power, iron and steel, machinery manufacturing, and chemicals. It also set a goal of doubling production in most sectors,[7] and each factory was given a quota to achieve.[8] Quotas were an important feature of this and all subsequent five-year plans, as Mao seemed fixated on implementing objective measures of economic progress.[9]

To ensure the success of his five-year plans, Mao told the nation that speaking or acting against the five-year plan was counter-revolutionary. "In 1953 the *People's Daily* echoed the chairman, telling its readers that 'only with industrialization of the state may we guarantee our economic independence and non-reliance on imperialism.'" [10]

The First Five-Year Plan was an apparent success. "Industrial output more than doubled, with an annual growth rate of 16%. Steel production grew from 1.3 million tonnes in 1952 to 5.2 million tonnes in 1957; the 16.56 million tonnes produced in 1953–57 was double China's combined steel production between 1900 and 1948. Coal production increased 98% between 1952 and 1957."[11] The average total factor productivity (TFP) growth was 4.3% in agriculture and 7.8% in non-agricultural sectors.[12]

Increased urbanization was another positive result of the

First Five-year Plan. China's total urban population grew from 57 million in 1949 to 100 million by 1957. Life expectancy increased from 36 years to 57 years, and salaries rose by 40%. Various infrastructure projects were also completed, notably the Wuhan Yangtze Great Bridge.[13]

Urban development came at a price, however. Implementing that aspect of the plan robbed the agricultural sector of workers. Grain production dropped, threatening the food supply. Furthermore, 88% of the development budget was pumped into cities, even though 84% of the population lived in rural areas. The government also diverted the bulk of the country's grain supplies to cities; by the mid-1950s, hunger was developing in parts of the country, leading to unrest and protests in rural areas.[14]

The 'Great Leap Forward'

The following five-year plan did not go as well as the first plan. In 1958, Mao announced the Second Five-Year Plan, better known today as "The Great Leap Forward."[15]

Inspired by the Soviet model, Mao planned to take China's underdeveloped agrarian economy and transform it into a modern industrial one.[16] What is more, Mao intended to overtake the Soviet Union in the shortest time possible.[17] Achieving this would be extremely challenging for China. Unlike Russia, which had been growing and developing for many years prior to World War I and World War II, China's Confucian society had long preferred the status quo to revolutionary change.[18]

Mao collectivized the farms and imposed ever increasing agricultural quotas.[19] To meet these strict production quotas, local government officials falsified crop reports. In 1958, actual grain production was 52% lower than that reported.[20]

The government then taxed the produce, taking a percentage of the reported harvest, leaving peasants with little or nothing to eat.[21] Some experts have calculated that, by 1961, as many as 45 million people had starved to death.[22]

This period of great suffering and enormous loss of life has come to be known as "The Great Chinese Famine," and has been more or less erased from China's official history. Discussion of the famine remains a taboo in China, where it is referred to euphemistically as the "Three Years of Natural Disasters" or the "Three Years of Difficulties."[23]

Later five-year plans

The early five-year plans focused mainly on agricultural and industrial production. The Fourth Five-Year Plan (1971–75), for example, set a goal of high growth and a doubling of steel production.[24] Subsequent five-year plans, however, were far more complex.

The Fifth Five-Year Plan (1976–80) featured similar production and economic goals, but differed in that it was created as part of a ten-year national economic development plan which would run from 1976 to 1985.[25] During the Fifth Five-Year Plan, Deng Xiaoping introduced the one-child policy and began the economic reforms that would lead China away from the Soviet-style system. The plan saw the beginnings of private enterprise and the first steps away from collectivization in the agricultural sector, moves which led to a period of unprecedented growth.

The Sixth Five-Year Plan to the Twelfth Five-Year Plan followed similar patterns of economic liberalization and growth. The Ninth Five-Year Plan called for the introduction of private property and corporation laws.[26] The Eleventh Five-Year Plan (2006–2010), during Wen Jiabao's premiership, adopted a scientific approach to development, and set a goal of doubling China's 2000 GDP by 2010.[27] Under reforms implemented in the sixth to twelfth plans, state assets were either corporatized or privatized as the country shifted toward a market-driven economy.

Like previous plans, the Twelfth Five-Year Plan – authored by President Hu Jintao and titled "Higher Quality Growth" – also focused on increasing GDP, but sought to decrease wealth disparities between rich and poor citizens and between the more-developed east and the country's impoverished west.[28] A common feature of all of these plans has been to set GDP growth targets of around 7%, meaning the economy would almost double in size the every ten years. In addition to direct economic growth, the eleventh plan set out a number of environmental goals such as reduced carbon emissions. It also included societal goals, such as increasing "life expectancy by one year, [and] reaching a goal of 3.3 patents per 10,000 citizens."[29] By the time the twelfth plan was released, Beijing had acknowledged that the country's high savings rate was actually hindering growth, particularly that of the service sector, and thus set a goal of increasing consumption.[30]

Five-year plans tend to include both economic and social goals because stability – be it economic, political or social – is a priority for the government. That these goals are interdependent is apparent in the Twelfth Five-Year Plan.[31] As the plans have developed, they have incorporated a greater number of environmental and social factors, as well as the original economic factors, in order to improve the lives of citizens and ensure they support the government and its programs.

The success of recent plans

From 1979 to 2009, China's economy grew at an average of 9.9% per year. One side effect of economic growth has been increased energy consumption, and the country's primary energy consumption grew at an annual rate of 5.6%. One of the goals of the Eleventh Five-Year Plan (2006–2010), was to reduce the country's energy intensity (energy consumption per unit of GDP). The plan was successful in achieving a decrease of 19.1%.[32]

Objective data often indicates the apparent success of China's five-year plans, but the spirit of the plans is often lost in achieving numeric goals set out in them. "It's not unusual for the plan's wider objectives to be thrown out the window in order to achieve an obscure data point."[33] This is essentially what happened in the Great Leap Forward, where stated goals of numerical production were achieved on paper, but the spirit of the plan – feeding the populace – was lost, and millions died of starvation.

A more recent example of this loss of focus is China's affordable housing initiative, a major component of the Twelfth Five-year Plan. The plan was successful in that the number of subsidized housing units built exceeded the quota of 36 million. However, a closer examination shows that only the letter, not the spirit, of the program was achieved.

The spirit of the twelfth plan was to provide low-cost housing to needy families. Instead, China's state auditor discovered that approximately US$1.47 billion had been diverted to pay salaries and office expenses, or invested in wealth management products. An additional US$77 million was obtained by companies constructing housing and offices which did not qualify under the scheme.[34] Investigators also discovered that as many as 26,000 people used fraudulent documents to reside in low-cost housing units.[35]

The Thirteenth Five-Year Plan

Faced with slower growth and an increasing wealth gap, the Thirteenth Five-Year Plan (2016–2020), focuses on economic growth, improved governance, and reducing state intervention.[36] In particular, the plan calls for the government to intervene less in the economy and to open the economy more to market forces."[37]

China's current five-year plan is focused on the following areas: increase of both GDP and family income, increases in innovation, increased consumption, the Internet Plus program, the reform of state owned enterprises (SOE), social security, and financial markets, as well as green development.[38]

Increasing both GDP and family incomes

Previous five-year plans did well at boosting China's GDP, but the country's people remained relatively poor, with average incomes about a quarter of those in the US. Increasing personal income is one of the goals of the latest five-year plan,[39] and Xi projects 6.5% GDP growth.[40] It is hoped that both GDP and household income will rise to such a level that China can be "a moderately prosperous society."[41] Specifically, Beijing plans to increase household incomes to US$12,000 per year, becoming a "low high income" economy by 2020.[42]

Greater innovation

Xi is calling for an increase in innovation and a movement away from heavy industry, so that China can move up the value production chain.[43] This goal appears to be in line with the government's plan for "Made in China 2025," whereby manufacturing productivity, quality, and profitability will increase through the use of technology. Greater use of technology will also create more highly-skilled jobs which pay better; these salaries will then bolster consumption in China's developing service sector.[44]

Greater consumption

Realizing the need to increase consumption as a function of GDP, the Thirteenth Five-Year Plan encourages extra consumption, as the current household savings rate of 25–50% of income has become a sticking point in the country's development and could prevent the government from achieving its goal of 7% growth.[45] Increased consumption should also result in a larger service sector.[46] This will achieve the twin goals of helping China move up the value chain and of creating much needed jobs for the seven million young people who graduate from universities each year.[47]

Internet Plus

There will be an expansion of Premier Li Keqiang's Internet Plus program with companies encouraged to increase their internet usage.[48] This program appears to be in keeping with the government's pledge to increase jobs in the tertiary sector and to promote China's movement up the value chain.

SOE Reform

Even after nearly 40 years of economic reforms, China still has 110 SOEs under central government control and 150,000 under local government control. Combined, "SOEs have assets worth US$15.7 trillion and last year generated profits of US$2.48 trillion."[49] SOEs still account for 20% of employment nationwide.[50] As discussed in the previous chapter, SOEs have long been criticized for underperforming and being overstaffed.

The new reforms call for further corporatization of SOEs, and placing them under more entrepreneurial managers. Experts such as Thomas Luedi, a managing partner at A.T. Kearney, believe the timing for further SOE reforms is exactly right.[51] Millions of workers were already let go during previous SOE reforms. "From 1998 to 2004, six in ten SOE workers were laid off."[52] At that time, labor costs were low, so there was no need for further layoffs which would have increased unemployment. Today, however, as labor costs are much higher, these reforms are both necessary and justified.[53]

Social Security Reform

Social security, pensions, and health insurance coverage will be increased. Under the thirteenth plan, 50% of costs for the treatment of critical illnesses will be covered. As part of pension reforms, government workers will contribute 8% of their salaries to the pension fund.[54]

Financial market reforms

The government has vowed to be less involved in setting the yuan exchange rate. These reforms are in keeping with the yuan being accepted as a Special Drawing Rights currency (SDR) by the IMF[55] (for more on this topic, see Chapter 7). Furthermore, the government will be reducing its intervention on such aspects of the economy as gasoline prices and bank-account interest rates.[56]

Green development

The government has proposed a real-time, online environmental monitoring system whereby factories are required to report air emissions and wastewater discharges on an ongoing basis. Water management systems will also be implemented to reduce the price and scarcity of water.[57]

Measurable impact of the current plan

Beijing faces a number of obstacles trying to achieve the goals of the Thirteenth Five-Year Plan. For example, the plan repealed the one-child policy, so now families in China can have two children.[58] The one-child policy prevented a population explosion, but – as mentioned in Chapter 1 – it had the negative result of decreasing the working-age population. "The proportion of working-age people (16 to 59) declined from a peak of 74.5% in 2010 to 66% last year."[59]

Few believe repealing the one-child policy will cause a baby boom. Surveys suggest that one child is now the norm for Chinese families and that expenses, particularly the cost of education, will prevent most families from having two children.[60] Some economists estimate that it will be nearly twenty years until the repeal of the one-child policy offsets the number of people in retirement.[61]

As China's economy grows so does its debt. Experts warn that China is in danger of becoming a debtor nation. "The country's debt-to-GDP ratio, by some estimates, is now 250%."[62] Other Asian tigers – specifically South Korea, Taiwan, and Japan – followed a similar pattern of rapid growth over a short period of time, and all eventually ended up in debt.[63]

Contained within the Thirteenth Five-Year Plan are potential challenges to achieving the GDP growth targets. For example, shifting from manufacturing to service sector means output per worker will decrease. Similarly, achieving the plan's environmental goals may also be in direct conflict with increasing the GDP. Xi's anti-corruption campaign has slowed the decision-making process for new projects.[64]

On the one hand, Beijing is pledging to allow market forces to control the economy with less state intervention. However, when the stock market took a hammering drop last summer, the government injected US$200 billion to prop it up. And contrary to the stated goal of SOE reform, Xi has said he wants SOEs to continue to play a central role in the economy.[65]

In the fourth quarter of 2015, China's stock market continued in a steady downward spiral as the economy slowed down. The US financial crisis, which became the global financial crisis, was exacerbated by the crash of the mortgage market. China's economy is similarly propped up by an ever rising real-estate market and exposed to similar risk if the real-estate bubble should burst. In the US the problem was caused by individual borrowers not being able to repay their home loans. In China, infrastructure projects have been financed through "local government financing vehicles" (LGFVs). Using highly inflated land as collateral, local governments are able to obtain loans from China Development Bank. After the first round of long-term borrowing, which is used to start a project, the local government can then borrow short-term loans from commercial banks or raise funds by selling bonds. To keep property prices high, it is in the interest of local governments to continue to expropriate land and drive the market up. At the same time, the central government is both buying up local government debt and setting a cap on government debt. This regional debt, plus China's US$570 billion national stimulus package in 2008, are factors which could lead China's economic bubble to burst.[66]

A credibility gap?

Many economists think China is publishing distorted GDP growth figures. Most economies go up and down, but China's economy seems to move continuously forward more or less in a straight line.[67] Observers have noticed that the production and growth numbers of local governments or trade numbers recorded by international trading partners do not always correlate with Beijing's figures. Part of that may be because of the obvious difficulties associated with collecting accurate data on such a large economy. It may also, however, involve direct trickery by local officials who inflate their figures in order to receive compensation and rewards.[68]

China's economy has become accustomed to growth rates in excess of 9%. If the real number is 7% or 8% but the government claims it is 9% or almost 10%, no one notices or cares, because 7% or 8% is still tremendous growth. When the real number drops to 5%, however, it will be harder to cover up, and that risks social unrest.[69] Faced with a slowing economy, increased unemployment, and an unhappy populace, Beijing could be tempted to increase debt to finance an economic stimulus package which would further exacerbate China's growing debt problem, and also violate Xi's stated goal of decreasing public debt.

Some experts believe China's real growth has already dropped to these worrying levels. "Many economists, moreover, have proven beyond a reasonable doubt that China's economy is currently growing much more slowly than it's been saying – in the 4% to 4.5% growth range versus the official 6.9%."[70] With slowing growth rates it may be impossible for China to reach its target of doubling the economy in five years. Furthermore, if the government's promises diverge too far from reality, this could create a credibility gap.

"Harry Wu, an economist at The Conference Board, an independent research institute, concludes that, from 1978–2012, China grew at 7.2% a year." During the same period the government's official estimate was 9.8%. According to Wu, in 2008 China's GDP only grew by 4.7%, although the government claimed it had grown by 9.6%. Similarly, in 2012, he calculated a growth rate of just 4.1% as opposed to the official rate of 9.7%.[71]

Research firm Capital Economics utilizes economic proxies to measure China's real economic growth. Proxy measures include looking at factors which should increase as real GDP increases. For example, electricity, rail cargo, and bank loans should increase if factories are actually producing more and if new factories are being built or hiring more workers. To make their calculations Capital Economics use an "activity proxy." Other proxies include freight movement, sea shipments, electricity use, property sales, and passenger travel. One advantage of using these measures is that they measure volume and are not affected by prices or exchange rates. Based on proxy measures, it was estimated that second quarter growth was 4.3%, not 7% as official estimated. According to Capital Economics, proxy measures are not 100% accurate and the real number was probably somewhere between the proxy measure and the official number.[72]

Movements within the Chinese economy support the government's claims of greater liberalization. The People's Bank of China, the central bank, "said it would allow foreign entities to open settlement accounts at domestic banks and test free convertibility in the free-trade zone at Shanghai."[73] The government has taken other real steps such as decreasing mandatory bank-deposit reserve levels to create more liquidity, and removing the cap on bank-account interest.[74]

Conclusions

Since the beginning of the economic reforms initiated through five-year plans, China's economy has grown tremendously, with GDP increasing from US$202 billion in 1980 to US$9.2

trillion in 2014. During the same period Chinese citizens have seen per capita GDP rise from US$205 to US$8,522.[75] Even if growth data has been exaggerated, China's progress is still impressive. Whether Beijing can achieve its ambitious growth goals of 6.5% per annum over the next five years remains to be seen. However, even if China grows at half the projected rate, the country will be much wealthier five years from now, as the world's second largest economy slowly makes its way to first position.

CHAPTER 5:

GOING OUT

"In the old days you built armies. Now you build a sovereign-wealth fund," says Jayne Bok, head of sovereign advisory in Asia for consulting firm Towers Watson.[1]

During the early years of China's economic transformation, China's engagement with the rest of the world was generally in the form of received foreign investment. Initially, China allowed limited foreign investment in special economic zones (SEZs), the most famous of which was in Shenzhen. Later, other SEZs were established, and the scope of foreign investment increased. Foreign joint ventures eventually became commonplace. At the beginning of the 21st century, however, investment began to flow in the other direction, as China became a source of outbound direct investment (ODI).

The Tenth Five-Year Plan (2001–05) outlined a "going outside" strategy that encouraged Chinese corporations, both privately-owned enterprises (POEs) and SOEs, to make direct investments overseas in order to gain access to foreign markets, secure natural resources, and acquire advanced technology.[2] Eventually, China's outbound investments became more strategic, focusing on mergers and acquisitions to strengthen domestic brands and eliminate competition, as well as infrastructure investment in foreign countries to solidify political alignment. In addition to strategic goals, investments were increasingly motivated by a desire to earn profits.

In the wake of the global financial crisis of 2007–08, the Chinese government seized the opportunity to purchase undervalued assets in developed countries.[3] Today, Chinese outbound investment ranges from owning hotels in New York and film studios in California, to investing in energy production facilities in Vietnam, farms in Cambodia, and oil refineries in the Middle East. Much of the funding for China's overseas investments comes through the government's sovereign wealth fund, the China Investment Company (CIC).

China's Sovereign Wealth Fund: the China Investment Company (CIC)

Sovereign-wealth funds are financial vehicles owned by governments which invest a government's cash reserves, national retirement pension funds, or revenues from the sales of commodities such as oil or other natural resources. In addition to increasing the returns on a country's reserves and diversifying its investments, sovereign wealth funds often invest in foreign countries to obtain political influence.[4]

China Investment Corporation (CIC) (中国投资有限责任公司; *zhōngguó tóuzī yǒuxiàn zérèn gōngsi*) with US$746.7 billion under management, is the world's fourth-largest sovereign wealth fund. Established in 2007 to diversify the investing of China's currency reserves, CIC is a wholly state-owned enterprise (SOE) and maintains very close ties to the Chinese government.[5] Although China has four sovereign wealth funds, the PRC's Ministry of Finance, which oversees CIC's management, has designated CIC as China's primary outbound investor. The corporation leads government efforts to reduce the cost of, and ensure the country's control over, raw materials and natural resources.[6]

About 25% of CIC's assets are invested outside China in many different countries.[7] In order to increase China's food security, the corporation has invested in agriculture in Asia, Africa and Latin America. In Europe, it holds a 10% stake in London's Heathrow Airport.[8] China has also been accepted into the European Bank for Reconstruction and Development. This will facilitate Chinese investment in the central and eastern European states which will be part of China's "Silk Road Economic Belt."[9]

CIC investments in North America

In the United States, CIC has made a number of real-estate investments, such as purchasing a skyscraper on New York City's Madison Avenue from The Carlyle Group.[10] In 2009, the corporation announced plans to invest heavily in distressed US real estate, in coordination with the US Treasury Department's Public-Private Investment Program (PPIP).[11] Beyond real estate, it has taken a seat on the board of US energy giant AES and several other foreign firms.[12] CIC has purchased small stakes in News Corp., which owns *Wall Street Journal*, American International Group Inc., and Apple Inc. CIC has also taken major stakes in investment banks Morgan Stanley and BlackRock Inc.

In addition to these direct investments, CIC owns shares in an array of US companies, purchased through external money managers who handle a portion of CIC's investments.[13] Overall, nearly half of CIC's equity investments are in the US.[14] CIC has also been building relationships with buyout firms, and "CIC said it plans to raise between US$50 billion and US$100 billion for the creation of a new unit to specialize in making overseas direct investments."[15]

CIC's first overseas office was in Toronto, but after racking up heavy losses in Canada, that office was relocated to New York.[16] According to a CIC spokesperson, the move was made to maintain CIC's existing relationships with New York investment banks, and to look into new investment opportunities in the US.[17] Some US politicians, however, oppose CIC's increasing investment in the US on grounds of national security.[18]

Wall Street Journal reported on concerns that sovereign wealth funds investing abroad "might be directed by political agendas in addition to financial goals."[19] For years, US politicians have been expressing concern about foreign entities buying US real estate.[20] Similar fears have been expressed about Chinese entities, particularly CIC, buying US properties. In 2005, political opposition prevented the state-owned China National Offshore Oil Corporation (CNOOC) from buying Unocal Corp.[21]

China has been investing all over the world. Below are a few highlights of Chinese investment, beginning in Southeast Asia, then moving to the Middle East, Africa, and Latin America and the Caribbean.

Chinese investment in Vietnam

In December 1987, Vietnam's National Assembly passed a law allowing foreign investment.[22] In 1991, China normalized relations with Vietnam. Chinese FDI began that same year when a firm from Guangxi invested in a joint venture to open a restaurant in Hanoi.[23]

Do Tien Sam, editor-in-chief of *China Research Journal* (published by Vietnam Academy of Social Sciences) told Xinhua News Agency that stable relations between the two countries have led to greater Chinese investment in Vietnam.[24] Since 1987, Chinese investment has risen steadily,

73

peaking in 2013. Most likely because of a combination of political stability and sound economic fundamentals in Vietnam, Chinese investment in Vietnam soared from a mere US$71 million in 2002 to US$2.3 billion in 2013, in which year there were 89 new projects and money was added to 11 previously established projects.[25]

Chinese FDI has tended to flow into the two major cities, Hanoi and Ho Chi Minh City, as well as the provinces of Binh Duong, Bac Ninh, and Hai Phong. Chinese money has gone into processing, agriculture, fisheries, manufacturing, steel, real estate, construction, textiles, appliances, fertilizers, building materials, fodder, and mining. Real estate and textiles are the most important of the 17 sectors of the Vietnamese economy that China has invested in; China has also engaged in building infrastructure and capacity-expanding projects in Vietnam, such as coal fired power plants.[26]

Vietnam is in dire need of better infrastructure. According to the World Economic Forum's Global Competitiveness Report, "Vietnam ranks 99th out of 140 in terms of overall quality of infrastructure, 93rd in quality of roads, and 76th in quality of port infrastructure."[27] An example of Chinese infrastructure investment in Vietnam would be the 120mw An KhanhI Thermoelectric Plant in northern Vietnam, one of four built by Chinese contractors.[28]

Chinese investment in Vietnam's garment industry is also drawing infrastructure investment in the form of industry capacity expansion. For example, Chinese garment and textile giant Jiangsu Julun Textiles Group Co. Ltd is set to invest US$68 million in a manufacturing facility in Bao Minh Industrial Park in Nam Dinh province. A Hong Kong company, Luenthai, is involved in a joint venture with the Vietnam National Textile and Garment Group (Vinatex) and China's Sanshui Jialida Textile Company to construct a garment manufacturing facility in the same industrial park.[29]

China has also been investing in raw materials such as rubber, fossil fuel and coal, as well as manufacturing plants producing wood products and finished goods such as cigarettes. As commodities become less profitable, Chinese investment has been shifting to the real-estate, insurance, financial, and technology sectors.[30]

Over the last two years, China's economy has slowed down considerably. One would expect this to adversely impact Chinese ODI, but the opposite has happened. Chinese ODI continues unabated; many economists believe that Chinese investors are searching for returns higher than those offered by the slowing Chinese economy. Consequently, in 2016, there was a dramatic surge of Chinese investment in Vietnam, which is reaching record levels. [31]

Problems with Chinese investment in Vietnam

In spite of Vietnam's advantageous demographics and solid economic indicators, Chinese investment in Vietnam has not been immune to setbacks. *Hanoi Times* reported that due to past business failures, Beijing has advised its SOEs to only take minority shares in new ventures, and to partner with local companies so they can benefit from local market knowledge.[32]

Corruption in Vietnam is an ongoing problem. Transparency International's 2014 Corruption Perceptions Index ranked Vietnam as the 119th most corrupt country, out of 175 in the world. GAN Integrity's 2015 Vietnam Corruption Report claims that "Companies are likely to experience bribery, political interference and facilitation payments."[33] The report goes on to state that corruption exists in the courts, among the police, public services, land administration, tax administration, and customs. GlobalSecurity.org has said that "Corruption and administrative red tape within the government has been a vast challenge for governmental consistency and productivity and for foreign companies doing business in Vietnam."[34]

The PRC and Vietnam are two of the last five remaining communist countries on Earth, yet their relationship has been anything but amicable. The Sino-Vietnam War of 1979 left scars on the relationship which could reopen at the slightest provocation. In 2014, there were violent protests in Vietnam against Chinese companies and citizens as a result of the "HYSY 981 oil rig fiasco, which not only sent protesters out into the streets, but also ended with Chinese-funded factories being burned."[35]

Vietnamese citizens as well as government officials worry that China could wind up controlling significant sectors of the Vietnamese economy and believe some restrictions should be set, particularly with respect to natural resources. *Hanoi Times* also reports concerns about China's unilateral benefits from Vietnam trade: "there needs to be a bilateral investment deal to place reasonable limits on China's involvement in Vietnam."[36] Vietnam runs a trade deficit with China, prompting some to say that China benefits more from the relationship than Vietnam.

According to another report, Vietnamese people worry that their country is becoming too dependent on China. The same report went on to say that Bui Xuan Khu, Vietnam's former minister of industry and trade, feels that Vietnam should nonetheless embrace all forms of foreign investment because of the technology transferred, the jobs it creates, and the taxes it generates. By this logic, Vietnam would absorb Chinese technology in order to create its own independent textile and garment manufacturing industry, which would then be globally competitive.[37]

"Buy Vietnamese" campaigns have arisen in Vietnam in the wake of squabbles between the two countries, particularly after sovereignty disputes in the South China Sea. Within Vietnam's government there is fear that Vietnam will become too economically dependent on China. While Vietnam runs a trade deficit with China it runs a surplus with both the US and the EU, driving Vietnam to embrace the Trans-Pacific Partnership (TPP).[38] The TPP, one of the largest trade deals in history, was signed by 12 countries: Australia, Brunei, Canada, Chile, Japan, Malaysia, Mexico, New Zealand, Peru, Singapore, the United States, and Vietnam. The exclusion of China is significant. The treaty was expected to boost Vietnam's exports by as much as 28%.[39] However, as soon as he took office, US President Donald Trump ordered his country's withdrawal from the deal.

With tensions high, and widespread fears about economic overdependence on China, any problem with a Chinese project in Vietnam becomes a threat to bilateral trade. For example, the Chinese-built Cat Linh–Ha Dong railway in Hanoi has fallen behind schedule. As a result, some Vietnamese officials have suggested abandoning the China contract in favor of a new agreement with a Japanese company. "Prime Minister Nguyen Xuan Phuc publicly scolded the company. One transportation expert quoted in local Vietnamese news suggested that Vietnam should entrust such projects to more experienced nations like Japan."[40] In spite of the above-mentioned difficulties, China pledged in 2016 to increase its overseas direct aid to Vietnam, building schools and hospitals.[41]

Chinese investment in Cambodia

In recent years, China has become one of Cambodia's largest donor countries, a major source of FDI, and a key trading partner. According to the Cambodian-Chinese Economic Trade and Investment Five-Year Plan (2013-2017), bilateral trade between the two countries was expected to total US$4.31 billion in 2016.[42] Between 1994 and 2015, Chinese companies invested in 543 projects worth a total of US$10.1 billion.[43] Relations between Cambodia and China date back centuries, but it is within the last twenty years, during China's economic rise, that the relationship has grown in importance.

The Council for the Development of Cambodia reported that, between 1994 and 2012, China invested US$9.17 billion in Cambodia.[44] Bilateral trade tripled between 2009 and 2011, "driven by imports of garment raw materials, machinery, motorcycles, cars, foodstuffs, electronics, furniture, medicines and cosmetics."[45] Chinese investment in Cambodia in 2013 alone was US$427 million, up 62% compared to the previous year. Chinese companies have invested in the kingdom's garment and manufacturing industries, and sectors including banking and finance, mining, energy, real estate, tourism, telecommunications, transport, and agriculture. China has also provided Cambodia with millions of dollars of military assistance.[46]

Chinese investment projects in Cambodia include the rebuilding of National Road 8, the construction of buildings for the Council of Ministers and the Library of the Senate in Phnom Penh, as well as providing computers for the library of the Royal Academy of Cambodia.[47] One of the most publicized Chinese projects in Cambodia is the Naga City Walk, an underground luxury mall which will be built to connect Phnom Penh's two NagaWorld Casinos, which cater largely to Chinese clientele. The project is being funded by China-Duty Free Group, an SOE.[48] Economic ties between the two countries have become so significant that the Cambodian government has publicly stated their wish to increase the use and free flow of the Chinese yuan.

China, an economic powerhouse, finds it beneficial to trade with and invest in Cambodia. Cambodia, of course, is grateful for the income, but there are concerns that with an export-oriented economy based largely on raw materials, Cambodia may find it difficult to move up the global value chain. Cambodia runs a trade deficit with China. In 2011, Cambodian exports to China totaled a mere US$184 million, mainly farm produce, rubber, fish, timber, and textiles.[49]

Why China invests in Cambodia

Among the main reasons for Chinese investment in Cambodia are a desire to secure natural resources, expand export markets, garner political support, enhance regional security, balance US political influence, and spread Chinese culture.[50]

Another attraction for Chinese investors is the fact that the Cambodian economy uses US dollars for most transactions, and many Chinese are interested in storing their wealth in dollars rather than yuan. For individual investors, the Cambodian economy represents easy, essentially unregulated access to US dollars.

Property taxes are low in Cambodia, and moving cash in and out of the kingdom is relatively cheap and easy.[51] Cambodia's economy is robust, growing at more than 6% per year, and this growth generates more US dollars for Chinese investors. In 2015 alone, "Chinese cross-border capital outflows into commercial real estate have grown rapidly, reaching US$11.7 billion."[52] And while Beijing is trying to reduce capital flight, the government itself benefits from Chinese investment in Cambodia. For China's government, profits earned in Cambodia can be added to China's growing foreign currency reserves.

Another reason for Chinese investment in Cambodia is the ease of doing business there. Chinese nationals find it easy to do business in Cambodia because a large percentage of the population have Chinese ancestry. Sino-Khmers have always played a major role in Cambodia's economy, preceding even the French colonial period.

"Mandarin is the second most popular language in Cambodia after English. There are approximately 56 schools offering Chinese-language classes to some 30,000 students nationwide."[53] Not only is there a Confucius Institute in Cambodia, housed at the Royal Academy of Cambodia, but they have created Chinese textbooks printed in the Khmer language. Currently, there are 500,000 Chinese and Sino-Khmers in Cambodia.[54] At the same time, more and more Khmer students are studying in China. "Between 2002 and 2004, the number of Cambodian students in China grew by nearly 20%."[55] Educational exchanges like these ultimately strengthen the economic ties between the two countries.

Currency fluctuations are another factor driving Chinese investors to Cambodia. To maintain China's competitive advantage in manufacturing, the government has devalued the yuan, keeping Chinese exports cheap. As a result, many Chinese have seen their savings shrink overnight. A lot of Chinese small and medium-sized investors have found investing in Cambodia attractive. In particular, purchasing Cambodian US-dollar-denominated real-estate can hedge against a falling yuan.

Turmoil in China's stock market may be another cause for increasing Chinese investment in Cambodian real estate, which many people see as being more stable.[56] In the first nine months of 2015, money poured into Cambodia from China following the stock market crash there."[57]

Chinese banking in Cambodia

China's ambitious plans for Asia include creating the Asian Infrastructure Investment Bank (AIIB), which it hopes will circumvent US-dominated international organizations, such as the World Bank and the IMF. Cambodia invested US$62 million by purchasing 623 shares of the AIIB, a body which is meant to invest in regional infrastructure projects. Cambodia joined the AIIB after "the World Bank placed a freeze on all new lending to the country to protest a Chinese-backed real estate project that forced some 3,000 families out of their homes around Phnom Penh's Boeung Kak Lake."[58] One advantage of the AIIB is that it frees up Asian Development Bank funds for other projects. However, critics claim, the AIIB may not make the moral and good-governance demands made by the World Bank and other institutions.[59] No-strings financing from China could undermine US efforts to promote political reform in Cambodia.

In 2010, Bank of China (BOC) became the first Chinese commercial bank to open a branch in Phnom Penh, and Cambodian officials hoped BOC would bring new capital and technology to the kingdom. At the same time, they hoped competition from BOC would stimulate Cambodia's banking sector.[60] In 2011, Industrial and Commercial Bank of China (ICBC), the largest of China's big four state owned banks, became the second Chinese bank to open a branch in Cambodia. Use of the Chinese yuan has been increasing in

Cambodia, particularly since the BOC branch opened in the Kingdom, offering products such as yuan deposit accounts and bonds. BOC has also assisted local banks in purchasing RMB bank products to hold as part of their reserve requirements.[61]

Chinese investment in the Middle East

In 2004, PRC President Hu Jintao visited Egypt. With Arab League Secretary General Amr Moussa, Hu signed the "Declaration of the China-Arab States Cooperation Forum."[62] Energy cooperation is central to the relationships between China and the Arab world, and the Energy Cooperation Conference is a key part of that relationship.[63] Much of China's commerce with the Middle East is based on China trading developmental loans, direct investment, infrastructure construction, and weapons, in exchange for oil.

Seizing on new economic opportunities, Chinese companies – along with Chinese experts, workers, and individuals – have been moving to the region in droves. In 2012 alone, Chinese enterprises signed US$19.94 billion in contracts in the Arab world and Chinese investment reached US$1.39 billion.[64] There are so many Chinese working and living in the Middle East that when fighting broke out in Libya in 2011, more than 37,000 Chinese nationals had to be evacuated. The United Arab Emirates is now home to approximately 200,000 Chinese residents.[65]

On the face of it, the relationship between China and the Middle East is based on the Gulf States trading oil to China, and China providing finance for infrastructure and capacity-building in the region. The reality is much more complicated, however. The Middle East has historically been a region whose political landscape was dominated by external forces, including global and colonial powers such as Britain, France, Russia, and the United States. In the last several decades, the US has been the major player in the region; US relationships with Israel, Iran, and Saudi Arabia – and US policy toward Iraq, Syria, and Palestine – have had a direct impact on global oil prices and oil availability, as well as flows of arms and money into and out of the region.

As China develops economically and expands its interests further and further beyond its borders, its growing need for energy has forced China into the Persian Gulf. Beijing's Middle East policy places it right at the heart of global affairs. China's relations with Middle Eastern nations are closely related to its relationship with the US, and its engagement with the global community.

China trades economic development for oil

China's economic ties to the Middle East have been steadily increasing with China importing petroleum and exporting infrastructure investment.[66] "China is the largest importer of oil from the Gulf region."[67] In fact, China purchases half of the oil produced by Iraq. Chinese national oil companies have been spearheading investment in local energy companies in the Middle East. In Iraq, they own significant stakes in the al-Ahdad, Halfaya and Rumaila oil fields.[68]

China's plan with the Silk Road Economic Belt and the 21st Century Maritime Silk Road is to establish what they refer to as the 1+2+3 cooperation pattern which has energy cooperation as a base, and then expands to trade and investment as well as technology.[69] Beijing's Arab Policy Paper also states that China plans to "be actively engaged in cooperation covering the whole nuclear industrial chain, and promote cooperation between the two sides in basic scientific research, nuclear fuels, and research reactors."[70]

China has helped cooperating governments to develop technology and capacity in the oil sector. They also finance the training of local business managers, engineers, technicians and workers. In the Sudan, for example, Chinese-funded projects have led directly to a dramatic increase in the number of jobs for Sudanese nationals.[71]

One component of China's bilateral cooperation agreements with 21 Arab countries has been the establishment of the Economic and Trade Committee to oversee trade and technical exchanges. Beijing has also signed investment-protection agreements with 16 Arab states, as well as dual-taxation avoidance agreements with 11 Arab countries.[72]

The "oil and gas plus" cooperation model is at the forefront of China's Middle East policy. This policy has led to the development of numerous interlocking trade and finance agreements, such as the so-called Petroleum Triangle which includes China, Saudi Arabia, Iran, and Russia.

Various banks and financial institutions have been created to fund infrastructure investment. One is the AIIB which, together with China, was founded by Turkey, Iran, and seven Arab states. China plans to set up a US$25 billion fund to grant special loans and commercial loans in the region. China will also pool resources with the UAE and Qatar to launch a US$20 billion joint-investment fund to support infrastructure development and high-end manufacturing industries in the Middle East.[73] One of the world's largest sovereign wealth funds, The Qatar Investment Authority, has signed a US$10 billion investment contract with Beijing's China International Trust and Investment Corporation (CITC).[74]

China profits from bilateral trade with the Middle East

Since the China-Arab States Cooperation Forum was launched in 2004, China has been courting the Middle East, extending low-interest lines of credit, investing massively in local infrastructure, and in some cases even forgiving billions of dollars' worth of loans. In 2010, for instance, China forgave roughly 80% of Iraq's debt.[75] While China may appear to be losing money on some of these transactions, there is actually a payoff. As the largest importer of oil from the Persian Gulf, China has benefited hugely from falling oil prices. Since mid-2014, oil prices have been in steady decline, resulting in China's import costs falling by almost 50%. As a result, China has been able to stockpile petroleum to ensure its future energy security.[76]

China's trade with the Middle East is not limited to oil. Tourism represents another source of income for both China and Arab countries. Consequently, China has signed tourism cooperation agreements with several Arab nations, making Egypt, Jordan and Tunisia major destinations for Chinese tourists. Nonstop flights now link Beijing and Shanghai with Dubai, and Beijing with Kuwait and Doha. To further support tourism and economic cooperation, the Bank of China now has an office in Bahrain.[77]

Bilateral trade agreements have also opened new export markets for the PRC. Chinese exports to the Middle East include light industrial equipment, textiles, food, clothing, grain, oil, food, metals and minerals, chemicals, and electronics. Imports to China from the Middle East include oil, fertilizer, chemicals, steel, copper, and aluminum.[78] Low-quality, low-cost Chinese exports are now extremely common in Iraq and Iran. China now exports more to Egypt than the US.

It is not just cheap products that China sells; they are also selling technical know-how. Algeria, where Chinese firms have constructed a 1,216-km highway, has become a market for Chinese engineering services. China maintains a trade surplus with some Arab nations. "Morocco's trade deficit with China in 2012 was also very large, with the North African country buying US$3.13 billion in Chinese goods and services while only exporting US$558 million to China."[79]

Chinese investment in Iran

Trade between China and what is now Iran has been going on for 2,000 years.[80] In the days of Zheng He (1371–1433), the famous Chinese seafarer, China and Persia were trading partners. After the 1979 Islamic Revolution, Iran broke ties with Western countries and began forging relationships with nations such as the Soviet Union (and now Russia), North Korea, and China. In 1980, Iran began purchasing weapons from China.[81]

Since then, China has become Iran's most important trading partner and the no. 1 buyer of Iranian oil. China is also Iran's largest investor. Iran is important to China because of its geostrategic location on the narrowest point of the Persian Gulf. Iran serves as a gateway for oil from other Middle Eastern nations, and grants China access to the Arabian and Caspian seas, as well as the Indian Ocean. China's New Silk Road project will connect Iran with China's existing pipelines and trade routes, which is likely to benefit both countries. On the whole, however, Iran needs China more than China needs Iran. Because of Western sanctions against Iran, Iran has been forced to adopt a "Look East" economic strategy, making China one of Iran's very few powerful allies.[82]

The relationship between Beijing and Tehran is one of mutual benefit. In China, Iran has an ally who is a permanent member of the UN Security Council. As a customer and an investor, Iran steers clear of internal political affairs and human-rights issues. For China, Iran represents both a trading partner and a market where China need not compete against Western countries.

In fact, Iran's longstanding difficulties with the West may create a strategic advantage for China, as Iran provides a monopoly market for Chinese weapons.[83] For example, when Western nations steered clear of arms sales to Iran, China saw an opportunity to make money by trading oil, weapons, and technology with Iran. "Supreme Leader Ayatollah Ali Khamenei said, 'The Islamic Republic will never forget China's cooperation during [the] sanctions era.'"[84] Today, Iran is the Middle East's largest purchaser of Chinese weapons.[85]

More than 100 Chinese companies are registered in Iran; apart from the oil industry, they are active in the extraction of aluminum, copper, and coal. Within the petroleum sector, Chinese companies – including state-owned Sinopec and China National Petroleum Corporation – are building a refinery in Hormuz and expanding an existing one in Abadan.[86]

One difficult facet of China's relationship with Iran is the fact that China is a member of the UN Security Council, and has actually voted in favor of some of the sanctions against Iran. This may have been to maintain good relations with the West or to support China's other Middle Eastern trading partners, such as Israel and Saudi Arabia, both of which want to see Iran contained.[87] China-Iran trade is significant, but a mere one-fortieth of China's trade with its three largest trading partners, the US, the EU, and Japan.[88] This puts China in an awkward position. On the one hand, it wants to support

Iran; on the other, hand, China does not want to alienate more important trading partners.

Chinese investment in Africa

Economic growth in Sub-Saharan Africa (SSA) has averaged roughly 5% per year for the past decade. Much of this growth can be attributed to foreign investment, including investment from China. During this period, China's economic exchanges with Africa have expanded dramatically, from 2.3% of SSA trade in 1985 to nearly a quarter of SSA trade in 2013. Presently, China is SSA's largest export and development partner, with China acquiring approximately one third of its energy from SSA.[89]

Chinese investment in Africa has skyrocketed in recent years, moving from US$7 billion in 2008 to US$26 billion in 2013. In 2015, President Xi Jinping promised African states US$60 billion in loans, aid, and export credits.[90]

Angola, South Africa, Sudan, and Nigeria have become China's largest bilateral trade partners on the continent.[91] Between 1998 and 2012, around 2,000 Chinese firms invested in roughly 4,000 projects in 49 African countries.[92] China has provided infrastructure assistance in the form of roads, railways, stadia and other official buildings. China has also contributed to healthcare programs. China exports heavy machinery and electrical equipment to Africa; its no. 1 import from Africa is minerals.[93]

Economists and politicians outside of China have raised concerns about China and Chinese SOEs investing so heavily in Africa. Some see these investments as a form of modern economic colonialism, whereby China trades soft loans and infrastructure investment in exchange for natural resources and energy. It has even been said that China's investments in

Africa, often carried out by large SOEs, are not motivated by a desire to make profits, but to bolster Beijing's geopolitical influence.

A closer look at China's Africa investments paints a different picture, however. The majority of Chinese investment in Africa is being carried out by private enterprises rather than SOEs. Most of the 2,200-plus Chinese companies investing in SSA are POEs.[94]

There continue to be large investment projects which can be characterized as attempts to gain a geostrategic edge, or infrastructure or soft loans, in return for natural resources. However, the main motive for Chinese investment in Africa appears to be profit. "The reason the Chinese go there is because of cheap labor, since labor costs in China itself are rising."[95] China invests in Africa in order to establish a solid base of critical raw materials, and to extend its geopolitical influence in the undeveloped nations.[96] Additionally, there are good opportunities to do profitable business. These profit-driven investments range from restaurants to hotels and consumer products.

Another concern is that China sometimes seems willing to trade with unstable governments which Western nations shun. Once again, this is not exactly true. While China seems unconcerned with the rule of law in some places, China generally confines its trading to politically stable countries. "Chinese ODI is indifferent to the rule of law measure, but on the other hand is positively correlated with political stability."[97]

Quantifying Chinese investment in Africa

Economists agree that Chinese investment in Africa is increasing, but no one knows the total value. Loans and grants from the PRC government are easy to quantify, but much of the investment is small, carried out by Chinese individuals investing in restaurants, hotels, Chinese medicine clinics, and other businesses. In 2012, China's ambassador to South Africa, Tian Xuejun, estimated this type of direct investment at US$14.7 billion.[98]

At the same time, some large investments have come from China's state-owned oil companies, which have invested in energy, mining, construction and manufacturing throughout the continent. China National Petroleum Corporation invested nearly US$6 billion in Sudan's oil sector, and the China Power Investment Corporation is planning to invest US$6 billion in bauxite and aluminum projects in Guinea.

Other large investments come from Chinese POEs. Huawei and ZTE, for example, have become the principal telecommunications providers in a number of African countries.[99] POEs are also investing in finance, aviation, agriculture, and even tourism. China is moving into Africa's financial sector: In 2007, ICBC purchased a 20% stake in South Africa's Standard Bank for US$5.5 billion.[100]

The largest investor

While China is Africa's largest trading partner, it is important to separate FDI from total investment, loans, aid and other activities. Total Chinese FDI in Africa in 2013–2014 only accounted for 4.4% of Africa's GDP and only around 3–5% of total FDI.[101] By 2002, annual Chinese investment in Africa had grown to approximately US$2 billion per year.[102] Between

2005 and 2014, Chinese direct investment in Africa increased to US$3.2 billion.[103] During the same period, the total value of all Chinese investment in Africa grew to US$32 billion.

China also accounts for 13% of loans to Africa. One fundamental difference between loans from Western countries and loans from China is that the latter charge interest, whereas many of the former do not.[104] Although China forgives many of its loans to less developed nations, most African countries run a trade deficit with China.[105] European countries, particularly France and the UK, are the largest investors by a tremendous margin, with the US not far behind. Even South Africa invests more on the rest of the continent than China does. Most of this investment, whether from China or from other sources, tends to focus on countries rich in natural resources.[106]

Much of China's economic engagement with Africa has been related to resources. Between 2000 and 2012, China has undertaken around US$30 billion in infrastructure investment projects in Africa.[107] While much of this investment was connected to the exchange of natural resources, such as oil or cocoa, investment also goes into other sectors and resource-poor countries.[108] Both resource-related and resource-unrelated trade are discussed in the Forum on China-Africa Cooperation (FOCAC) which includes delegations from 50 African countries, the African Union, and China. It addresses China's trade not only with countries which are rich in natural resources such as Nigeria and South Africa, but also with resource-poor countries such as Ethiopia, Kenya, and Uganda. In the latter places, service-sector investments dominate, including restaurants, hotels, and import-export furniture companies.[109]

Financing Chinese investment in Africa

Infrastructure investment projects in Africa have been financed through the People's Bank of China, the China Development Bank, and Exim Bank. Much of China's financing activity on the continent has focused on FDI. FDI, however, is only one piece of the puzzle. An FDI investment would involve a Chinese entity investing directly in an African entity resulting in the Chinese entity obtaining a proportion of the voting rights in the African entity. As such, much of China's financial activity with Africa cannot be classified as FDI; instead many of China's pledges to Africa are financed by government-owned policy banks in China. These financings represent a wide array of structures. China promised US$5 billion to the China-Africa Development Fund, a private equity and venture capital investment arm of the China Development Bank, as well as US$5 billion for the Special Loan for the Development of African SMEs, another branch of the China Development Bank, and US$10 billion for the China-Africa Production Capacity Cooperation Fund.[110]

Bilateral trade between China and Africa exceeded US$106 billion by 2008 with the terms, nature, and shape of these deals largely determined by the banks which provide the financing. The diversity and scope of this trade, the related investments, and its financing represent a new approach in China's global economic strategy.[111]

Chinese financing not only seeks advantageous geographical locations, but Chinese banks are also looking for "locations with relatively low efficiency in the banking system and with relatively light regulation."[112] These conditions make it possible for Chinese banks to open local commercial branches serving the banking and finance needs of not only Chinese companies, but also local enterprises and entrepreneurs.

Some of China's funding activities in Africa are tied to oil. The government of Angola arranged several billion US dollars' worth of credit with Exim Bank which was linked (directly or indirectly) to making oil concessions available to Chinese companies.[113] Additional Chinese government funding will go to the China-Africa Industrial Cooperation Fund.[114]

The Ethiopian government tried for years to obtain financing from the World Bank and the African Development Bank for the Gibe III Dam project. Both refused because of armed conflicts in the region. Finally, ICBC granted a US$500 million loan for a turbine to be constructed by the Dongfang Electric Company. "In September 2012, China Development Bank signed a memorandum of understanding with the Ethiopia Sugar Corporation for another loan of US$500 million for the construction of sugar factories in the Lower Omo Valley."[115]

Large, conventional project financing is conducted through banks which have close ties to China's government, such as China Development Bank. These banks are also involved in financing the activities of the China-Africa Development Fund.[116] This fund is a principle funding vehicle for China-Africa economic cooperation, and was the first Chinese fund to promote investment in Africa.[117] Another fund, the China International Fund, is engaged in joint ventures in Guinea and Zimbabwe.[118]

Additional financing comes through policy banks, such as Exim Bank which has partnered with the World Bank and the African Development Bank. The world's largest bank, ICBC, has become a principal financier in such projects as the Morupule Power Station expansion in Botswana, as well as numerous other projects.

In addition to pipeline and banking finance projects, ICBC

and Standard Bank are now expanding into retail banking. The privately-held China Merchant Bank is also moving into African operations. Stanley Ho's Macao-based banks are moving into Portuguese-speaking countries such as Mozambique and Angola.[119] The expansion of Chinese banks into the retail sector is motivated by the needs of local markets, which are going unserved by local banks. "To date the presence of Chinese banks in emerging markets like Africa has been limited, with these (local) institutions unable to handle basic activities, such as remittances and advances, in African countries."[120] Both local and foreign businesses have more confidence dealing with a Chinese bank or a local bank partnered with a Chinese bank than with a purely local financial institution.[121]

China investment in Latin America and the Caribbean

Over the past two decades, China has steadily increased its investment in Latin America and the Caribbean (LAC), with bilateral trade growing twentyfold since the year 2000.[122] More recently, Chinese investment in the region has increased from US$7 billion in 2011 to US$29 billion in 2015.[123] To support their increased economic activity in the region, China has been participating in LAC trade organizations, becoming a permanent observer in the Organization of American States in 2004, and a member of the Inter-American Development Bank in 2009. Additionally, China participates in the Economic Commission for Latin America and the Caribbean (ECLAC).[124]

At a 2015 meeting of Latin American presidents, hosted in Beijing, President Xi Jinping pledged US$250 billion over the next decade.[125] This money will come in various forms, such as the purchase of agricultural products, raw materials, and energy, as well as lending, infrastructure investment, and exporting finished products to Latin America.

China currently imports 40% of the world's soybean production, 75% of which it buys from Brazil and Argentina. China also imports a third of the world's iron ore and a fifth of its copper, much of which comes from LAC countries. China buys oil from Venezuela, copper from Chile, and both copper and fishmeal from Peru.[126] "China is staying close to Latin America because they have many of the raw materials the Asian nation seeks, including iron, oil and food."[127]

Other Chinese economic activity in the LAC region involves lending. In 2015, China loaned a total of US$30 billion to Latin American governments, double the previous year's total. This figure exceeds monies loaned to Latin America by the World Bank and Inter-American Development Bank. Some of these loans are coupled with infrastructure construction projects being handled by Chinese firms, and China has offered an additional US$35 billion for infrastructure investment.[128]

China's economic involvement in Latin America is not just about China making loans and extracting natural resources. China's exports to Latin America have grown year on year, reaching US$130 billion in 2014. According to IMF data, "China has become the top trade partner of Brazil, Chile, and Peru" and has free trade agreements with Chile, Costa Rica, and Peru,[129] as well as institutional arrangements with several other LAC countries.[130]

However, Chinese investment projects are not always successful. In 2014, a Chinese-led business group was awarded a contract to build a high-speed railway in Mexico, but the contract was later rescinded because of protests against local government corruption. In 2011, Chongqing Grain Group began building a US$2 billion soy processing plant, but as of 2016 the site remains empty.[131]

95

Why China invests in LAC

China's goals in Latin America include securing energy, raw materials and export markets. China also utilizes global trade to solve problems faced at home, such as ensuring the continued growth of its own economy. Investment in overseas infrastructure projects creates opportunities for Chinese firms and contractors.[132]

More than half of China's FDI has gone into energy and oil companies, with mining, particularly copper and iron ore, accounting for another 25%. Some of this investment is driven by China's insatiable need for raw materials. A second motive for heavy investment in raw materials is to build reserves and lock in current prices. Many other investments are related to food. China is a net importer of food, and Beijing seems to be searching for various sources of staples to ensure the country's food security. Therefore, China is investing in Brazilian soy and other foodstuffs from Latin America.

Early Chinese investment in Latin America focused on importing commodities China needed. The newest wave of Chinese investment has focused on "a need to maintain economic growth by exporting its industries into other world regions."[135] By investing in large projects, China is exporting both workers and pollution to LAC. Over the past two decades, wages in China have increased by between four- and ninefold, and this threatens to price Chinese manufacturing out of world markets. Seeking employment for its younger generation, China sends many of its workers to other countries, including LAC, where they construct highways, dams, and railroads.[136]

To further support the growth of China's economy, the PRC uses its overseas investments to create markets for Chinese goods. This market-seeking behavior provides

Chinese companies with numerous advantages. Chinese firms can avoid Chinese import restrictions and can flood LAC markets with cheap goods from Southeast Asia and Africa.[136]

By exporting industrial projects, Chinese companies can avoid domestic regulations which may increase the cost of doing business. China also benefits by exporting pollution to LAC. Raw-material processing is extremely polluting, and China can avoid environmental problems by processing its raw materials in LAC countries.[137]

Quantifying Chinese investment in Latin America

Today, LAC is China's fourth largest trading partner, as of 2014 accounting for 12% of LAC's total global trade.[138] The two economies are so closely tied that "A World Bank analysis estimates that for every 1% decline in Chinese economic growth, LAC's overall growth rate is reduced by 0.6%."[139]

In January 2015, the First Ministerial Meeting of the Forum of China and the Community of Latin American and Caribbean States (CELAC) was held in Beijing.[140] CELAC has 33 member countries including every country in Latin America and the Caribbean.[141] At the meeting, President, Xi Jinping announced the CELAC-China Five-Year Cooperation Plan, which calls for bilateral trade to grow to over US$500 billion annually and for Chinese FDI to increase to more than US$250 billion over the next decade. The Cooperation Plan also established 12,000 scholarships and training programs for citizens of CELAC states.[142]

During the same meeting, Xi also announced the 1+3+6 cooperation framework and the 3×3 cooperation model.[143] The 1 refers to China and CELAC,[144] while the 3 refers to the three drivers of economic growth: trade, investment, and financial cooperation. The number 6 refers to the six Chinese industries which will be involved: energy and resources, infrastructure construction, agriculture, manufacturing, scientific and technological innovation, and information technologies.[145] The 3x3 refers to "Chinese and Latin American enterprises, societies, and governments" which will cooperate in "logistics, power generation, and information technology."[146]

Over the past five years, Chinese investment in LAC has averaged nearly US$10.7 billion per annum. FDI has also increased steadily, with 87% coming from SOEs. Some 57% of FDI relates to raw-material acquisition.[147] Most of China's FDI has been through mergers and acquisitions, over four-fifths of which was in raw material extraction, with oil and gas accounting for 70% of this figure.[148]

Chinese FDI, while significant, is considerably less than that of some Western countries: 20% less than the Netherlands, 17% less than the United States, and 10% less than Spain. "The UN Economic Commission for Latin America and the Caribbean highlights that 13% of Chinese outward FDI is directed to LAC—are highly misleading. Much of Chinese (and Korean) assets have been parked in the offshore tax havens of the Cayman Islands and the British Virgin Islands."[149] Even without discounting Chinese FDI for money parked in Caribbean banks, Chinese FDI in the region is still dwarfed by US FDI, the latter being estimated at US$350 billion.

The US has long been the dominant power in LAC and it still overshadows China's influence. China's regional importance, however, is growing steadily. In 2000, China accounted for only 2% of Latin America's foreign trade, while the US "was 53%. As of 2010, the Chinese share had grown to 11% of the total, while that of the United States had dropped to 39%."[150] As much as Chinese influence in the region is growing, US economic dominance continues. In fact, US exports to the whole of Latin America are still three times those of China.[151]

Transition to the Belt and Road Initiative

The "going out" strategy was made redundant in 2013, when Xi unveiled the The Silk Road Economic Belt and the 21st-century Maritime Silk Road, later called One Belt One Road, and eventually dubbed the Belt and Road Initiative (BRI). The BRI will be explored in greater detail later in this book.

CHAPTER 6:

CHINA'S MIDDLE CLASS

In 2001, 41% of Chinese lived in poverty, but by 2011 that number had dropped to 12%.[1] Over the same ten-year period, China's middle class grew by 203 million.[2] The growth of the middle class in China and elsewhere in Asia is of great importance to the global economy. In fact, the World Economic Forum chose the growth of Asia's middle class as the eighth most significant global trend in 2012.[3] These sentiments were echoed in a 2011 Brookings Institution report.[4]

Since 1980, the average Chinese worker has seen their income grow tenfold. Even more incredible is that, as recently as 2000, the average annual income in China was only US$760.[5] According to the IMF, between 2001 and 2011, China's middle class jumped from 3% to 18% of the population. Additionally, the upper-middle income segment increased from below 1% to 5%.[6]

The income for a Chinese middle-class family of four ranges from US$14,600 to US$29,200.[7] In this book, however, the middle class is defined not by their income in dollars, a statistic which means little without a full analysis of the cost of living. A better definition is the one used a CNN Money report which identifies the middle class as those with discretionary income equal to one third of their income. By this definition, the PRC now has the world's largest middle class.[8]

This chapter will examine China's middle class, who they are, where they are located, and how they became middle class. It will also look at how the middle class spend their money and, finally, the impact China's middle class is having on both China and on the world economy.

History of China's middle class

Americans take the term "middle class" for granted because they come from a country where nearly everyone is middle class. But even in the West, the concept of the middle class has existed for less than 150 years.

While the earliest reference to a middle class in the West can be traced back to Aristotle, the Western middle classes did not actually begin to develop until the 19th Century. In China, by contrast, the middle class only began to emerge in the 1980s, but this demographic has experienced major growth over the past decade.[9]

Defining the middle class is not easy, as the term has different meanings to different people and in different cultures. In the 19th and early 20th centuries, the Western middle class consisted largely of entrepreneurs who were able to generate wealth independent of an employer. However, the perception of the middle class has changed. In the US now, most people who have a job – particularly a white-collar job – and who have neither inherited wealth nor receive welfare payments from the state, consider themselves middle class.[10]

During the Mao era, when the economy was strictly planned, a communist middle class existed. It was composed of well-placed factory managers and cadres who received higher salaries and better benefits than ordinary people. At that time, it was unusual for anyone to change one's job, location, or social status; poor people stayed poor, and those with positions of advantages retained their advantages. Beginning in the early 1980s, as China transitioned toward a free market economy, the already-advantaged government workers and entrepreneurs became the new middle class.[11] Many researchers refer to this group as "the new rich," but US researchers identify them as China's "new middle class."[12] A truly private and independent middle class is very new concept in China.[13]

In the West, the middle classes were a product of the Industrial Revolution. They were the managers and entrepreneurs of the companies which developed as the population moved away from agricultural work. A similar class developed in China, but did not grow dramatically until the 1990s. The first generation of China's middle class included the same entrepreneurs and professionals as the American middle class, but in China, the middle class also extended to government cadres. A large proportion of China's middle class was government and former government employees; even many of those who could be called entrepreneurs had come from the state sector, as previously every factory had been state owned. In many instances, managers of formerly state-owned factories remained in their posts, but now ran those factories as private enterprises.[14]

Under the strict communist system of the 1970s, belonging to the upper or middle class was stigmatized.[15] Landlords, bosses, and professors were considered enemies of the people. For a period, the Chinese Communist Party effectively did away with the concept of social class. However, as economic reforms progressed, the government relied on the growing middle class to move the economy forward.[16] The PRC government sees the development of a middle class as a key factor favoring modernization.[17] The government now seems to recognize that the future expansion of China's GDP is dependent on the middle class, as they are generally more entrepreneurial and possess greater human capital than other strata in society.[18]

The Chinese middle class generally purchase durable goods, such as household appliances, in greater quantities than other classes. Most middle class households own a TV, a refrigerator, and a washing machine; many have luxuries like a car, a piano, a computer, or a video camera.[19] Many economists outside the PRC hope China's middle class will boost global consumption and help the world return to kind of growth rates seen before global financial crisis. Similarly, Beijing is pinning its hopes on the middle class to rescue China's economy.

Where and how much?

Many of the new middle class are entrepreneurs or white-collar workers, yet others are government employees who have been able to parlay their positions into very lucrative *guanxi* networks of connections and influence. The sources and amounts of family income can be a very sensitive topic, and reports on the average income of China's middle class may not reflect reality. Additionally, both government workers and white-collar executives may receive perks which are not common in the West, but which boost their income and amplify their ability to consume ability. For example, they have a company car or get a preferential loan for a house, thus freeing up income to be spent elsewhere.[20] Much of the accumulated wealth of the middle class today comes from economic advantages they derived as government employees during the economic transition of the 1990s. One research team examining China's middle class interviewed a government worker who was able to buy his primary residence directly from the ministry where he worked; as a result, he was later able to invest in a second property.[21]

Researchers have identified education, industrialization, urbanization, and globalization as factors driving the development of the middle class in China. All four components have accelerated since the economic reforms of the 1990s.[22] The urban workforce grew from 20% of the country's total workforce in the 1970s to 40% in 2008.[23] Globalization through FDI has helped create many white-collar jobs. Additionally, capacity-building programs among multinational corporations have provided training for Chinese managers, further increasing the level of talent in the country. These changes have been most prominent in urban areas. Not surprisingly, these areas are where most of the middle class can be found.

Over the past decade, 200 million Chinese migrated from the countryside to the cities. By 2012, China had more urban than rural residents for the first time in its history.[24] As of 2012, two thirds of China's middle class were living in urban areas, and it is expected these urban residents will contribute to China's consumption growth in accordance with the government's plan to move the country away from its dependence on manufacturing, and toward a consumption-based economy.[25]

Consumer spending in China only makes up 35% of GDP, far behind that of developed economies.[26] Historically, China's economy has been characterized by high levels of savings and low levels of consumption. Much of the reluctance to consume is because government-supported healthcare programs and education is lacking; education alone can cost a family 30% of its income.[27] Although consumption as a function of GDP in China is comparatively

104

small, the Chinese middle class is so large that their spending has a real influence on world GDP. In 2012, Chinese consumers accounted for 7.12% of total global consumption, valued at US$3 trillion.[28]

One side effect of China's economic rise has been a glut of college graduates, making competition for jobs fierce. As a result, parents are willing to spend money on supplemental courses and tutoring sessions to give their children an advantage when competing in a tight job market.[29] The economy appears to be suffering from a vicious circle: Consumption is low because parents save for their children's education, and because there is a surplus of educated young people, parents are under pressure to increase their spending on education to bolster their children's job prospects. Increased savings, of course, translates to lower consumer spending. Additionally, young people without jobs also spend less – and this strata of the society is growing rapidly.

Recognizing that the economy cannot continue to grow without increased consumer spending, the government has announced plans to improve state education and healthcare coverage so citizens will be free to allocate more of their income to consumption.[30]

It is hoped that the growth of China's urban population will fuel the expansion of China's consumer and service sectors, which is the only way forward for the country's economy. Modern, developed economies, such as those in North America or Western Europe, are largely dependent on consumption. "The old model of economic growth based on exports and big government-spending has become unsustainable."[31]

Profile of the middle class

A significant part of the middle class is made up of government workers who supplement their government salaries with "fees" extracted from the public they are meant to serve.[32] These "fees" – which researchers refer to these as the "gray economy" – include "red envelopes" (filled with cash) and gifts given to functionaries to expedite government services.[33] Wang Xiaolu, an economist and deputy director of the National Economic Research Institute, thinks that this "gray economy" may account for as much as 15% of GDP.[34]

A typical middle-class Chinese couple may include a husband working as an engineer and a wife in real estate, earning a combined US$10,000 and living in a US$37,000 condominium. Their wedding, costing around US$4,000 including lunch for 150 people at a nice hotel, would have been another signal of having reached middle-class status. In Shanghai, where salaries are higher than in other parts of the country, a middle-class family might have a combined income of "US$18,000 a year and live in a three bedroom apartment, furnished with foreign brand-name furniture."[35] They would drive an imported car, eat in restaurants, use their air-conditioning whenever they felt like it, and buy a US$250 phone for their 12-year-old daughter. A middle-class single, by contrast, would earn about US$1,000 a month and spend their free time shopping in trendy malls and frequenting restaurants. A couple earning "more than US$32,000 a year can live in a nice suburban townhouse or home, vacation in Thailand or Europe, and drive a Buick."[36]

Although many current middle-class households originated from the state sector, there is also a direct correlation between education and income. Household heads in the lower middle class typically have 10 years of formal education, while those in the upper middle class have 12 or more.[37] But it is not strictly education which defines the middle class.

To define the middle class or understand how they define themselves, one must consider the dual Chinese concepts of "One World One Dream" and "The Chinese Dream."[38] Both signify that the Chinese today view themselves as citizens of a nation which is quickly developing and becoming a global economic power. Alongside the dream of national development, there is a personal dream of achieving a middle-class lifestyle.[39] Being middle class in China is about having options and making choices.

The middle classes in developed Western countries have existed for decades or even for a century, but in China the concept is fairly new. A significant percentage of middle-class people in developed countries come from middle-class families, whereas the Chinese middle class may come from generations of poverty. In the US, industrialization helped a middle class gradually develop.[40] In China, industrialization was part of a planned economy and did not give rise to a middle class; this segment of society did not even begin to appear in China until after the economic reforms of 1978.[41]

A significant factor in the development of the middle class in more developed countries was job specialization. Choosing to be an accountant or an engineer meant instantly moving into the middle class.[42] In pre-reform China, however, there was no such freedom of job selection and no consequent shift into the middle class. In developed Western countries, the middle class may make up 80% of the population, creating an actual social group of middle-income earners which one joins when one begins to earn enough money.[43] In China, by contrast, the middle class is still too small and too new to have a well-defined culture.[44]

China's middle class differentiate themselves through their purchases. Again the issue of choice comes into play. Being middle class in China means being able to choose how to dress.[45] From 1949 until the late 1990s, nearly everyone in China wore a uniform and had similar hairstyles. Purchases were regulated through the use of ration coupons, and under the controlled economy people consumed the same goods and services. The government even dictated when and how people would spend their leisure time through state-sponsored sports events, dances, concerts, and theater performances.[46]

Previous generations of Chinese were confronted with very basic products designed for mass consumption. Now, the middle class express their individuality through their consumption choices.[47] In the late 1990s a consumption economy began to develop, with state banks being told to make personal loans to citizens for the first time. To promote consumption, the government even increased the number of national holidays. This new freedom of consumption has resulted in increased personal choices and an expansion of the personal sphere.[48]

Changing tastes of the middle class

Housing is the single largest expense for the middle class, so moving from communal housing with shared bathrooms to a personal apartment is a major signal that one has joined the middle class. In China, apartments come bare, and kitchen and bathroom fixtures must be purchased separately. These purchases, which often add up to 30% of the cost of the apartment, are another way for middle class people to express their individuality.

When China's economy first began to grow, the middle class distinguished themselves by purchasing foreign goods.

Chinese styles were considered old fashioned; anything foreign was considered new and exciting. The new trend, however, is to purchase high quality, expensive goods with a Chinese design. Restaurants featuring Chinese regional cuisine are becoming increasingly popular, as is furniture with ornate animal carvings reflecting either classical Chinese or classical Western styles. Chinese-style fashions are also growing in popularity, as are classical Chinese-style pottery, handbags, and baskets.[49]

In the early days of economic growth, the middle class and the wealthy showed off by wearing and using brand name products with huge labels. Currently, this trend has reversed and labels are generally getting smaller. Among the truly well off, there is a perception that large, gaudy labels are favored by those who wish to appear wealthy, but who have no taste. Where luxury travel used to be a mark of distinction, today experiential travel and backpacking are held in higher esteem. Four-wheel-drive or hiking adventures in remote regions of China have become new badges of the middle class.[50]

One BBC report profiled a typical Chinese middle-class family called the Zhangs. The husband is an entrepreneur and his wife has a good job. Their combined income is US$40,000 per year. They own the apartment they live in, as well as a Japanese car, and their only child attends a private school.[51]

Most of China's middle class lives in cities, and many of them own cars. They are young entrepreneurs or white-collar professionals, under the age of 50, often working for multinational companies which pay better than local companies. China's dynamic economic growth over the last 20 years has created a lot of opportunities for people to start businesses. Some middle class individuals are employed by SOEs, and have seen their wages triple over the last 15 years.

Whereas their parents' generation typically saved 30% of

their salary, the new middle class do a lot of shopping. This drives the retail sector, especially the luxury goods segment.[52] "Now that conspicuous consumption is the official policy, the wealthy and mid-range consumers are snapping up luxury brands."[53] Many people under the age of 30 save nothing at all, preferring instead to buy brand-name products from Europe and the US.[54]

Psychologically, China's middle class are caught in a conundrum. On the one hand, life in China has taught them that they have to fend for themselves. Without government programs, personal savings are a necessity to ensure their and their family's financial security. Because social and healthcare systems in China are still inadequate, they try to save 20% of their salary each month for their retirement.[55] On the other hand, being middle class necessitates making certain purchases, such as homes, cars, designer clothes, and watches.

A third problem this new social class faces is the lack of disposable income. China's middle class earns roughly a quarter of what the US middle class does, but they try to keep up appearances by buying expensive imported goods.[56] Face is an important motivator in China; "The individual is looking for society's endorsement and qualified stamp of approval that they have mastered the rules and have been able to climb society's predefined hierarchy."[57] In other words, conspicuous spending on luxury goods is necessary to achieve true middle-class standing in China.

Historically, Chinese consumers were very price sensitive and unwilling to spend a lot of money on home appliances which no one would see them use. They generally purchased cheaper home products because they did not throw dinner parties or entertain guests.[58] Chinese people felt, "There is no point in paying a lot of money for a brand if no one knows what you own."[59] For the same reason, Häagen-Dazs restaurants were more popular than Häagen-Dazs take home ice cream. Much of the allure of spending money on Häagen-Dazs was to be seen eating it.[60] Similarly, a marketing survey discovered that foreign luxury beer brands were purchased by managers and drunk in expensive restaurants rather than at home.[61]

These spending habits are now changing and Chinese consumers are increasingly interested in higher quality products, for both home and outside use. Travel is becoming an important part of middle-class spending. In the past, travel was not something your neighbors could see you consuming, so it held a low priority in consumer spending. Now, possibly because of social media, travel is becoming a popular status symbol. Shopping trips abroad, particularly to buy luxury goods such as Louis Vuitton handbags, have become very popular.[62] Overseas shopping adds to the status of the shopper as he or she returns from Paris, London, or New York sporting new, imported items of the latest style. Both overseas travel and education fit well with the pattern of China's middle class becoming both more Western and more global.[63]

The entertainment choices of China's middle class are also becoming more global. The Chinese Fosun Group recently bought stakes in both Cirque du Soleil and Club Med, while the Shanghai Disney Resort opened in 2016. The National Basketball Association, the National Collegiate Athletic Association, and Arena Football have all organized sports events in the PRC. Western-style movies are also popular, and Oriental DreamWorks, a joint venture involving DreamWorks Studios and Chinese investors, plans to make blockbuster movies in China.[64]

How the middle class spend their money

The new middle class are "globally minded" and are expected to heavily influence world markets.[65] Some see the queues outside Apple stores in cities in China as being indicative of the country's growing middle class.[66] Chinese consumers spend an average of 10 hours per week shopping.[67] In absolute terms, however, salaries in China are low and rents in urban areas, where most of the middle class live, are high. "The average city resident can afford to rent a 700-square-foot apartment, spend 35% of their income on food, and still put 20% aside in savings, as is customary in China."[68] Typically, both husband and wife work full-time and the wife makes most decisions about household spending. Foreign brands such as Procter & Gamble and Unilever are popular among the middle class.[69]

The emerging middle classes in developing countries represent a growing market for high value foods; this trend is true of China as well. Historically, good food has been a status symbol in China, as it still is among its modern middle class;[70] they enjoy eating in restaurants, and can afford to do on average twice a week. What is more, the increasing wealth of China's middle class has created a market for foreign foods and brands.[71] China's middle class is beginning to eat like Americans, consuming more and more meat. In fact, China already consumes half of the world's pork.[72]

The adoption of packaged foods and even grocery stores, as opposed to traditional markets, can also be traced to increased affluence. Other interests of the middle class are losing weight, exercising, and learning English. While many of these traits appear to have been borrowed from the west, some are distinctly Asian. For example, China's middle class enjoys going to posh, expensive karaoke bars, but attending pop concerts – which many Westerners like to do – is much less common.[73]

China's middle class like Western brands such as Pizza Hut and KFC.[74] Many people in the US or Europe seen these as cheap places to eat, but relative to the low wages in China, they are something of a luxury.[75] For this reason, KFC branches in China have larger seating areas than in the US, because Chinese consumers want the experience of dining out.[76]

The middle class in China exhibits cultural characteristics which may seem unusual to Western observers. For example, although China's middle class has a much smaller income than their US counterparts, a study by the Boston Consulting Group indicates Chinese consumers were prepared to pay a 30% premium for iPhones.[77] China's middle class can be portrayed as desiring "novelty," and are continuously on the lookout for new styles or new products. Chinese consumers do not have strong brand loyalty;[78] they like shopping online and they share their purchases and experiences on social media in order to gain status, show off, or warn others about the poor services or products of particular retailers.[79] As a result, they are willing to pay extra for the novelty or status of being the first person to have the newest iPhone. Adoption rates for technological goods are higher among China's middle class than almost any other population in the world.[80]

Status is so important to Chinese consumers that people earning unimaginably low incomes often own luxury goods. According to CNN Money, a doctor in a small city earning roughly US$36,000 per year devoted around US$800 per month to consumption. Among the luxuries she allowed herself were a Gucci watch costing US$4,700, a US$1,600 Burberry coat and a US$320 Hermes silk scarf. The article went on to say that buying Louis Vuitton, Apple, and other imported brands was an important status symbol in China.[81]

Luxury goods for children also enjoy a huge market in China, as the majority of middle-income families indulge their only child. A great many couples pin all of their hopes on their child and spare no expense when it comes to that child's education and development.[82] Because of the notoriously bad air quality in Beijing, air filters are a popular item purchased for the home, as are water filters and face masks.[83] Keeping their one child healthy is a major priority for Chinese families.

Many young, skilled, English-speaking middle-class people have relocated to other countries. In 2010 alone, 508,000 Chinese emigrated to OECD member countries, with the US receiving 87,000 Chinese immigrants. Others purchase real-estate in the US or the EU in order to obtain a second passport as insurance against a worst case scenario in China.[84] The final aspiration of the middle and upper class, after achieving all of the material trappings, is to emigrate. Many cite the the education and legal systems, as well as the environment, as reasons for moving abroad.[85] Those who stay in China have to pay the exorbitant rents, educational costs, and healthcare costs of raising a family there, and often find themselves cash poor.

Financial pressures

The two largest expenses for China's middle class are real estate and education. The middle class invest heavily in domestic real estate, buying properties in developments with names like Thames Town, Napa Valley, Soho, Central Park, Palm Springs, Beijing Riviera, Vancouver Forest, and Up East Side Manhattan.[86] Although housing is usually the largest single investment for most families, under PRC law they are not permitted to own the land on which the house stands.[87]

Education is expensive because middle-class parents pay for their children to attend private schools and tuition centers in China and abroad. They also purchase supplemental English lessons for their children. Among the upper middle class, 34% have at least a bachelor's degree and 26% can speak English.[88] Upper middle class parents also send their children to boarding schools in the US and the UK, often securing citizenship for them.[89]

The combination of high costs, low wages, and feeling they need to spend heavily on luxury goods to maintain status, means many middle-class people are heavily in debt. The concept of "house slaves" (*fáng nú* in Mandarin) appears frequently in reports about the middle class.[90] "The middle classes in big cities often accumulate vast debt to pay for their apartments."[91] Financial pressures are so great that fear of losing their jobs prevents workers from taking sick days or going on vacation.[92]

A *Daily Telegraph* report told of a family in a second-tier city, Wuhan, who bought their apartment for 2,500 yuan per square meter; eight years later, it was worth 9,000 yuan.[93] Appreciation helped those who got in early make fortunes, but carrying a mortgage based on 9,000 yuan per square meter is a burden for many in the middle class. Adding to their economic woes, Chinese couples can also expect to pay 40,000 yuan per year for their child's university education.[94]

'Nothing left at the end of the month club'

China's middle class can be divided into generations, whereby Generation 2 is expected to have the greatest future influence on both China's economy and the global economy.[95] Generation 2 consumers were born after 1980, and raised in a

China which was relatively wealthy compared to previous generations. Because they were born after the one-child policy was launched, they do not have brothers or sisters. Despite China's population policy, Generation 2 is nearly three times the size of the baby-boomer generation in the US.[96]

The post-1980 generation can also be called Generation Y, and they are now mainstream consumers supporting much of the country's consumption spending.[97] Those born before the millennium are in a very unique position. On the one hand, as only children, they are pressured to succeed in education and career; on the other hand, they are unrestrained when it comes to spending money. They enjoy spending money in order to gain face.

An even more extreme subset of Generation Y are those referred to as the spend-all-your-salary clan (Mandarin: *yuèguāng zú*). Market researchers have gone so far as to say that Chinese under the age of 32 have a savings rate of zero. This age strata demonstrates unprecedented optimism, assuming a salary increase is on the horizon, and that they will somehow be richer than their parents. *Financial Times* interviewed a typical office lady who claimed she spent 70–80% of her salary every month, mostly on apparel and cosmetics.[98] She had three credit cards (extremely unusual in China, where there are just 0.13 credit cards per person), compared to 2.6 credit cards for the average American.[99]

One reason this demographic is able to spend recklessly is that many of them live at home and do not pay rent. Also, as only children, they have their parents and grandparents, often six adults, providing financial support.

The impact of China's middle class

Each year in China, November 11 is Singles Day, and usually the single most lucrative day each year for retailers. In 2013, online sales alone reached US$4 billion, making it one of the largest retail events in history. By contrast, Cyber Monday in the US generated US$1.5 billion in sales.[100] Purchases of electronics, apparel, fashion, and other goods were driven largely by China's middle class, and some researchers believe, "This could be the century of the Chinese consumer" as China becomes one of the most important consumer markets on the planet.[101] Simply as a result of their numbers, "China's new consumers hold the potential to become a new long-term source of global aggregate demand."[102]

China's economy can be described using various superlatives. The biggest boom in auto sales in history occurred in China. By 2007, China had become the world's no. 2 market for cars, with sales of over 7.2 million autos.[103] By 2014, China had become not only the world's largest market for luxury goods, but also the world's no. 2 market, behind the US, for luxury autos. In 2014, BMW AG's China sales hit 456,732 units. In the same year, Daimler saw record sales of 281,588 units in China.[104] In 2012, 50 million flat screen TVs were sold in China, compared to 42 million in the US. In the same year 27 million laptops were sold in China.[105] China is the world's largest cellphone market.[106] China is already the world's largest consumer of energy, and is on pace to become the world's second largest consumer economy.[107] The country is already the world's largest emitter of greenhouse gases,[108] and many worry about the environmental consequences if China's middle class becomes as acquisitive as the American middle class.

History has demonstrated that the middle-income group of

a country helps drive the country's consumption. Because of its size, and the fact it is still growing, China's middle class could become an important driver of the global economy.[109] A McKinsey report on China's middle class suggests that their growing income and buying power will drive various sectors. The report predicts that the spending power of the urban middle class "will soon redefine the Chinese market segment."[110]

The high savings rate shown by many middle-class people is not only slowing China's economic growth, but causing imbalances in the world economy. Economists have gone so far as to say that this "savings glut" has had a profound impact on the global financial crisis. "A large amount of savings funneled into OECD countries with deep capital markets has lowered long-term interest rates to extraordinarily low levels and helped to fuel a property price bubble which subsequently burst with devastating results."[111]

"Li Qiang, a sociologist at Tsinghua University, says the expansion of middle stratum people is conducive to social development."[112] Westerners often equate the growth of the middle class with a push for democracy, but neither China's middle class nor the wealthy appear to want to challenge the existing political system.[113] However, the middle class has changed Chinese society in other respects.[114] Income has become more closely correlated with educational attainment, for instance. Managers feature prominently among the new middle class, and many of them have university degrees from China or abroad. Recognizing the relationship between education and income encourages the middle class to pay for top-quality private education for their children, which again raises the bar for the rest of society.

Research has found that the middle class was unwilling to challenge authority due to fear that it might disrupt their personal economic situation.[115] Additionally, the middle class feel uncertain of the permanence of their position. Bearing the burden of car loans and educational expenses for their children, they dub themselves "mortgage slaves" and "child slaves."[116] China's overinflated real-estate market has left many married couples with no choice but to rely on their parents for loans.

In spite of major economic growth, the middle class appears to support the Chinese Communist Party. The new system is frequently referred to as a socialist market economy. In China, "About 40% of entrepreneurs are members of the Chinese Communist Party,"[117] Some of China's entrepreneurs emerged from the state sector as they were the people best placed to benefit from housing and ownership reforms. Many businesspeople maintain close ties to the state because of the business advantages it provides them. Others simply believe that maintaining a close relationship with the state is the right thing to do.[118]

The continued growth of China's middle class

Economic reforms have lifted hundreds of millions of PRC citizens out of poverty.[119] There is concern, however, that this trend may slow and eventually stop. The middle class can be divided into five groups: entrepreneurs in high-tech companies; managerial staff working in foreign firms; managers in state-owned financial institutions; professional technicians; and some self-employed private entrepreneurs.[120] Gaining entry to one of these segments requires a college degree or enough money and know-how to establish your own business. As a result of these high barriers to entry, some experts believe that China's middle class will stop growing. Factors such as which private or foreign school your child attended will determine social mobility, and these advantages are unattainable for those born into poor families.[121]

While the middle class is likely to continue growing, the impoverished class may become further entrenched as they lack access to the education needed to join the middle class. The impoverished are located largely in rural areas where people have less access to education and government services compared to urban residents. One of the many problems facing rural Chinese and preventing them from moving to the city and joining the middle class is the hukou system (explained in detail in Chapter 1). Because it is difficult for country folk to move to big cities,[122] the middle class will likely continue to expand in China's second-, third- and even fourth-tier cities.[123]

Emigration of the middle class

Part of China's middle class is leaving China, emigrating to such countries as Australia in search of a better, slower way of life, and an environment with less air and water pollution and safer food.[124] Surveys have found that food safety and air pollution are among the greatest concerns of China's middle class.

The modern Chinese emigrant is generally a professional with good career prospects who may be leaving China forever, or just seeking a foreign residence permit to facilitate business investment or as an emergency fall back ("just in case").[125] Others study abroad to establish residency on the path to obtaining citizenship. Australia and Canada attract many immigrants, but the US remains by far the most popular.[126]

Is China's middle class really middle class?

By 2018, China has seen a definite urbanization of the middle class, with countryside people and migrant workers being left out. Even a second-tier city such as Chengdu – where the average income is just over US$13,000 a year – has a large enough middle class to support the world's biggest shopping mall. The average urban salary in the PRC is 2.7 times the average rural salary. Urban households in the US tend to be 4% richer than rural households; in China, they are 63% richer. Some 43% of China's population is still rural, so this means hundreds of millions of Chinese – about one and a half times the population of the US – is poor.[127]

What about the middle class? Are they also poor? McKinsey defines the middle class in China as households that have incomes between US$9,000 and US$34,000 per year.[128] With purchasing power parity, some would argue that these families should be living as well as their Western counterparts. However, Andrew Collier of Orient Capital Research in Hong Kong estimates that the top 1–3% of China's population holds a full half of the total savings in China's banks.[129]

Because certain expenses in China are so much higher than in the US, even with purchasing power parity reducing other costs, middle class people in China have considerably less disposable income than their US counterparts. A two-bedroom apartment in Beijing, depending on its location, goes for between US$1.5 million and US$3 million.[130] In New York's Brooklyn, homes go for an average US$788,529; in Queens the average is US$452,304;[131] in Manhattan, it is US$1,312,814.[132]

A report by CKGSB Knowledge presented a typical story of a Chinese soldier and his wife whose income would qualify them as middle class. After purchasing a basic apartment in Beijing for US$500,000, they found they could no longer afford the mortgage repayments, so they rented out the apartment and moved into the husband's barracks.[133] Due to the lower incomes in China, some middle-class families cannot afford to live in the apartments they have purchased. The income to rent ratio for Beijing tends to be roughly 45.1/1, whereas in New York it is 12.5/1.[134]

Middle-class families in both the US and China pay taxes. In return, US families generally receive free primary and secondary education for their children, provided by government schools. Healthcare is expensive, but many have employers who provide health insurance. Also, their retirement will be partially funded by Social Security and partly by their employer in the form of a pension or a 401K plan. China's middle class spends heavily on their children's education. A 2001 news item states that many families spends a third of their income on education;[135] a much more recent report puts the proportion of total outlay on children's education at 55%.[136]

Inadequate government health insurance forces PRC citizens to not only pay for private insurance, but also utilize and pay for private hospitals. State retirement provisions are minimal.[137] To make matters worse, private health care and education are often more expensive in China than elsewhere, but the quality is low.[138]

All of these factors contribute to China's rising household debt, which now stands at 44% of GDP. It is no wonder that debt is growing, because consumer spending – which increased 10.55% between 2015 and 2016 – is expanding faster than GDP growth. From 2016 to 2017, consumer debt rose 30% and mortgages increased by 23%.[139] With higher expenses and spending growing faster than GDP, China's middle class is very likely to be considerably poorer than many previously believed.

Conclusion

Although there are different ways to define the middle class, China now appears to have the largest middle class in the world. In fact, there are now more middle-class people in China than the entire population of the US. While their average income is much lower than their Western counterparts, the economic power of the Chinese middle class is global in magnitude. Due to their sheer numbers, they impact everything from the market for luxury goods to greenhouse-gas emissions, making China no. 1 in both categories.

There has been a great deal of talk about China's economic miracle, about how China went from being one of the poorest countries in the world to one of the richest in such a short period of time. However, numerous economists have pointed out that China's economic rise is nothing new: China had the world's largest economy for 19 of the last 20 centuries.[140] The growth of China's middle class represents a rebalancing of the world economy, with the wealth of the East relative to the West reverting to pre-industrial levels.[141]

Outsiders and the Chinese themselves hope that China's middle class will save the world economy by increasing consumption and driving up global GDP. Westerners frequently equate increase prosperity in a country with demands for democracy or political reform. China experts have determined, however, that the Chinese middle class are very unlikely to challenge the political status quo.

The spending power of China's middle class is considerably less than that of the middle class in other countries. In addition to earning less money, they have to spend a higher percentage of their incomes on housing, primary and secondary education, and health care. Home mortgages and consumer debt are rising at a rate many times the rate of GDP growth.

CHAPTER 7:

CHINESE CURRENCY VALUATION

China's national currency is called the renminbi (RMB) or the yuan, with the FX symbol CNY (Chinese New Yuan). In the fourth quarter of 2015, the IMF announced it was adding the yuan to its basket of currencies called Special Drawing Rights (SDR). The yuan become the fifth currency in the basket, alongside the US dollar, the Japanese yen, the euro, and the British pound.[1]

China's inclusion in the SDR is a victory of prestige for the country, as the IMF stamp of approval signifies that the yuan is now an international currency convertible in the basket of global hard currencies. The inclusion is also a step toward China challenging the US domination of international exchange.[2]

The SDR system was has been in place since 1969, when it replaced its predecessor, the Bretton Woods system.

The Bretton Woods system

The Bretton Woods system was the prevalent monetary system used between the end of World War II and the early 1970s. The name refers to the site of the 1944 convention in Bretton Woods, in the US state of New Hampshire, where the

IMF and the World Bank were born.[3] These institutions were established to "monitor exchange rates and lend reserve currencies to nations with trade deficits." as well as support international free trade and fund postwar reconstruction.[4]

The original 44 member nations agreed to fix their exchange rates by pegging their currencies to the US dollar, which was then still backed by gold. At that time, US$1 equaled roughly 1/35 ounces of gold. "Nations also agreed to buy and sell US dollars to keep their currencies within 1% of the fixed rate."[5]

The Bretton Woods system was both historic and revolutionary as it was the first international monetary authority formed to help regulate exchange rates.[6] To participate in the Bretton Woods system, each member state would pay a prescribed amount of currency and gold or gold equivalent into the fund, depending on the relative size of the country's economy. Countries could then borrow from the basket as needed to increase their liquidity.[7]

Although the IMF was established as an international body, in practice, it was heavily dominated by the US, which had by far the largest economy. In addition to the fact that the US made the largest donation to the fund, the dollar was given another boost: Countries were allowed to use US dollars to substitute for up to 25% of their gold contribution. The reason why the US dollar could be substituted for gold was because the US was the only member nation still on a gold standard at that time. Voting rights of member nations were determined by the percentage of currency they had in the basket; this gave the US tremendous veto powers.[8]

Through the 1960s, the US dollars held in the IMF were the main source of liquidity of currencies around the world. Eventually, however, the US was no longer able to support the gold reserves required.[9] In 1971, President Richard M.

Nixon announced that the US was going off the gold standard.[10] This marked the end of the Bretton Woods system. Therefore, a new system was proposed. Liquidity would in future be backed by a basket of currencies, so the Special Drawing Rights (SDR) concept was created.[11]

The new system gave countries greater freedom as to how to regulate their exchange rates. In addition, "By 1973, most major world economies had allowed their currencies to float freely against the US dollar."[12] "Since the collapse of the Bretton Woods system, IMF members have been free to choose any form of exchange arrangement they wish (except pegging their currency to gold): allowing the currency to float freely, pegging it to another currency or a basket of currencies, adopting the currency of another country, participating in a currency bloc, or forming part of a monetary union."[13]

Special Drawing Rights (SDR)

"The Special Drawing Right (SDR) is an international reserve asset, created by the IMF in 1969 to supplement the existing official reserves of member countries."[14] Today, SDRs are used to calculate transactions with the IMF and some other international organizations. Members can exchange SDRs for hard currency, with their value based on a basket of currencies. Although the IMF has 185 member states, to date, only 144 have been given SDRs.[15]

Governments invest their reserves in foreign currencies such as the euro or US dollar by buying government bonds issued by those countries. The current SDR currencies account for 93% of the world's total foreign reserve investment, with the following breakdown: US dollar 64%, euro 20%, pound sterling 5%, and Japanese yen 4%.[16] In 2016, the Chinese yuan was given a 10.92% share.[17] This means that the yuan came in higher than both the pound sterling and the yen, and that the euro's share was decreased, while the US dollar's percentage remained largely unchanged.[18]

Implications for China's economy

Inclusion in the SDR currency group demonstrates the effectiveness of China's economic reforms and its successful integration into the global monetary system.[19] It also means that the IMF selection board felt that the yuan met the requirement of being freely tradeable, as evidenced by being used in international transactions and being freely traded on foreign currency exchanges.[20]

China lobbied long and hard for its currency to be accepted into the SDR, both as a point of prestige and as a way of challenging the US dollar as the main currency of international exchange.[21] The yuan's upgrading should encourage more countries to hold their money in Chinese currency, either as a means of diversifying their portfolios, or to challenge the dominance of the US dollar.[22] The dollar's position as the world's top currency is a symbol of US status and power, which China would like to challenge. Other countries also opposed to US economic dominance may move assets into yuan as well. Between 2010 and 2014, 37 central banks added yuan to their currency reserves.[23]

Not only central banks, but also individual and institutional investors – as well as fund managers around the world – may now diversify their portfolios by adding yuan and yuan-denominated assets, reflecting the currency's new status.[24] By some estimates, "US$1 trillion in global currency reserves will switch into Chinese assets" and as much as US$6.2 trillion in yuan-denominated bond offshore purchases.[25]

However, experts believe that until China "fully liberalizes capital controls or allow the currency to float freely" investors will be cautious.[26] Until then, the yuan cannot be considered a truly hard currency.

The yuan as a hard currency

To be considered a hard currency, a country's monetary units must be "widely accepted around the world as a form of payment for goods and services."[27] Additionally, it must be expected to remain relatively stable in the short run.[28] It must also be highly liquid in foreign exchange markets. The US dollar is an excellent example of a hard currency, as it is both the most traded currency and the world's preferred reserve currency. Around 70% of the all international trade is conducted using the US dollar.

Currently the world has seven other hard currencies; the next most traded currencies are (in descending order): the euro (EUR); Japanese yen (JPY); British pound (GBP); Swiss franc (CHF); Canadian dollar (CAD); Australian dollar (AUD) and South African rand (ZAR).[29] Conspicuously absent from the list is the Chinese yuan (CNY). Although the yuan is one of only five currencies to be included in the prestigious IMF Special Drawing Rights, it still does not qualify as a hard currency.

Other attributes of a hard currency are that it is issued by a politically stable government and by a country with a large GDP. China is certainly politically stable and its GDP is the world's second largest. However, the yuan fails to meet other metrics of usability and acceptance as a reserve currency by central banks.

The following example clearly demonstrates how little the yuan is used outside China: although the yuan is the fifth most used currency globally, it only accounts for 2.5% of all international payments tracked by SWIFT, as opposed to 43.3% for the US dollar, and 28.7% for the euro. Additionally, 70% of international transactions involving the yuan are between Hong Kong and the Chinese mainland. If Hong Kong is excluded, then the yuan only accounts for 0.8% of global SWIFT payments.[30]

The US dollar accounts for 61% of total foreign currency reserves, while the euro is in second place, accounting for 25%.[31] One reason why central banks are not holding significant quantities of yuan is that "Central bankers also tend to maintain currency reserves in proportion to their actual use."[32] As Chinese currency accounts for a mere 2.5% of global transactions, the percentage of yuan kept by most central banks is quite low.

The one continent where use of the yuan is expanding rapidly is Africa.[33] Zimbabwe is deep in the grips of a currency crisis stemming from hyperinflation. According to the Cato Journal, in November 2008, inflation reached a whopping 79.6 billion %. Zimbabwe has added the yuan to a basket of currencies now used in the country.[34] The addition of the yuan, tied to a loan agreement between China and Zimbabwe, does not seem to have changed the fact that the country still uses the US dollar as its primary currency.[35] Other African nations who also borrow from China have agreed to keep small proportions of their reserves in Chinese currency. For example, in 2014, the Central Bank of Nigeria agreed to keep 2–7% of its foreign reserves in yuan.[36]

Opposition to the yuan's selection for SDR

Selection for the SDR is based on "two criteria, the size of the country's exports and whether its currency is freely usable."[37] As recently as 2010, China's application to have the yuan accepted into the SDR was rejected. Although China met the export criteria, the IMF felt that the currency was not sufficiently freely usable.[38]

"Before 2009, very few international investors were interested in the country (China) because of the government's control over everything from investments to currency valuations."[40] Since then, however, Beijing has instituted further economic reforms in order to meet IMF requirements, such as: "including better access for foreigners to Chinese currency markets, more frequent debt issuance and expanded RMB trading hours."[41] The government has also further liberalized how the yuan is valued, and the central bank has doubled its allowable trading range.[42] The central bank also announced that the midpoint would be based on the previous day's closing.[43] These reforms are a clear indication that the value of the yuan will be more market driven, which is one of the criteria for inclusion in the SDR. As of November 2015, the Chinese government also began to allow direct exchange between the RMB and the Swiss franc,[44] thus further strengthening Beijing's view that the yuan is an international currency.

Despite recent reforms, some economists continue to highlight the degree of control China's government has over its currency.[45] "China's central bank still sets its daily exchange rate, allowing the RMB to fluctuate within a fixed range."[46]

The relationship between the yuan and the US dollar

Among China's foreign cash reserves are unprecedented quantities of US dollars and US government securities, and it uses these to regulate the value of its own currency. Because China is so dependent on foreign trade, Beijing does not want the value of its currency to climb too high and thus make Chinese exports expensive. For the last decade, as China's economy grew, its currency steadily gained in value.[47] As a result, the government frequently steps in to regulate the value of the currency, such as in August 2015 when the People's Bank of China (PBoC, China's central bank) chose to devalue the yuan by approximately 4.4% over a period of several days.[48] This was the largest devaluation since China's modern exchange rate system began in 1994.[49]

To prevent the yuan from sliding further, Chinese state-owned banks sold off US dollars, decreasing foreign-currency reserves. "'Apparently, the central bank does not want the yuan to run out of control,' said a trader at a European bank in Shanghai."[50] The PBoC used the dual techniques of selling US dollars and buying yuan on currency markets to stem capital outflows from China.[51]

Analysts were unsure how to interpret the move. Some believe that the significance goes far beyond a one-off correction. In a webcast, Tom Orlik, the chief Asia economist at Bloomberg Intelligence, said this shift "wasn't just about devaluation of the currency, this was also about a shift in the way China manages its exchange rate."[52]

Setting the yuan exchange rate

The value of the world's most actively traded currencies are generally expressed in terms of their value against the US dollar. The exchange rates for the major currencies are market-determined and based on the value of daily trading in the world's foreign exchange markets.[53]

The value of the yuan, however, is not strictly market determined. In effect, it is controlled by China's government. Prior to 2005, Beijing maintained an artificial peg rate which

131

required close monitoring of international currency markets. In order to maintain the rate, the government had to sell off foreign currency or buy up yuan. When the peg was removed in 2005, the yuan was immediately revalued, going from the peg rate of 8.27 to 8.11 against the US dollar.[54] Since then, the currency has been able to exist in a more market-driven scenario, with the value floating within a narrow range of 0.5% around the central parity published by the PBoC.[55] After the August 2015 devaluation, Beijing said it would allow further liberalization, thus allowing market forces to have a greater influence on the yuan's value.

The yuan is currently valued in this manner: Largely ignoring daily trading activity, a reference rate is set each morning by the PBoC.[56] Using this rate as a mid-point, the bank allows the yuan to move no more than 2% higher or lower.[57] The yuan is closely tied to the US dollar because China manages the exchange rate against the US dollar: when the US dollar rises against other major currencies, the yuan also rises.[58]

In recent years, the PBoC has progressively allowed the yuan to fluctuate more and more over the course of each trading day.[59] Part of the fallout of the August 2015 devaluation is that Beijing said they will permit more market information to influence the yuan's value. The fixing point, for example, will be influenced by the level at which the yuan closed in the previous day's trading.[60] This should allow the currency to rise or fall more rapidly.[61]

A drop in the yuan creates more competition for US exporters, as Chinese exports become cheaper. Some experts warn that opening the yuan to market forces could weaken the yuan, putting even more exchange-rate pressure on the US, as Chinese goods would continue to become cheaper.[62]

The currency conundrum

When setting the valuation of the yuan, Beijing is confronted with two conflicting goals. On the one hand, a cheaper yuan helps Chinese exporters by making Chinese products cheaper overseas. But, on the other hand, opening the yuan to market forces could weaken the currency, and lead to capital outflows. By artificially buoying the yuan, China can help curtail capital flight which would weaken the economy as a whole.[63] Other concerns for Beijing include avoiding a trade war with the US which could happen if the PBoC chose to dramatically weaken the yuan. This could also lead to other countries devaluing their currencies to keep their exports competitive with China-made products. The conflicting benefits of both a stronger and a weaker currency present China with a currency conundrum.

Impact on the yuan becoming an international currency

Some US Congressmen have accused China of artificially depressing the yuan to gain a competitive edge for their exports.[64] Consequently, the devaluation was called an unfair tactic by US lawmakers, who saw it as an attempt to save China's slowing economy.[65] The US has typically been one of the biggest critics of the PBoC's policy of keeping the yuan pegged to the US dollar, as a result of this policy is an artificially low yuan that gives Chinese exports a price advantage. Since the peg to the US dollar was removed in 2005, the yuan has steadily appreciated.[66]

Although it was tight government control that allowed the move to happen, some saw the devaluation as a sign that China is moving toward a more market-driven economy.[67] In addition, as China allows the exchange rate to be more influenced by the market, devaluation is an unavoidable consequence.[68] Adjusting the yuan exchange rate is not necessarily the first step in causing an exchange-rate war;[69] it may simply be the effect of normal market forces.

The IMF has commended China's devaluation of the yuan.[70] The IMF "told Beijing Friday it wants the yuan to float freely within three years, and applauded the Chinese central bank on this basis."[71] China's subsequent decision to allow a wider band of exchange rates for the yuan will increase the flexibility of the yuan, which is a necessary step if China wishes to integrate its currency into global financial markets.[72]

Almost in compliance with the wishes of the IMF, the Chinese side has vowed to allow the yuan exchange rate to be more market-influenced with the reference rate being based on the closing rate of the previous day's inter-bank foreign exchange markets.[73]

In addition to the prestige factor and increasing China's economic influence worldwide, being included in the SDR currencies could have some very real economic benefits for China. For example, it could make borrowing cheaper for Chinese businesses. It could also mean that raw materials and commodities can be purchased in yuan. But to get to that status, more of the world's central banks will have to hold reserves in yuan, and this would help to stabilize its value.[74]

Some saw the devaluation as fulfilling two goals with one move, as both a desperate act to control a falling economy, and a move that might help convince the IMF that the yuan will now be more closely controlled by market forces.[75]

Poor economic indicators prompting the devaluation

Just as there are many theories about the long-term impact of the devaluation, there are various theories as to why the PBoC decided to devalue the currency. Some analysts, such as Albert Edwards of Societe Generale, believe the answer is simple: The yuan had been overvalued for years and that needed to be corrected.[76] The fact that the yuan dropped after increased exposure to market factors suggests that it was in fact overvalued, which is not Beijing's fault.[77] While some saw the devaluation of the yuan as either proof of the Chinese economy's instability or the government's inability to control it, others see the move as not only justified, but as a positive indicator of Beijing's ability to transition to a market-driven economy.

Another theory is that the Chinese authorities were concerned about a slowing economy leading to lower demand for commodities.[78] In recent years, consumption growth in China has slowed, as has export growth.[79] "Exports fell by 8%, followed by a 6.6% drop in car sales and slower business investment in July. Factory output for the month of July fell short of the 6.6% projected growth, coming in instead at 6% year-on-year."[80] In addition to a general economic downturn, Chinese stocks have dropped significantly over the last several months, with the Shanghai index losing 32% of its value.[81] This forced the government to act to stabilize the economy, and a currency devaluation is one response.[82] Currency devaluation is a sign that the government is concerned about slowing growth rate.[83]

Capital outflow is another worrying sign of a softening Chinese economy. China has seen an outflow of US$500 billion in foreign currency reserves.[84] These outflows of foreign capital reserves have resulted in the spot rate for the yuan trading weaker than the rate set by the PBoC.[85] One of the factors contributing to foreign currency outflows has been the bank selling US dollars to prop up the yuan.[86]

A weak property market combined with lower domestic demand and exports have caused the Chinese economy to register growth of only 7%, the lowest in six years. To counter the economic slowdown, the government is planning to offer tax breaks and interest rate cuts to companies.[87] Some foreign analysts do not believe the government's reduced growth numbers, believing that the truth is even more grim. "Some economists believe China's economy is already growing only half as fast as official data shows, or even less."[88]

While China closely monitors and controls the yuan's exchange rate to the US dollar, it does not as tightly control the yuan against other currencies such as the euro. A rising yuan, against the US dollar has caused China's exports to the EU to become more expensive, and consequently fall by 12% compared to a year ago.[89]

Since Deng Xiaoping launched the reform process, many in the West have held some type of faith in Beijing's ability to manage the complexities of a fast growing, modern economy, in terms of currency, debt, interest, and other aspects of a market-driven economy.[90] But what many outsiders forget, and what is demonstrated by the drop in value of the yuan, is that now the government has not even a fraction of the control over the economy it did back when China had a "command economy."[91]

Those who favor free markets in China have been calling for less government intervention, but many of those same voices will now be calling for greater government control. The question is, do these reformist voices call for free-markets in China only when it is good for their own bottom lines, but not for China's?[92] Rather than seeing the devaluation of the yuan as grounds to panic or criticize, one could also see the yuan devaluation as a perfectly reasonable measure for a government to take, given the current economic climate. The devaluation served to help grow the economy by increasing exports.[93]

"William Dudley, head of the New York Federal Reserve, also said an adjustment to the yuan was probably appropriate if the Chinese economy was weaker than the authorities had expected."[94] Economic data would suggest that the PRC economy has indeed been weaker than expected, in spite of government spending on infrastructure projects.[95] In fact, a 24.1% increase in fiscal expenditure was not enough to pull the economy out of its downturn.[96] State-owned banks were also being pressured to lend money to companies for investment in factories.[97]

Impact of the yuan devaluation in China and Hong Kong

The effects of a currency devaluation in a country the size of China were immediately felt throughout the world.

For China, a drop in the yuan means an increase in the cost of servicing foreign debt, calculated in US dollars.[98] The manufacturing sector would also be impacted by the higher cost of raw materials. Commodities, which are priced in US dollars, immediately became more expensive for Chinese manufacturers, who are some of the world's largest importers of oil, copper, and coal.[99] In fact, Chinese demand for raw materials is so significant that when the economy first began slowing down, in summer 2014, world oil prices dropped significantly, from US$110 per barrel to US$50. Other commodities, such as nickel, copper, and aluminum dropped to lows not seen since 2009.[100]

137

Chinese airline stocks immediately dropped as investors estimated the effect higher fuel prices would have on the airlines' profit margins.[101] Chinese exports suddenly became cheaper for international consumers. However, those exported products are now being made with more expensive commodities, a reality that negatively impacts Chinese manufacturers.[102] While a drop in the yuan will make Chinese products more competitive overseas, Bloomberg estimates that the higher cost of commodities and raw materials will have a net negative impact on China's economy.[103]

One industry hit particularly hard by the devaluation has been the automotive industry, which is heavily dependent on imported metals. Less than 5% of vehicles manufactured in China are sold overseas. Therefore, the less expensive yuan does not help gain market share abroad. Meanwhile, a slowing economy combined with higher raw material costs are hurting domestic sales. Auto sales in China experienced the first year-over-year drop in more than six years.[104] A weaker yuan should depress auto sales even further.

Back in 2000, it was predicted that a devaluation of the yuan could have an impact on the Hong Kong dollar. Now that the yuan has dropped, it is unclear if the fall was dramatic enough to impact the Hong Kong dollar.[105] Nonetheless, the effects will be felt in certain parts of Hong Kong's economy; the retail sector could suffer if Chinese tourists do less shopping in the special administrative region. If retailers begin earning less, landlords may be forced to reduce rents.[106] Hong Kong money changers and banks are benefitting from the yuan depreciation, however, as Chinese from the mainland scramble to move their cash out of the country. Hong Kong has always been a gateway for cash from China to move abroad.[107]

Impact on the US

US stocks fell, as did prices for commodities which China imports in large quantities, such as copper and oil. There was much speculation that the yuan devaluation was a sign that China's economy had slowed and that demand for raw materials would remain low.[108] The US dollar has been strong recently, making US exports less attractive. A falling yuan makes US dollar-priced products even more expensive, which could result in decreased demand for American goods. At the same time, Chinese products have become even cheaper in the US, perhaps negatively impacting domestic sales of US products. "Some analysts worry that China's devaluation may be exporting deflation around the world."[109] Many reports used the term "currency war," as there were fears that countries would begin devaluing their own currencies to compete with China. At the same time, manufacturers in other countries may cut prices for goods sold overseas. Falling incomes, on top of cheaper goods from China, could drive prices down further and result in deflation.

The US dollar has already risen against the currencies of many of its trading partners, such as Europe and Japan, lifting the price of US goods overseas; the drop in the yuan will further exacerbate this problem. However, many US manufacturers maintain factories and suppliers across Europe and in emerging markets as a hedge.[110]

In short, there is evidence both in favor of and against the yuan devaluation having a strong impact on the American economy. Of course, fears still remain that this cut may be the first of many. A steadily dropping yuan could make many of the negative outcomes discussed above become reality.

Impact on the UK and Australia

Stock exchanges across both Asia and Europe suffered losses of about 1%, with the London FTSE 100 dropping almost 2% at one point, with a net loss of 1.4%.[111] The slowdown in China is expected to negatively impact mining companies, and to put further pressure on British stock indexes.[112] Makers of luxury goods, as well as British retailers dependent on Chinese consumers, have been hard hit, as a drop in the yuan made luxury imports more expensive. Shares in Burberry, which has 65 sales outlets in China, fell 4.4%.[113]

China is a large commodity importer and Australia's no. 1 trade partner. A weaker yuan makes raw materials from Australia more expensive, which may negatively impact Australia in the form of reduced demand.[114] Immediately after the yuan devaluation the Australian dollar plunged to a six-year low.[115] Analysts at Credit Suisse consider the yuan to be 5–10% overvalued, and consequently predicted additional devaluation, which will put further pressure on the Australian dollar, as well as US and Japanese exports.[116] Declining stock exchanges throughout Asia could also affect Australia, as many of the nations hit are among Australia's major trade partners.[117] Analysts in Australia also believe that a weaker yuan will result in decreased demand for raw materials, and this will drive commodities prices down even further.[118]

Impact on Southeast Asia

While some experts believe that the yuan's devaluation will have very little net impact on the US, they believe it may have a great impact on other countries that do a lot of trade with China. The devaluation may force countries such as Australia,

Malaysia and South Korea to devalue their currency as well. While the drop impacted those currencies immediately, a larger drop in the yuan and the consequent impact had already been predicted by some experts, prior to August 2015. "An analysis by Morgan Stanley in March predicted that a 15% drop in the yuan, much larger than today's move, would cause a 5–7% drop in other Asian currencies."[119] This multiplier effect, if true, could be very worrying, particularly if the PBoC allows the yuan to drop further.

Immediately after the yuan devaluation, commodities indexes declined to 2003 levels. "Broad indexes of Asian stocks, excluding the Japan market, fell 2%, plunging to a two-year low."[120]

Other Asian currencies were also impacted. The Vietnamese dong was hit especially hard. Vietnam, like China, is moving from a centrally-planned economy to a more market-driven economy. This transition is reflected in the handling of exchange rates: the exchange rate for the dong is officially considered a managed floating rate, but is also similar to a crawling peg.[121] Vietnam also widened the exchange band for the dong. "Vietnam's move means 'a currency war started almost immediately,' said Marshall Gittler, head of Global FX Strategy at IronFX, based in Cyprus."[122]

Two of Southeast Asia's most vulnerable currencies are the Malaysian ringgit and Indonesian rupiah, both of which dropped significantly due to the devaluation.[123] In fact, the Malaysian ringgit dropped by 4.2% within days of the yuan's fall, hitting its lowest point since 2009, (Patterson). At the same time, the rupiah hit a 17-year low. The Australian and New Zealand dollars fell to six-year lows.[124] Other Southeast Asian currencies, such as the Thai baht, hit lows not seen in years.[125]

Impact on India

Some experts believe that India is largely insulated from downturns in the Asian markets and that India's bull market will continue. "'The rupee is relatively less impacted in Asia as India is less export dependent," said Sue Trinh, head of Asia foreign exchange strategy at RBC in Hong Kong. "A weaker yuan is arguably beneficial for India."[126] But contrary to bullish predictions for India's stock market, the currency was also hit hard, dropping by one rupee to the US dollar.[127] Indian manufacturers, particularly in the textile and chemicals sectors, will have trouble competing with a cheaper yuan.[128] A further drop in the yuan would most likely result in cheaper Chinese exports to India,[129] mainly in the sectors of iron and steel, bulk drugs, and chemicals.[130]

India has long run a trade deficit with China. "India's trade deficit with China has almost doubled from US$25 billion in 2008–09 to US$50 billion in 2014–15." China accounts for 35% of India's total trade deficit.[131] A cheaper yuan will tip these numbers further in China's favor. Indian importers of Chinese goods may derive a slight benefit from a cheaper yuan. India imports all sorts of cheap products from China, everything from shoes to electronics; because of the yuan's devaluation, these imports just became a little cheaper.[132] On the other hand, Indian textile manufacturers and chemical producers will now have a harder time competing with Chinese manufacturers.[133] India's exports have been steadily decreasing; if they decrease further because of the yuan's drop, it could worsen India's trade balance.[134]

Impact on Africa and Brazil

The yuan drop was keenly felt in Africa. China is not only many African countries no. 1 trade partner, but some African nations have even added the yuan to their foreign exchange systems.[135] "In 2011, the Nigerian Central Bank pledged to store between 5%-10% of its foreign reserves in yuan, alongside US dollars and euros."[136] Nigeria and some other African countries hoped the yuan would protect their local currencies from volatility in the petroleum sector.[137] Africa, like Australia, exports commodities to China which will now be more expensive for Chinese manufacturers. This could have a long-term impact on African currencies.[138]

China is Brazil's main trading partner. Normally, a drop in the yuan would be devastating for Brazil, but because Brazil's economy had already fallen to lows not seen in 20 years, the impact from the drop in the yuan was less significant.[139]

China's new petro yuan

According to some media, China's 2018 introduction of the petro yuan marked the beginning of the end of the US dollar as a key currency. "Death of US dollar? China launches petro yuan to challenge greenback's dominance,"[140] ran a headline in RT (formerly Russia Today) on March 26, 2018. Headlines in other media read "China Prepares Death Blow To The Dollar"[141] and "Washington May Be Speeding Up The Death Of The Dollar With Increased Sanctions On Iran."[142] These alarmist headlines all referred to China's launch of the petro yuan and the impact that some doomsayers predict this will have on the US dollar.

The petro yuan is designed to provide an alternative to the petro dollar. In loose terms, the petro dollar refers to oil revenue denoted in dollars. Since the 1970s, oil has been priced in US dollars.[143] Commodities in general are usually priced in US dollars so prices can remain stable and both buyers and sellers can be protected from exchange-rate risks.

Much of the power and internationalization of the US dollar comes from the fact that commodities – oil being perhaps the most important – are priced in US dollars. Countries which are not US allies resent having to use the dollar to conduct international business, and have tried to undermine the dollar's dominance. In 2000, Iraq, which was under an embargo, received permission from the UN to accept oil payments in euros rather than US dollars.[144] At that time, the UN estimated that switching over to the euro would cost Iraq US$270 million because purchasers would pay US$0.10 less per barrel to compensate for the difficulty of dealing with euros rather than dollars. This loss in revenue was something Iraqi officials were willing to accept, calling the dollar "the currency of an 'enemy state.'"[145] Similarly, Libya's Muammar Gaddafi once unveiled a plan for a pan-African "gold dinar," but it never took off.[146]

Since 2012, Iran (China's largest supplier of oil) has been accepting yuan in exchange for oil, because US sanctions against Tehran have made it difficult for Iran to transact business in dollars.[147] As of 2016, Iran is demanding euros from its other customers, saying that it wants to free itself from the control of the US dollar.[148] The US decision to back out of the Iran nuclear agreement in 2018 further tightened restrictions on Iran. Anticipating this move, Tehran declared it would replace the US dollar with the euro in official financial reporting. Iran has also conducted the first ever swap of the Iranian rial and Turkish lira.[149] As China is Iran's no. 1 customer, and now that Beijing is urging SOEs to value oil imports in yuan, it is possible that Iran and China may begin using the yuan as a medium of exchange.

In 2017, China established a means of circumventing dollars in its dealings with Russia by creating a payment-versus-payment (PVP) system to facilitate transactions involving the Chinese yuan and the Russian ruble.[150] China has stated that it would like to utilize PVP systems (which allows for the clearance of two currencies at the same time) for other currencies along the Belt and Road Initiative (BRI).[151] "Russia, Iraq, Indonesia, and other countries, many of which play a vital role in the BRI, have already engaged in non-dollar trades."[152]

In 2018, the US suspended US$900 million in security aid to Pakistan.[153] Pakistan's central bank approved the Chinese yuan for use in trade with China, and to allow the yuan to replace the dollar in projects associated with the China-Pakistan Economic Corridor (CPEC), which is expected to cost US$50 billion.[154]

China's latest move away from the dollar and toward the internationalization of the yuan, was announcing the launch of the petro yuan in 2017. Apart from strengthening the yuan, China, as the world's largest importer of oil, wants to be able to price oil in yuan.[155] To this end, China has established yuan-denominated oil futures which "will be fully convertible into gold on the Shanghai and Hong Kong foreign exchange markets."[156]

BRICS countries have expressed their support for the petro yuan at their 2017 conference in Xiamen. Venezuela has also said it supports the petro yuan.[157] Other countries suffering under US sanctions include Russia and Venezuela; both would like to stop using the US dollar, and both are moving closer to China in both the political and the economic sense.[158]

The world beyond Beijing's allies has been skeptical about the yuan as an international currency, because of what is seen as heavy-handed government intervention in the currency's value. According to CNBC: "The yuan is not yet fully convertible, it's fixed daily, prone to intervention and subject to capital controls."[159] Another issue is that a benchmark would have to be established by which to price oil. Current dollar-denominated benchmarks including the West Texas Intermediate and Brent, are widely accepted by both sellers and purchasers. There are concerns that a yuan benchmark would be controlled by Beijing, rather than the market. Many experts believe Beijing may force SOEs to conduct transaction in yuan, but that these may be the only companies which do so.[160]

Some have called China's petro yuan an attempt to destroy the dollar. This seems unlikely, as China still holds over US$1 trillion in foreign currency reserves, and would not want to see it devalued.[161] Another point is that the petro yuan actually poses very little, if any threat to US currency hegemony. Because the US dollar is easily exchangeable, has a track record of nearly a century, and is supported by US taxpayers, it remains the reserve currency of choice for foreign governments as well as the currency of choice for international business transactions.[162] The existence of petro yuan oil futures do not mean that oil producers are agreeing to accept yuan as payment. It simply means transactions will be priced in yuan, but payment will probably still be made in dollars.[163]

CHAPTER 8:

SHADOW BANKING

When people hear the term "shadow banking," they think it refers to something mysterious or nefarious. In reality shadow banking simply means lending and other financial activities conducted outside the scope of banking regulations, often by non-banks. Shadow banking activities in China include off-the-balance- sheet transactions by such entities as insurance companies. Because the PRC's state-owned banks tend to favor loans to large SOEs, shadow banking is an important source of funds for small SOEs and private enterprises. For investors, shadow banking offers higher interest rates but at higher risk. Generally, there is no depositor's insurance. For borrowers, shadow banking requires a lower degree of creditworthiness. The institutions themselves exist outside of the banking system, so they are not subject to loan-to-deposit (LTD) ratios; this means they can lend a greater proportion of their deposits.[1]

China's shadow banking industry was estimated to be worth US$15 trillion in 2018.[2] In Western countries, shadow banking activities are largely carried out by institutions other than banks and in particular institutions separate from the government. In China, however, shadow banking has historically been dominated by state-owned banks which operate in unregulated areas of shadow banking. In 2014, it was estimated only 12% of total banking capital was private money.[3]

In 2015, Brookings Institution published a report outlining types of shadow banking products and arrangements in China, including:[4]

Loans and leases made by trust companies.

Trust loans and entrusted loans made to corporations account for the largest proportion of shadow credit to end borrowers.[5] Trust products total about US$3.8 trillion in credit provided to debt-ridden property developers and local governments, who lack good credit and cannot obtain bank loans.[6]

Bankers' acceptances is a form of short-term credit generally lasting a few months, which pay a fixed amount at maturity. It is often used for non-financial transactions, such as purchasing goods.

Microfinance companies are separately licensed financial institutions authorized to make extremely small loans, usually to small or rural borrowers.

Financial leasing encompasses forms of leasing which are not on a bank or trust company's balance sheet.

Guarantees provided by guarantee companies in China provide financial guarantees for financial transactions, including for shadow banking.

Pawn shops and various unofficial lenders which make small collateralized loans to households and businesses.

Trust Beneficiary Rights (TBRs) are a type of derivative, whereby the investor receives a stated proportion of the returns accruing to a trust.

Wealth management products are a debt obligation or pool of obligations which provide a return based on the success of the underlying projects being funded. WMPs can be close-ended (with a finite life span) or open-ended, where investors can withdraw their money at any time. Closed-end products are the more common of the two, accounting for around 57% of the total in mid-2016.[7]

Inter-bank market activities. Under this arrangement both banks and corporations can loan money to banks, in a deposit like agreement.[8]

Peer-to-peer (P2P). Small investors invest their money with a P2P firm who then makes small loans to private borrowers at high rates of interest.[9] Some professional P2P platforms have been established such as Alibaba's Ant Financial and Tencent, which specialize in making loans to small and medium-size enterprises. Although not fully licensed as banks, these firms are still subject to some government restrictions, such as borrowing limits for "individuals (a maximum of 200,000 yuan) and institutions (a maximum of 5 million yuan)."[10]

Informal credit by small private lenders. This is another type of shadow banking activity which is difficult to quantify.[11]

Large corporations often participate in shadow banking as lenders. Many firms have excess savings which they can lend through the shadow banking system to other firms. Large SOEs sometimes receive credit from banks at low interest rates and use shadow banking to loan the money to their subsidiaries.

One of the primary reasons for the borrowers to engage in shadow banking is because they lack creditworthiness to follow more traditional avenues of obtaining loans. By definition, this makes the loans more risky. Shadow-banking investment funds pool investments from multiple investors which is then lent to companies with low credit ratings. If the companies go bankrupt or fail to make payments, the investors could lose their investment, so the default risk is quite high.[12] Investors, however, continue to invest under the impression that these products, particularly those sold through banks, are guaranteed.

Having unregulated products sold through banks is confusing enough but the legality becomes even more murky when one considers that banks are often the borrowers in these transactions. Banks will borrow through shadow banking products to obtain more capital they can lend out at a higher rate of interest. By obtaining capital in this way, banks can skirt LTD ratio requirements. They can also loan to risky, overinflated sectors, such as the real estate, property development, or mining industries. The loans can be processed through a complex chain of intermediaries such as trusts, securities companies, other banks and asset managers, in order to obscure the true nature of the loans. The bank can then purchase the product from one of these intermediaries and pay the interest to the bank itself. In this case, the product can be carried on the books as an investment, rather than a liability. A multiplier effect drives up the profitability of these investments because 100% of the principle could be invested, as there are no LTD ratio requirements. Normally, if the bank had X amount of money on deposit, they would only be permitted to lend 80% or 90% of it, holding the remainder to meet LTD ratios. This convoluted chain of purchases and resales of debt allows the bank to invest 100% of the money, thus earning a higher return.[13]

While shadow banking has existed for decades in China, it did not play as significant of a role as it does today until the 2011 credit crunch. Since then, it has become an important source of liquidity and financing.[14] Shadow banking assets doubled after 2011, and peaked in 2016 at 82% of GDP.[15] Since 2016, the total volume of the industry has decreased, but wealth management products (WMPs) and trust products have continued to grow.[16] Due to government regulations, 75% of WMPs must be invested in traditional debt instruments, including bonds, money market instruments, and bank deposits. WMPs allow private investors to gain access to the bond market, which would normally be prohibited under government regulations.[17] As a result, WMPs have become one of the primary sources of funding for bond issues, In 2016, WMPs accounted for roughly 25% of all funding.[18]

As the result of a government crackdown, and more stringent enforcement of the rules, shadow banking has become more complex, in order to avoid non-performing loan provisions, or LTD ratio ceilings.[19] By reclassifying shadow banking products as investments, rather than loans, a bank can reduce its apparent risk exposure, at least on paper. The shadow banking products and the chain of transfers and exchanges allows the bank to participate in the success or profit derived from the product while transferring the risk to another entity such as a trust company, or the bank's own wealth management arm.[20] This allows banks to demonstrate lower credit exposure as well as lower non-performing loan percentages.[21]

Banks are the primary players in shadow banking, participating directly or indirectly in shadow banking activities. They may, for example, act as intermediaries to facilitate loans between two non-financial institutions which would be illegal under Chinese law. The bank facilitating the transaction charges a handling fee to collect the principle and interest. It may or may not accept credit risk in the process.[22]

The debt and shadow-banking threat

The internet has driven down the costs of lending, and helped to fuel an increase in the use of credit in general. The outgoing governor of the People's Bank of China (PBoC), Zhou Xiaochuan, warned about the large amount of debt being used in China, stating that leverage is the reason for macro-financial vulnerability. At the end of 2016, China's leverage ratio was 247% of GDP, while corporate leveraging stood at 165% of GDP.[23] As financial leverage increases in China, so does the percentage of non-performing loans. This includes the liabilities of SOEs which equal 120% of GDP.[24]

Wealth management products are a particularly worrying area of debt. WMPs are short-term investments which mature in three to six months, at which point the money must be returned to the investor. The problem, however, is that the products are used to finance longer-term projects in real estate and mining which may take over a year to come due. This means the institution must sell more products and take in more cash in the interim in order to make payments to existing investors. Consequently, those responsible for selling WMPs are under tremendous pressure to find investors. They receive small salaries and large commissions, and are generally expected to sell over US$15 million per year. They are motivated by self-interest, and the banks and institutions which employee them need these products moved in order to bring in much-needed cash.[25]

Historically, defaults in the trust industry have been low because borrowers could count on issuing new debt to pay old debts. But now, as the government cracks down, borrowers are less likely to be able to rely on new issues to pay off the old ones.[26] By early 2018, at least two such products had been forced to delay payments. This was the result of markets tightening, making it difficult to refinance maturing issues with new ones. Zhongrong International Trust Co. was meant to pay US$141 million, which it finally paid, but several days later than promised.[27] One of the doomsday scenarios that could harm China's future is that if too many WMPs go bust, new investors will stop putting money in, creating a chain reaction, whereby the banks will lack money to pay off old investors. The big question is whether the government would, or even should, step in with a bailout, and if that bailout should go to the investors or to the banks.

The government has been strengthening laws and cracking down on shadow banking. Since December 2017, the China Banking Regulatory Commission has been discouraging banks from referring their clients to invest in trust products, which accounted for about 66% of total trust assets.[28] As a result, there has been a noticeable decrease in the number of trust products offered. So far in 2018, only 229 new products have been issued, versus 666 in the same period last year.[29]

In November 2017, Beijing set up the Financial Stability and Development Committee, to police the restrictions and tighten loopholes that allow risky lending. "Days later, the People's Bank of China and financial regulators jointly issued new draft rules to govern the wealth management industry."[30]

Tighter government regulations on shadow banking has led to the industry finding creative way to circumvent restrictions. One example would be the use of negotiable certificates of deposit, a kind of debt instrument which can be carried as equity on the balance sheet.[31]

Experts agree that China has a debt problem and that shadow banking is potentially dangerous. But a decrease in shadow banking does not necessarily mean things are improving, as the decrease in shadow banking has been accompanied by an increase in traditional debt.[32] In January 2018, banks issued US$458.3 billion of new loans.[33]

China's debt will be analyzed in the next chapter.

CHAPTER 9:

PUBLIC DEBT

Bloomberg estimated that at the close of 2017, China's outstanding debt amounted to 266% of GDP.[1] Largely due to increasing debt, in May 2017, Moody's downgraded China's government's credit rating to A1 from Aa3.[2] One of the country's largest asset management firms, China Huarong Asset Management, estimated that the total volume of non-performing loans at China's banks could reach US$476 billion by 2020.[3]

China, with the world's largest foreign currency reserves, is a country where both the people and the government are famous for being prodigious savers. The question then arising is: Just how did China accumulate so much debt?

The growth of debt stems from one of the same sources as the growth of non-performing loans – namely the vast infrastructure projects undertaken by the government in order to stimulate the economy. Using loans to finance large infrastructure projects helped keep China's GDP growth between 9.5% and 10.5% between 2008 and 2011, and has kept GDP growth in the black ever since. Non-performing loans have not been repaid, and interest payments have not been made; many fear those loans never will be paid back. Many experts claim that no one actually knows the total volume of China's non-performing loans because official figures focus mostly on banks; debt held within the shadow banking system is difficult to quantify. In some instances, conventional banks have even sold their non-performing loans to shadow-banking institutions to get them off the balance sheet.[4]

Another major source of debt in China is household borrowing, which has grown steadily over the past 10 years. Private debt in the PRC has grown to US$6.7 trillion, or 50% of GDP.[5]

Part of the reason for swelling consumer debt is that the government has been encouraging consumerism as a way of buoying the GDP. Another reason is that the younger generation seems more willing to increase their debt so they can buy more. Soaring house prices are also to blame; home buyers are forced to use a larger percentage of their income to service their mortgages, and so have to use credit to finance the rest of their consumption.[6]

Stunningly rapid real-estate appreciation is making it very difficult for many Chinese to buy a home. In Beijing and Shanghai, housing prices have increased by 25% over the past two years. By the end of 2017, home mortgages stood at more than US$3.6 trillion, representing the largest proportion of household loans.[7] The second largest component, accounting for 22% are operating loans, are given to small businesses. Consumption lending, including credit cards and auto loans, accounted for 19%. Other forms of household credit, including margin lending, peer-to-peer loans and micro-lending, are difficult to quantify, but most likely also account for a significant proportion of the indebtedness of the average household in the PRC.[8]

Until now, the mortgage market has helped the economy grow, not only through home sales, but also through increased expenditure on electrical appliances, home furnishings, and other items. More recently, however, there are concerns that the increasing cost of mortgage payments may force homeowners to spend less in other areas, and this will slow down the country's economic growth. It may also cause Chinese consumers to use credit to make other purchases, thus driving up total indebtedness. Consequently, some sources claim the household debt-to-disposable income ratio has climbed to 82%.[9] Other estimates have Chinese household debt at as much as 106% of disposable income.[10] This debt burden leaves the typical homeowner extremely vulnerable to increases in interest rates or inflation.

The property loan-to-value ratio in China has reached 50%, the same level as in the US before the global financial crisis. This means that both borrowers and banks are depending on home prices remaining high. Should prices come down, both banks and individuals would see their wealth wiped out. Another ratio, the mortgage instalment to monthly income ratio, has reached 67%. Any ratio above 50% is generally considered a warning sign.[11]

US household debt is about 105% of disposable income, so whether one takes the Chinese figure of 85% or 106%, China is at least approaching, if not exceeding, American levels of household debt. A significant difference between the two countries, however, is that US household debt has not grown appreciably for several years, whereas China's is rising steadily. Although Chinese households have seen their income increase by an impressive 12% in an average year, their indebtedness has increased by an alarming 23% per annum.[12] The trend appears to be continuing, as by the end of January 2018, China's households had already borrowed a total of US$143 billion.[13]

Meanwhile, central government debt continues to grow. Beijing has relied on infrastructure investment to drive the economy, and each year has created new debt to cover some of the previous year's expenditure. Currently, infrastructure investment contributes 45% to GDP. Rather than decreasing this amount, China's planned US$100 billion investment in the Silk Road Fund, in addition to other pledges used to finance the US$1 trillion Belt and Road Initiative (BRI) could cause a major increase in debt. Economists have already stated their belief that BRI investments will not be profitable and that they will eventually just serve to increase the percentage of non-performing loans.[14]

China's non-performing real estate loans have been surging in 2018 and are expected to reach US$13.59 billion by the end of the year.[15] The non-performing loan ratio at Chinese commercial banks at the close of 2017 was 1.74%, totaling US$264 billion.[16] This data has been questioned, however, after the China Banking Regulatory Commission discovered fake reporting by some local lenders. The commission found that Shanghai Pudong Development Bank Co. illegally lent US$12 billion over many years to 1,493 shell companies so they could take over bad loans made by its Chengdu branch, which then reported zero bad loans.[17]

The China Development Press under the State Council Development Research Center describes several types of chicanery in relation to the reporting of non-performing loans. Banks have been known to dispose of bad loans as a way of passing on operational losses, as well as to cover up illegal activities. In other instances, banks have colluded with asset management companies in order to set up fake deals which disguised non-performing loans made to SOEs. Bad loans are sometimes sold in illegal transactions involving insider trading and related parties. Additionally, the value of non-performing assets is often set arbitrarily. The assets are then sold through fake auctions, with phantom bidding, designed to distort the market.[18]

In a recent report, the Bank of International Settlement

named China as one of the countries at greatest risk of facing a banking crisis. Other economists, such as Shen Jianguang, chief Asia economist at Mizuho Securities Asia Ltd. in Hong Kong, estimates that while China's debt is high, the peak has already passed, and that a combination of higher corporate profits and government intervention should help to reduce it in the future. One positive indicator is that interbank lending slowed in 2017, reducing the growth of the M2 broad money supply to a low not seen since 1996. Curbing debt, however, is expected to lead to a reduction in the construction of housing, bridges, tunnels, and other infrastructure.[19]

One reason why companies, consumers and even local governments are willing to amass large amounts of debt is their belief that the central government will bail them out.[20] The era of central-government bailouts may be over, however. President Xi Jinping told Xinhua that he will prioritize those problems which threaten economic stability. He has referred to the reduction of debt as a "critical battle" and has asked local governments and companies – both POEs and SOEs – to accelerate their plans to reduce debt. The rules on debt creation and credit ratings for local government financing vehicles (LGFVs) have been tightened and some of these may be permitted to default on their existing debt. Meanwhile, total debts of SOEs had reached US$17 trillion as of the end of February 2018.[21]

Another wrinkle in the China debt problem is the possibility of a trade war with the United States. Nearly 20% of China's exports go to the US and exports are still fundamental to the country's economic growth. The IMF has warned that a trade war could decrease China's GDP growth; this would in turn increase its debt as a percentage of GDP.[22]

US-China trade difficulties will be explored in greater detail in the final chapter of this book.

CHAPTER 10:

THE BELT AND ROAD INITIATIVE AND CPEC

China's New Silk Road Project – also called the Belt and Road Initiative (BRI) and formerly known as One Belt One Road (OBOR) – was launched in 2013 by President Xi Jinping and Premier Li Keqiang.[1] BRI is composed of two components: the "Silk Road Economic Belt" and the "21st Century Maritime Silk Road." The project is a major components of Xi's sweeping reforms, and is clearly meant to be his greatest legacy.[2]

The New Silk Road is intended to strengthen ties and increase economic exchanges between Europe and China; trade has already grown 168% over the last ten years.[3] Other goals include: strengthening policy communication; increasing economic and monetary cooperation; eliminating trade barriers; and improving transportation from the Pacific Ocean to the Baltic Sea, from Central Asia to the Indian Ocean, and eventually from East Asia to West Asia and South Asia.[4]

Chinese media predict that BRI will eventually involve two-thirds of the world's population and account for one-third of global GDP.[5]

Development of BRI

Xi first announced his five-point proposal for the BRI, which he then referred to as the "New Silk Road Economic Belt," during a 2013 speech in Astana, Kazakhstan, and reiterated them during a Shanghai Cooperation Organization (SCO) summit.[6] The BRI is a continuation of Deng Xiaoping Theory, a series of economic reforms which began in the late 1970s and which emerged in the form of the Shenzhen Special Economic Area. Reforms were continued during Jiang Zemin's term in office as part of his 2002 "going out" strategy. The BRI can be seen as the pinnacle of "going out," as China seeks to become a world economic power.[7]

Over the last two decades, as its foreign trade has grown, China has expanded its regional economic and political participation. In Southeast Asia, for example, China is already a member of ASEAN+3, a trade group that includes the Association of Southeast Asian Nations (ASEAN) as well as China, South Korea, and Japan.[8] In Europe, China became a shareholder of the European Development Bank in order to gain entry into the region and further assist its projects in Central Asia, particularly in Kazakhstan.[9] China is also a member of the New Development Bank, formerly referred to as the BRICS Development Bank, an organization whose membership comprises Brazil, Russia, India, China and South Africa.

The New Silk Road will begin in China's northwestern territory of Xinjiang, also called the Uyghur Autonomous Region. Xinjiang borders the Central Asian countries of Kazakhstan, Kyrgyzstan, and Tajikistan, and China hopes to benefit from cultural similarities between China's Uyghur population and the population of Central Asia, most of whom share the religion of Islam and speak related Turkic languages.

The New Silk Road will allow China to expand its economic influence over these countries, which were formerly dominated by Russia. Kazakhstan, Kyrgyzstan, and Tajikistan, as well as Russia, are already members of the SCO.

Xi's "China dream" of the "great rejuvenation of the nation" is meant to bring economic development to Xinjiang, China's gateway to Central Asia. It is hoped that greater prosperity will help prevent radicalization of China's Muslim minority. An additional benefit of these overland routes through the Central Asian nations is that they will allow China to bypass Russian territory, a country with whom China's relationship is unstable.[10]

After Central Asia, the westward route is planned to run through Iran, Iraq, Syria, Turkey, then Bulgaria and Romania, linking eventually with Czechia, Germany, the Netherlands, and Italy.[11] The overland route is one means of decreasing US control of international trade, bypassing the US Navy and its dominance of the high seas.[12]

The overland routes will mainly use rail connections. Currently there are only three rail links between China and Europe: One ends in Germany, another terminates in Poland, while the third is the experimental Madrid-Yiwu route. Construction of a fourth route – a high-speed railway connecting Beijing and Moscow – has been announced.[13]

The BRI will also have multiple maritime routes, many of which are already in use.[14] The maritime segments of the New Silk Road will give the PRC's navy access to both the Black and Mediterranean seas, which are significant routes for energy transportation.[15] Infrastructure investment in Africa has already begun with the construction of harbors and ports which are to be combined with railroads to landlocked African countries.[16]

China's need for energy

A primary goal of the BRI is to improve China's energy security. Much of China's energy comes from Central Asia, hence that region being a key geographical component of the initiative.[17] During the same trip to Central Asia that Xi first announced the BRI project, he also signed a joint operation contract with Turkmenistan for one of the world's largest gas fields, Galkinish. This project is to be led by China National Petroleum Corp. Additional contracts were signed to increase the volume of gas purchased by China, and commit Beijing to helping Turkmenistan construct a new gas line.[18]

Since 1993, China has been a net energy importer.[19] As a result, the original intent of the "going out" strategy was to encourage Chinese companies to go abroad and secure energy assets for China.[20] Oil-producing nations such as Iran were key targets of the "going out" strategy, and are now an integral component of the BRI. Beijing sees Iran as a counterbalance to US domination in the Middle East, and consequently admitted Iran to the SCO as an observer.[21] The BRI now plans to connect Iranian producers with the Turkmenistan-China pipeline and the future Kazakhstan-China oil pipelines.[22] In addition, pre-existing hydrocarbons contracts with Iran, totaling US$120 billion, will give China access to the Caspian Sea and the Persian Gulf.[23]

The BRI will also bolster economic ties between China and Saudi Arabia, long Washington's primary ally in the Middle East. Saudi Arabia is already China's leading trade partner in the region, and China has supplied the kingdom with nuclear capable missiles.[24] Bilateral trade between the two countries is significant; Saudi Aramco owns refineries in Qingdao and Fujian in China. Meanwhile, "Chinese firms have begun to invest in Saudi infrastructure and industry."[25] Beijing is also the top oil and gas investor in Iraq, with long-term service contracts for the al-Ahdab, Rumaila, Halfaya, and Maysan oil fields.[26]

In Europe, the BRI has given COSCO, a Chinese state-owned shipping company, the opportunity to assume managerial control and operation of Piraeus, a major port in Greece. Greece "controls one-fifth of the world's merchant fleet and is the largest client for Chinese shipbuilding yards."[27] This will increase China's trade with Greece, as well as helping China access the Black and the Mediterranean seas.[28]

Additional benefits of the BRI

The BRI project is designed to achieve both strategic and economic goals, as well as secure energy for China. At the same time, economic goals seem to be the main driver for the project.[29] If successful, the initiative should keep China moving toward its development goals.[30] The project will increase markets and provide jobs and investment for all of China's regions, hopefully propping up China's slowing economy.[31]

Every one of China's provinces is in some way involved in the project and will see direct economic benefits.[32] China plans to use labor from China as much as possible, thereby creating jobs for Chinese workers.[33] The BRI will provide China's regional governments with a way of remedying over-capacity problems as well as a method of paying off the non-performing loans which could potentially cripple the economy.[34]

Financing the BRI

The initiative is expected to cost up to US$1 trillion, and so have a negative impact on China's current cash reserves.[35] Much of the financing will be done through China's state-owned banks and China International Trust and Investment Corporation (CITIC), a state-owned investment conglomerate. Additionally, in December 2015, the Silk Road Fund was established with a government injection of US$40 billion.[36]

Lack of infrastructure is a major factor hindering the economic progress of developing nations.[37] To remedy this problem, a network of financial institutions has been created. The Silk Road Fund – together with CITIC, Exim Bank, and the China Development Bank – will cooperate with institutions such as the China-ASEAN Investment Cooperation Fund and the China-Eurasia Economic Cooperation Fund, as well as the new Asian Infrastructure Investment Bank (AIIB), to fund development projects which fall within the scope of the New Silk Road.[38]

The Asian Infrastructure Investment Bank

AIIB, which was launched with capital of US$100 billion, is a parallel project operating within the framework of the New Silk Road. AIIB has a range of strategic, economic, and political goals. In Europe, AIIB will undertake financing and infrastructure projects, eroding the importance of the EU.[39]

In Asia, AIIB will help develop infrastructure, particularly in the sectors of "energy and power, transportation, telecommunications, rural infrastructure and agriculture development, water supply and sanitation, environmental protection, urban development and logistics, etc."[40] According to *The Economist*, building roads and mobile-phone towers are among prospective projects.[41]

Asia already has the Asian Development Bank (ADB) and the World Bank. Nonetheless, Beijing sees a need for AIIB because of funding gaps in the ADB, and also because ADB funds all manner of projects. AIIB, by contrast, will focus exclusively on infrastructure. Another aim of AIIB may be to counteract Japanese influence, as Tokyo has historically had the greatest influence over the ADB.[42]

AIIB will also counterbalance US dominance of the World Bank and the IMF.[43] China's veto power within AIIB is like that of the US within the World Bank.[44] Washington is concerned that AIIB will decrease US influence over the global economy. They cite specific problems with previous PRC financing projects, such as "China's existing record of loans to unstable governments, construction deals for unnecessary infrastructure, and villagers abruptly uprooted with little compensation."[45] Unfortunately for the US, most of their closest allies have already joined AIIB. "In early 2015, Washington publicly rebuked its Western European partners, including France, the United Kingdom, and Germany, for joining the China-led multilateral bank, citing concerns about AIIB's lack of adherence to best practices in governance and accountability."[46]

"The calculation for joining is simple. China, with its vast wealth and resources, now rivals the US at the global economic table."[47] While China has made concessions about board makeup, it is clear that AIIB will be under Chinese control, and that Beijing and AIIB will not be involved in discussions about labor rights or environmental issues as other international banking institutions often are. "The new bank, China promises, will not be bogged down in oversight."[48]

166

Chinese investment in ASEAN

Much has been written about the component of the BRI which runs through the ASEAN countries, as it seems a clear example of China's economic expansion beyond its own borders. As China grows in economic strength, they are increasingly becoming the dominant economic player in the Asia Pacific.

Over the last decade, trade between China and ASEAN has more than tripled, making China ASEAN's no. 1 trading partner. Chinese FDI in ASEAN hit US$8.2 billion in 2015.[49] China is among the top five trading partners of each ASEAN member taken individually.[50]

Notable Chinese investment projects in ASEAN include the joint venture between China's Shanghai Automotive Industry Corporation and Wuling Automotive Company, and General General Motors of the USA, that saw construction of a U$700 million car plant begin in Indonesia in 2005.[51] In addition, Beijing Auto International Cooperation has set up a plant in Malaysia, and Zhongce Rubber has opened a tire plant in Thailand. Several PRC companies are involved in energy infrastructure projects in the region. In the telecommunications sector, Huawei and ZTE are among the top players in the region.[52]

The economic relationship between China and ASEAN is expected to continue growing. At the 2014 China-ASEAN Summit held in Burma, PRC Premier Li Keqiang dubbed the next ten years a "diamond decade" for China-ASEAN relations.[53]

The following sections will examine the ASEAN economy, as well as its interaction with China. Next, it will examine China's independent interactions with a few, select ASEAN countries: Singapore, Thailand, Vietnam, Cambodia, and

Laos. Each is included for examination due to unique economic attributes: Singapore is the most developed but small; Thailand offers an interesting balance of size and development; Vietnam was selected because it is the no. 3 ASEAN member in terms of population, has one of the fastest growing economies in the world, and – as it borders China – it serves as a bridge between ASEAN and the Middle Kingdom; Cambodia and Laos are included as they represent two of the smallest and most China-dependent economies in ASEAN.

China and ASEAN economic interaction

Geographical and cultural proximity facilitate economic interaction between China and ASEAN. Another commonality is rapid GDP growth; from 2005–2014, ASEAN's GDP grew by an annual average of 5%, while China's grew at an average of 8%.[54] To put this growth in perspective, during the same period, Japan, a major trading partner of both, grew at an average rate of only 0.4%.[55]

ASEAN's dynamic growth comes largely from the concept of Regional Value Chains (RVCs), whereby the various member states have different comparative advantages and through division of labor are able to achieve a total productivity which is more than the sum of its parts.[56] ASEAN enjoys an advantage in terms of labor costs, as salaries tend to be much lower in ASEAN than in China, particularly in Cambodia, Laos, Myanmar, and Vietnam (CLMV).

Taking advantage of these lower production costs, Chinese companies shift labor-intensive processes from China to ASEAN countries.[57] In addition, advanced manufacturing can be done in the wealthier ASEAN countries. Therefore, electronics, car parts, and components are all subjects of RVCs between China and the more developed ASEAN countries, including Singapore, Malaysia, and Thailand. Lower end manufacturing can be done in the less developed countries, with Chinese companies manufacture clothing and textiles in CLMV.[58]

As both a manufacturing hub and an important source of capital, China has the potential to not only buoy the ASEAN economies, but also create structural imbalances that damage the region in the long run. Chinese investment and the jobs it brings are welcomed, but the jobs come with a price: local economies can become too dependent on China. Since the ASEAN-China Free Trade Agreement (ACFTA) took effect in 2010, ASEAN as a group has been running a trade deficit with China. Apart from Thailand and Malaysia, all ASEAN member countries run a trade deficit with China.[59]

Although China represents one of the largest FDI sources for some ASEAN countries, the total volume of Chinese FDI into ASEAN is small, accounting for only 2.3% of total FDI.[60] Chinese FDI compared to Chinese trade totals for ASEAN is also extremely small at only 10.7%.[61] Additionally, unlike the US, China runs a trade surplus with most of ASEAN. Some suggest that increasing their trade surplus is one of the motivations for China establishing so many free trade agreements with ASEAN.[62]

China-ASEAN trade agreements

China has in place multiple agreements and institutions which facilitate trade, investment, and lending to the ASEAN countries. Some of the major agreements and institutions include:

- China's office of Official Development Assistance –

which extends loans and exports credit to ASEAN partners, particularly in CLMV, through the China-ASEAN Investment Cooperation Fund (see below).[63]

- Regional Comprehensive Economic Partnership – which focuses on trade.
- New Development Bank – which funds basic services and grants emergency assistance in conflict-affected states; the bank also invests in infrastructure such as electricity, transport, telecommunications, and water and sewage.
- Asian Infrastructure Investment Bank (AIIB) – which funds infrastructure and communication
- China-ASEAN Investment Cooperation Fund – which funds infrastructure projects.
- Free Trade Area of the Asia-Pacific – which has been endorsed by all Asia-Pacific Economic Cooperation (APEC) members.[64]
- ASEAN-People's Republic of China Comprehensive Economic Cooperation Agreement, and the Asia-Pacific Trade Agreement.
- China also has individual free trade agreements with Thailand and Singapore.[65]

China-Singapore trade and investment

Singapore is a small nation with a population of just over 5.5 million. With a per capita GDP of over US$53,000 Singapore is considered a high-income country.[66] Its economy is heavily dependent on trade, with total trade, imports and exports combined, equal to 326% of GDP.[67]

Singapore is China's largest source of foreign investment, while Singapore is also the largest recipient of Chinese investment in Asia. Singaporean investment in China has mostly been in the service sector, including dental, education, and banking. Singapore is also a major player in China's real-estate market. In 2014, China was Singapore's largest trading partner and Singapore was China's third largest trading partner.[68] Consequently, the two countries' economies are closely aligned; in fact, China's sovereign wealth fund, the China Investment Corporation (CIC), which invests the government's reserves, was modeled on Singapore's sovereign wealth fund, Temasek Holdings.[69] In 2010, the Monetary Authority of Singapore established a bilateral currency swap agreement with the People's Bank of China (PBoC) which was a major step toward the internationalization of the Chinese yuan.[70]

China and Singapore have cooperated on a number of large projects, including development of Datansha Island in the provincial capital of Guangzhou as well as the Sino-Singapore Guangzhou Knowledge City, which supports technology development.[71] Other projects include the Sino-Singapore Tianjin Eco-City, a sustainable green city initiative.[72] Other, similar joint ventures include Guangzhou Science City and Guangzhou International Biological Island which, like Sino-Guangzhou Knowledge City, receive significant financing from Temasek Holdings.[73]

China-Thailand trade and investment

Thailand, with a population of just over 66 million, is the fourth largest country in ASEAN and has the second highest GDP. The country enjoys a relatively high standard of living, with a per capita GDP of US$5,778 per year.[74] In 2016, export trade accounted for around 68% of Thailand's total GDP.[75]

China is Thailand's second largest trading partner, behind the United States,[76] and the China-Thailand Free Trade Agreement was signed in 2003.[77] In addition, China is the no. 2

foreign investor in Thailand, after Japan. PRC companies are being offered bridge loans from Siam Commercial Bank to encourage their investment in 161 projects being promoted by the Thai government, such as the Eastern Economic Corridor development project. So far, the largest recipients of Chinese investment have been the sectors of automotive and auto parts, petrochemicals, smart electronics, agriculture and biotechnology, tourism, medicine, digital, robotics, aviation, and textiles.[78]

Since seizing power in 2014, Thailand's military government has stressed Thailand's economic relations with China, whilst pivoting away from the US.[79] In January 2016, the military government approved Thailand's entry into AIIB in order to finance its many plans for infrastructure expansion.[80]

Bangkok is hoping to use US$40 billion in Chinese investment to jump start the economy, but so far the cash has failed to materialize.[81] Plans to build a Thai-Chinese railway, for example, have not moved beyond the discussion phase.[82] The railway is expected to cost US$13 billion, for which China is offering financing at 2% per year. On top of the political uncertainty that may be hindering investment, there is opposition from inside of Thailand, some questioning whether Thailand needs or wants the railroad.[83]

Despite the projects which have failed to materialize, the country has attracted an increasing amount of Chinese investment from POEs and SOEs. For example, in the city of Rayong, the Thai-Chinese Rayong Industrial Zone was established in 2012. It now hosts numerous Chinese-owned solar, rubber, and industrial manufacturing businesses.[84]

As labor becomes cheaper in other ASEAN countries such as Cambodia and Burma, Thailand, like China and Vietnam, is trying to move up the value chain, leaving low-skilled manufacturing behind and increasing its competitiveness in the manufacture of computers and digital equipment. To achieve this, the Thai government is courting additional Chinese investment in the high-tech sector.[85]

Increasing Chinese investment and tourism has led to Thailand becoming home to one of the largest overseas concentrations of Chinese nationals. Chinese visitors in 2015 far exceeded seven million, and are expected to increase dramatically despite uncertainty following the death of Thailand's king. In some parts of the country, particularly in coastal cities such as Pattaya, Mandarin is spoken as much as or more than English.[86]

South China Morning Post estimates that one third of the Thai population is of Chinese ethnicity, but that acceptance of this group has only recently come about due to China's economic importance.[87] Traditionally, local Chinese have been influential in the Thai business sector, and historically China has been able to utilize these local ethnic connections to facilitate investment.

China-Vietnam trade and investment

Vietnam's 89 million inhabitants have a per capita GDP of US$1,685.[88] Vietnam has averaged about 6% GDP growth for the past five years, making it one of the fastest growing economies in Asia.[89] Vietnam has made impressive progress, nearly doubling per capita GDP since 2004.[90] A trade dependent nation, Vietnam's total trade equals 179% of GDP,[91] and the state still controls certain sectors such as the financial and banking sectors. As a result of state control of financial services, non-performing loans are at a high level; in 2016, across Vietnam's entire banking system, non-performing loans reached 5.84%.[92]

While the US is Vietnam's largest export partner, China is Vietnam's no. 1 trade partner overall. Imports from China are roughly triple the value of Vietnam's exports to China.[93]

China Daily reported that in 2015 China was operating 1,300 projects in Vietnam. Vietnam is expected to be a conduit for China to trade with ASEAN through China's Guangxi Province.[94] Chinese investment in Vietnam has increased, China going from the no. 8 source of FDI in 2016 to the no. 3 source in 2017.[95] However, this figure includes Hong Kong, Macao, and Taiwan, all of which are usually considered separate entities for investment purposes.[96]

Chinese FDI usually takes the form of Build-Operate-Transfer (BOT), Build Transfer (BT) or Build-Transfer-Operate (BTO) agreements.[97] Chinese investment in Vietnam tends to be focused on labor intensive industries such as garment and textiles, hydropower, steel production, chemicals, and cement production. The also produce a great deal of pollution.[98] Some major PRC investment projects in Vietnam include: Vinh Tan 1 Thermal Power Project in Binh Thuan Province; Hung Nghiep Formosa Dong Nai Textile Limited Company project in Nhon Trach Industrial Park, Dong Nai Province; Texhong Group's textile factories in the northern provinces; Viet Luan tire project in Tay Ninh Province; Tan Cao Tham rubber processing plant; the Vietnam-China Mining and Metallurgy Project in Lao Cai Province; the Thai Nguyen iron and steel plant extension; the Cat Linh- Ha Dong urban railway project; and the Da River water pipeline project.[99]

A blow to potential China-Vietnam trade and investment came when the US withdrew from the TPP. Chinese firms had been planning to establish manufacturing and assembly plants in Vietnam and export duty-free to the US.[100] Now that the US has removed itself from the TPP, this incentive for China investment in Vietnam has diminished.

China-Cambodia trade and investment

The Kingdom of Cambodia is a relatively small country with a per capita GDP of a bit more than US$1,000 per year and a population of just over 15 million.[101] Cambodia's economy is heavily dependent on trade, with a total trade volume (imports plus exports) equaling 142% of GDP.[102] The largest obstacles to economic development are corruption and lack of rule of law.[103]

Cambodia is sandwiched between two huge neighbors: Thailand, which has about four times the population; and Vietnam, which has around six times Cambodia's population. Throughout history, Cambodia has been a victim of repeated incursions or domination by one or the other of these relative behemoths. As a result, Cambodia's relationship with China, Asia's no. 1 power, helps to balance the region, enabling Phnom Penh to better negotiate with Hanoi and Bangkok. Chinese influence and money has made Cambodia less dependent on other countries. In 2015, Chinese investment in Cambodia exceeded all other sources of FDI,[104] accounting for 35% of total inbound investment.[105]

China is Cambodia's no. 3 trade partner, and no. 2 import partner.[106] Cambodia runs a trade deficit with China; China receives 4.4% of Cambodia's exports while 24% of Cambodia's imports come from China.[107] Cambodia's exports to the PRC are largely agricultural products and raw materials, such as wood, plastic, and rubber.[108]

Chinese investments in Cambodia has included infrastructure projects and steel industry projects. Guangxi Nonferrous Metal Group is constructing a steel mill in Preah Vihear Province. Cambodia Iron & Steel Mining Industry Group and the China Railway Group have agreed to construct a railway. Cambodia's Power Partner Profit Group has signed

MOUs with Chinese companies relating agricultural and mineral resources. The Civil Aviation Administration of China has signed an MOU with Cambodia's State Secretariat of Civil Aviation.[109] Other Chinese investment projects in Cambodia include: South East Asia Telecom Group, and the Russei Chrum Krom hydropower dam built by Huadian.[110] In addition, at a meeting in 2015 with Prime Minister Hun Sen, PRC President Xi Jinping promised US$500 to US$700 million in additional aid.[111]

The first Cambodia-China Business Forum and Financial Development Forum was held in Phnom Penh in December 2016 with the theme, "Cambodia: The Kingdom of Opportunity Along the 'One Belt, One Road'." In 2015, trade between the two countries increased by US$3.75 billion compared to the previous year to reach US$5 billion.[112] Chinese investment has gone into agriculture and agro-industry, manufacturing industry, tourism, energy, construction and real estate, and the financial sector.[113]

Cambodia has also established direct economic relations with individual Chinese provinces. In March 2017, an MOU was signed between Cambodia and China's Shaanxi Province, to strengthen ties and increase trade. Shaanxi Province alone accounts for about a quarter of China's total investment in Cambodia, focusing on irrigation systems, telecommunications, hydropower, and infrastructure. Cambodia's minister of commerce has underlined the importance of establishing a trade center in Xi'an, Shaanxi Province to facilitate Chinese investment in the kingdom.[114]

China-Laos trade and investment

The population of the Lao People's Democratic Republic is 6.8 million, with a per capita GDP of US$1,644.[115] The country's underdeveloped financial system– which suffers from too much government regulation, high credit costs, and lack of access to financing – has slowed economic development.[116] Exports account for 29.3% of Laotian GDP.[117]

China is Laos' no. 2 trade partner in terms both of exports and imports, behind Thailand and ahead of Vietnam.[118] Trade between China and Laos has increased steadily, nearly tripling from US$1.3 billion in 2011 to US$3.6 billion in 2014.[119] However, China's economic slowdown caused trade to contract to US$2.78 billion in 2015.[120]

In particular, Laos trades with China's Yunnan Province, accounting for 40% of Yunnan's total trade. China is also the top investor in Laos, with over 760 projects underway.[121] Yunnanese companies lead many of these investment projects, and they include roads, electricity transmission lines, water supply, and economic zone projects.[122] Chinese investment is also helping to modernize Laos' financial markets. The state-owned Lao Development Bank signed an MOU with China's Fudian Bank to facilitate trade and investment, country-to-country services, capital management, credit cooperation, and currency exchange.[123]

The Laotian economy has been growing at an average rate of 7% per year.[124] Voice of America credits China with being a major driver in the economic development of Laos, PRC investment being significant in sectors such as mining, energy, agriculture, banking and commercial real-estate construction. Credit extended by the Bank of China accounts for 40% of Laos' total foreign debt, with most of these funds being used in infrastructure and power projects. In Vientiane, Chinese investment is building a large office tower as well as the That Luang Lake residential and commercial complex. Another project already underway is a high-speed railway from Vientiane to the Chinese border.[125]

177

Other Chinese investors in Laos include: China International Water and Electric Corporation, China Huadian, China Electric Power Technology Import and Export Corporation, China Machinery Engineering Corporation, Far East Industrial (Hong Kong, China) and China Electrical Equipment Corporation, China National Electric Equipment Corporation, Harbin Power Engineering, Harbin Turbine and Harbin Electric China Machinery Engineering Corporation. The last of these is constructing two power transmission lines in the country. In addition, China Railway Group and Yunnan Provincial Energy Investment Group are backing the China-Laos railway project; and Yunnan Hai Cheng, a Chinese developer, is developing Boten Special Economic Zone.[126]

On the downside, the VOA reported that the Asian Development Bank believes that Laotian economy is too dependent on China, as demonstrated by the 2015 slowdown in China and its impact on Laos. The bank is recommending Laos diversify its economy, and focus more on regional connectivity and integration with ASEAN.

China-Pakistan Economic Corridor (CPEC)

The China-Pakistan Economic Corridor (CPEC) (Chinese: 中国-巴基斯坦经济走廊) is one of the most significant components of China's BRI. CPEC will link Xinjiang in China with Gwadar Port in Pakistan, and on to Iran. For China, CPEC will create a shorter, safer, and cheaper route for energy imports and open up new markets for its exports. For Pakistan, CPEC is meant to bring in much needed infrastructure upgrades and GDP growth.

Pakistan's economy has been mostly stagnant for the better part of two decades, plagued by high unemployment, low wages, and a lack of infrastructure. Beijing – and many

178

external observers – suggest that CPEC will stimulate the Pakistani economy.[127] The project is also meant to strengthen the so-called "Iron Brotherhood," linking China and Pakistan, a dynamic which will counterbalance the economic and political influence of the US and India in South Asia.[128] Other benefits to Pakistan include making Pakistan energy self-sufficient. "Supporters of CPEC say it is a one-time opportunity for Pakistan to resolve its crippling power-supply shortfalls, and for the first time to establish a nationwide network of logistical infrastructure."[129]

China-Pakistan economic activity

Over the last two decades, China has dramatically increased its outbound direct investment. Chinese ODI typically goes to developing countries,[130] and Chinese investment in Pakistan includes some of the earliest outbound investments made by the PRC. Sino-Pakistani friendship dates back to 1950, when newly independent Pakistan was one of the first countries to reject recognition of the Republic of China on Taiwan, instead recognizing the PRC. In 1951, relations between the two countries were normalized.[131]

Friendship and cooperation between Beijing and Islamabad has increased, in part due to China's worsening relationship with India, which came to a head in 1962 with the Sino-Indian War.[132] That same year, China and Pakistan signed their first trade agreement, as well as an agreement to build a road linking Xinjiang with Pakistan. They formed a strategic alliance to counter India and Russia, and China also supported Pakistan in its two wars against India in 1965 and 1971.[133] In 1982, they established the China-Pakistan Joint Committee of Economy.[134] PRC President Jiang Zemin's 1996 visit to Pakistan saw the beginning of a more comprehensive friendship. Bilateral relations were strengthened even further in 2005, when they signed a Treaty of Friendship, wherein both parties agreed not to enter any organization or agreement which infringed on the sovereignty of the other.[135]

Geopolitical cooperation between the two nations has been accompanied by significant investment. In 2002, China began helping with the construction of Gwadar Port, despite some reservations on the Chinese side.[136] Initially, China was not interested in building the port, but reluctantly agreed after being guaranteed sovereign usage rights.[137] In 2007, the Pakistan-China Free Trade Agreement was signed. Since then, China has also increased its investment in Pakistani infrastructure, such as building the PRC Tower in Karachi. Chinese leaders often visit Pakistan, including Premier Wen Jiabao in 2010 and Premier Li Keqiang in 2013.[138]

In addition to infrastructure, China also gives military aid to Pakistan. In 2011, Pakistan's prime minister asked China to construct a base for the Pakistani Navy at their port in Gwadar. Chinese military aid extends to money, construction and military hardware.[139]

The presence of Chinese investment (particularly the billions of dollars being invested in CPEC), has attracted other foreign investment into Pakistan, such as Turkish home-appliance maker Arcelik AS and Dutch dairy giant Royal FrieslandCampina. Chinese-funded power plants are expected to end Pakistan's frequent power outages, and thus boost the viability of additional foreign investment.

Over the past five years, Pakistani consumer spending has increased by 83.4%.[140] Due to this increased spending, consumer product companies are beginning to move to Pakistan to take advantage of the world's sixth largest population.[141] Pakistan is also growing as an auto market, with Renault entering negotiations with local companies to develop a new car brand.[142]

CPEC in detail

As a component of China's overall New Silk Road Project, CPEC will link with the new Maritime Silk Route (planned as part of a trans-Eurasian project) and connect three billion people in Asia, Africa and Europe.[143] The corridor will not only allow for the transportation of goods and people overland from China to Pakistan, but also information, technology, oil, and gas through a series of grids and pipelines.[144] Gwadar Port is one of the most important components of CPEC for Beijing, as PRC control of this port will reduce the time and money it costs to move Iranian oil to China.

CPEC is part of China's Thirteenth Five-Year Plan, with the stated goals of improving Pakistan's infrastructure while strengthening the economic relationship between China and Pakistan. The project is financed through concessional loans which Pakistan will have to begin repaying in 2020. A US$54 billion figure is often published, but some claim the final cost of the project for Pakistan may reach US$75 billion.[145] Pakistan is meant to pay these loans through revenues generated by the project, as the corridor is expected to increase Pakistan's GDP growth by 2.5%.[146]

Some of the infrastructure construction projects along the Silk Road will be carried out by Chinese SOEs, while private companies will construct US$33 billion of energy infrastructure.[147] Phase One of the project was the 2017 completion of Gwadar International Airport, as well as major renovations to Gwadar Port.[148] CPEC will also upgrade the Karakoram Highway linking China and Pakistan, along which 80% of China's oil is will eventually be transported. Currently, China imports oil via supertankers through the Strait of Malacca, a 16,000-km journey that takes two or three months.

Utilizing Gwadar Port reduces the distance to less than 5,000 km.[149]

CPEC includes constructing highways connecting Karachi and Lahore and Rawalpindi to the Chinese border. Other components include upgrading the Karachi-Peshawar main railway so trains can travel at up to 160 km/h by December 2019. The Pakistani railway network will also be extended to connect with China's Southern Xinjiang Railway in Kashgar. A liquefied natural gas pipeline will be built to transport gas from Iran to Gwadar and Nawabshah. From Gwadar, oil and gas could be transported along the corridor to China, reducing the current 12,000 km journey to 2,395 km.[150]

One of the unique aspects of the project is that it not only links countries through improved transportation, but also through digital connectivity. To this end, fiber-optic lines will be installed, improving communication between the two countries.[151] As CPEC is also an energy project, the Pakistani government intends to rebuild the Diamer-Bhasha dam on the Indus River, to provide hydroelectric power and a reservoir.[152]

In the early stages of the project, Pakistan is expected to benefit from a surge of Chinese FDI. However, much of CPEC is being financed with concessional loans and loans from state-owned Chinese banks which will have to be repaid. This looming debt could trigger an economic crisis for Pakistan. "Gross external financing needs of the country will jump almost 60% by then, from a projected US$11 billion for the current fiscal year, to US$17.5 billion in 2020."[153]

Financing the corridor

The China-Pakistan Joint Cooperation Committee (JCC) agreements earmarked billions of dollars' worth of soft loans for specific projects, such as three road projects overseen by the Chinese National Highway Authority.[154] Industrial zones will also be established along the corridor.[155] Financing for additional projects such as power plants, solar parks and wind farms, will be raised partly through Islamic finance instruments, such as Sukuk (Islamic bonds). The use of Islamic financing will represent cooperation between public and private financing in Pakistan that will largely benefit the country's Islamic financing sector. The funding of these projects will increase the country's liquidity, and indirectly benefit Pakistan's real estate, manufacturing, construction materials, and contracting sectors.[156]

Pakistan has been promoting Islamic (Shariah) financing in the country, and CPEC may provide opportunities to do this.[157] The government has transferred 20% to 40% of its debt financing to Islamic sources, and the same may be done with CPEC-related debt.[158] One Islamic financing instrument available is *Sukuk*, Shariah compliant bonds which are structured in such a fashion so as not to violate Islam's prohibition against paying or charging interest.

Apart from China's state-owned banks, the Asian Development Bank and AIIB will provide much of the funding for the corridor. Both the ADB and the AIIB have stated that they would consider utilizing Islamic financing.[159] Shariah-compliant funding agreements have already been reached for certain projects such as a coal-mining operation in Pakistan's Thar region. Other Shariah-compliant leasing contracts have been employed, such as a financing technique called *ijara*,[160] for temporary services or wages.[161]

Pakistan-India and Pakistan-Russia relations

There has been a great deal of enmity between Pakistan and India. Both China and Pakistan have fought wars against

183

India, making China a logical ally for Pakistan. CPEC is a major step toward solidifying the link between China and Pakistan, while more or less excluding India. As a reaction to the strategic alignment of Pakistan and China, India has formed its own strategic and economic relations with Afghanistan and Iran.[162]

Russia has always been a wild card in this region, periodically swinging towards or away from China. Russia initially declined to join the Belt and Road Initiative. More recently, however, the Russian ambassador to Pakistan announced that Russia is in discussions with Pakistan to merge CPEC with Russia's Eurasian Economic Union.[163] Russia has repeatedly assured India that Russia's increased involvement with Pakistan will not damage Russia-India relations. However, this has done little to alleviate Indian fears that Russia is choosing Pakistan over India, and, many experts say that Russia's support for CPEC could harm India's vital strategic interests.[164] In contrast, Chinese state-owned media group The Global Times took a more positive view, reporting that Russia's joining with CPEC creates an opportunity for China, Russia, and Pakistan to improve their relationship.[165] Conspicuously absent from that report was any mention of improved relations with India.

Due to increased cooperation between Russia, China, and Pakistan, Russia is now being permitted to use Gwadar Port for its exports. This current development is simply an improvement of existing Sino-Russian relations. Russia and China were already cooperating through BRICS agreements, and Russia is a member of the SCO. Additionally, China and Russia have been collaborating on the "the Belt and the Union" which links China's Belt and Road Initiative with the Russia-backed Eurasian Economic Union.[166]

India's current relations with Pakistan are troubled.

Furthermore, their relationship with China has deteriorated since Xi Jinping's 2015 visit to Pakistan and consequent announcement of CPEC. The Chinese have since further alienated India by reaching out to other neighboring countries, offering them participation in the BRI, and Iran has said it wants its harbor at Chabahar to be a sister port to Pakistan's Gwadar.[167] India has sought to counter China's growing influence by making efforts to increase its involvement with other countries in the region. However, countries such as Afghanistan and other Central Asian nations instead seek the benefits of collaboration with China and Pakistan, as it will give them access to much needed seaports and allow them to serve as a transfer point for Chinese energy imports.[168]

Another important global dynamic to consider are relationships with the US and UK. Increased Chinese investment through CPEC may reduce Pakistan's dependence on US support.[169] Irrespective of CPEC, Pakistani authorities are worried that US support may be at risk after Trump's election because of his pro-India stance.[170] While the US may be moving away from Pakistan and toward India, the UK has encouraged its companies to invest in Pakistan along with CPEC.[171] Being a former British colony and a member of the British Commonwealth, India cannot be happy about an apparent shift in British interest toward a Chinese-based project in Pakistan.[172]

Problems related to CPEC

While CPEC has the potential to bring investment, improved infrastructure and GDP growth to Pakistan, the project is also facing a number of difficulties. Some of the problems associated with the corridor relate to its impact on local communities.[173] Voices in Pakistan have expressed fears that CPEC may lead to widespread human displacement. Farmers are particularly susceptible, as the land they occupy could generate more profit if converted to energy or transportation infrastructure. A threat to farmland has deeper implications for the country's long term survival, as only a small percentage of Pakistan's land is arable. Significant loss of farmland may lead to Pakistan becoming dependent on food imports.[174]

Another problem associated with CPEC is the possibility Pakistan may not be able to repay the loans from China. An IMF report on the corridor, cited in *Dawn*, said problems relating to the business climate, governance, and security need to be addressed if the corridor is to generate sufficient revenues to cover loan payments.[175] If these problems are not resolved, Pakistan may find itself unable to pay its debts.[176] However, even if these problems are resolved, Pakistan may still struggle to repay the loans from the increase in its GDP. Estimates of the total revenues to be generated by CPEC include money earned by Chinese retailers along the New Silk Road, as well as Chinese construction companies, finance companies, telecom companies, and energy companies, and most of this wealth will likely be repatriated to China. As such, this money will not be available when Pakistan should begin making repayments. It is estimated that the profit repatriation plus debt servicing could reach about 0.4% of Pakistani GDP per year.[177]

Express Tribune reported that Dr. Kaiser Bengali, former adviser to the chief minister of Balochistan, has questioned the socio-economic implications of the corridor, and raised a number of issues which he feels need to be addressed in order to protect Pakistan's economic interests.[178] These questions include areas which the government has more or less labeled taboo, such as the protection of jobs and industries, CPEC's impact on Pakistan's balance of payments, and Pakistan's budgetary position.[179] Representing an extremely underdeveloped province, Dr. Bengali was also concerned about what (if any) benefit Balochistan would derive from the corridor.[180] A chamber of commerce representing three Pakistani regions (Gujrat, Gujranwala and Sialkot) has expressed similar concerns about the establishment of Chinese industries and warehouses in Pakistan.[190]

Dr. Bengali has also raised concerns regarding the financing terms of CPEC which have not been made clear to the public. He also expressed worry that the construction projects would damage rather than help local industries. "China is bringing goods, machinery, and labor for the construction of CPEC projects. The hope that these construction activities would generate economic activities is fading away."[182]

Initially, it was hoped that Chinese construction contracts would generate jobs and that raw materials and supplies would be sourced locally. Now it seems that much of the labor and other materials are being brought from China, thus reducing the benefit Pakistan derives from the project. Leaders of domestic chambers of commerce told *Dawn* that they have asked the government to brief the business community on the industrial activities of the Chinese.[183] They said that they were worried that Chinese industry could crowd out local industry, destroy Pakistan's ability to export, and leave Pakistan completely dependent on Chinese industry.[184]

These fears seem to be well founded, as CPEC has already increased Pakistan's trade deficit with China.[185] In addition, economists in Pakistan worry that the trade deficit will continue to expand, and Pakistan will become more and more dependent on China. Other voices in Pakistan are concerned that Chinese infrastructure construction activities could cause scarcity and drive up the domestic price of raw materials.[186] *Express Tribune* warns that the corridor may harm local manufacturing industry.[187]

Responding to these fears, Dr. Bengali has asked the government to disclose details regarding the balance of payments and the long-term capital inflows and outflows related to the loans.[188] CPEC agreements have granted a number of tax benefits to Chinese firms operating in Pakistan, reducing tax revenue for the Pakistani government. CPEC terms go as far as to waive taxes on the very Chinese financial institutions that are benefiting from CPEC financing. Recently, the Pakistani government has also begun granting Chinese companies tax-free operation for construction income.[189] "So far, PKR 150 billion worth of tax exemptions have been given to CPEC-related projects", according to sources in the Federal Board of Revenue.[190] Those PKR 150 billion would have gone a long way toward repaying Pakistan's debts.

Apart from potential economic problems, CPEC also raises security issues. In an academic paper, Dr. Siegfried Wolf, a South Asia expert at the University of Heidelberg, explained that there are significant security concerns regarding the portion of CPEC which runs through Balochistan. Local rebels believe Islamabad is exploiting their region for the benefit of the capital, without economic benefit for Balochistan. The Pakistani government has taken an extreme line in response, publicly declaring that not only is CPEC good for the whole country, but anyone who speaks out against it is a traitor.[191] This reaction by the government has raised warning flags in international circles in relation to freedom of speech and other human rights, which the Pakistani government seems willing to ignore in the name of economic progress.

Dr. Wolf also pointed out that Beijing now expects Islamabad to align both its military and political decision-making with Beijing, warning that such a move could turn Pakistan into Beijing's "client."[192] This type of public criticism is another major stumbling block for the corridor, as local protest – be it word or deed – is something that Beijing is unaccustomed to. China has a one-party system and follows a top down decision-making process when dealing with issues of national interest or foreign policy. Nearly all media in the country are owned by the state and follow the party line. As such, China is not used to the kind of public or media criticism which CPEC sometimes receives in Pakistan. In China, both the BRI and CPEC receive only glowing praise from the media.[193]

In contrast to China's top-down, single party system, Pakistan's political system is composed of provincial and federal governments, both of which are democratically elected. Provincial governments have dominion over particular aspects of governance, and can even veto the wishes of the federal government in some instances. Additionally, the press in Pakistan enjoys a relatively high degree of freedom and often criticizes or questions the government, even on sensitive issues.[194]

While various political entities within Pakistan seek to benefit from the corridor, the media has repeatedly demanded transparency and economic feasibility analysis.[195] Some in Pakistan are calling CPEC the new East India Company, invoking visions of Pakistan's colonial past and loss of self-determination.[196] China, or Islamabad (at Beijing's request), have reacted by labeling critics of the corridor as "enemies of Pakistan" engaging in "disinformation," "maligning" CPEC, and promoting a "hidden agenda."[197]

Unaccustomed to having to navigate this type of outspoken

democracy, and finding a need to appease various political parties, Beijing has become frustrated by the repeated need to send a mission to Islamabad to negotiate a consensus among multiple political entities. Zheng Xiaosong, a vice minister in the Communist Party of China's International Department, visited Islamabad and urged Pakistan's political parties "to resolve their differences and make CPEC a success."[198]

Security Threats to CPEC

The Pakistani government has vowed to provide security for all foreign investment in Pakistan, but the port of Gwadar, which is key to the entire CPEC, lies in Baluchistan, a region where Baluch locals oppose the port, labeling it an attempt by the Chinese to colonize them.[199] This opposition to CPEC led to the slaying in 2006 of three Chinese engineers in Baluchistan.[200] The Baluch also feel that Islamabad is capitalizing on their homeland and resources to enrich the capital at the expense of Baluchistan. What is more, the area where the port is located is an area claimed by Islamic State. As a result there have been repeated attacks, such as one at a Sufi shrine where 50 worshipers were killed.[201]

Additional security challenges come from the fact that the corridor runs through Gilgit-Baltistan, a semi-autonomous region in northern Pakistan bordering the disputed territory of Kashmir. It is feared that terrorists within Pakistan could seek to destabilize Indian-administered Kashmir through Gilgit-Baltistan.[202]

Potential terror threats also come from a Pakistani domestic group called Tehrik-i-Taliban Pakistan (TTP), as well as Islamic terrorist organizations that have declared jihad against China because of Beijing's perceived mistreatment of the Uyghur minority in China's Xinjiang region.[203] "Both

190

organizations worship the fight against the Chinese as their 'Islamic responsibility,' describing them as 'enemy of all Muslims'."[204] These groups may see CPEC projects as symbolic of China and strike against them.[205]

The possibility still exists that Uyghur terrorists, such as the East Turkestan Islamic Movement, will join forces with others to attack Chinese interests, as was ordered in 2014 by Mufti Abu Zar al-Burmi in a video entitled "Let's Disturb China." A similar message was put forth by a Uyghur terrorist leader, Abdullah Mansour, who in an interview vowed to carry out more attacks against Chinese targets.[206] China believes that the terrorism has spread from Pakistan into China, blaming terrorist activity within Xinjiang on groups connected with Pakistan. Chinese companies have expressed security concerns, prompting Beijing to pressure Pakistan to step up military patrols in Baluchistan.[207]

On the one hand, Beijing is anxious to see the corridor completed in as short a time as possible and to start earning returns on their investment. On the other hand, they are also concerned about the safety of Chinese nationals and Chinese projects in the region. Islamabad has assured Beijing that the army will protect Chinese interests; additional Pakistani troops have been deployed along CPEC; and new counter-terrorism policies and special laws have been implemented to empower the military and intelligence services to curb terrorism.[208]

Pakistan's assurances to China raise two questions: How sure can Pakistan be that it can control the problem of terrorism, and could terrorism delay or even stall CPEC?[209] Combating terrorism also creates the very real necessity for Pakistan-PRC military cooperation, which then feeds into India's fears of having PRC military forces stationed in South Asia, as well as Baluch fears of colonization. India fears an

191

expanding Chinese military, and has already expressed concerns about the military implications of China controlling Gwadar Port.[210]

The corridor as of 2018

As a direct result of CPEC, Pakistan's trade deficit has hit a record level of US$30 billion. The IMF has determined that the country's capital outflows, including loan repayments, profit repatriation, and imports of inputs, will peak at US$3.5 billion to 4.5 billion by 2025. The IMF warned that running such unhealthy current accounts risks the country's macroeconomic stability. There is also speculation that power generated by CPEC projects will be too expensive for Pakistani consumers.[211]

Pakistan is now facing a financial shortfall, unable to meet its 2018–2019 service payments for its foreign loans. If Islamabad were to ask the IMF for a bailout, the IMF would review Pakistan's finances and challenge Pakistan's participation in CPEC. "The IMF does not approve of the project in view of the poor health of the economy."[212] Consequently, Pakistan has sought help from China, and speculation is that China will grant the additional loans, so as not to threaten CPEC. Asia Times quoted a source from Pakistan's Finance Ministry as saying "China will have to meet Pakistan's demand because if they refuse, Pakistan will approach the IMF for a bailout package and if that happened the smooth sailing of CPEC would become extremely difficult – a scenario which Chinese would not like to see."[213]

This means that Pakistan's debt to China will increase, as Pakistan borrows money from China to repay its previous loans from China and other foreign countries.

The BRI as of 2018

The BRI has now been expanded to the Arctic, through the "Polar Silk Road," the Caribbean, and Latin America. To date, the only major economies which have not joined the BRI are the United States, Canada, Japan, and India.[214] But just what they have joined is unclear. The BRI is not an organization like ASEAN or NAFTA. Rather, it seems to be a loosely-defined Chinese project on a global scale.

There is no public list of projects associated with the BRI, so it is impossible to say which projects around the world are part of BRI, which have succeeded, or which have failed. Additionally, there is the question of what it means to be a member. There are similar Chinese projects in non-BRI countries. The list of activities which bear the BRI name seems to be growing continuously, even including such spectacles as fashion shows, concerts, and art exhibits.[215] The initiative has no specific time-frame, and no estimated completion date has ever been made public. What is more, some of the "successes of the BRI" that are cited date back to 2002, long before the BRI was launched and well before Xi Jinping became the PRC's president.[216]

International criticism of the BRI and CPEC continues to grow. In 2018, 27 of 28 EU ambassadors to Beijing signed a letter, denouncing the BRI as hampering free trade and favoring the interests of Chinese companies who are given preference in awarding contracts.[217] The letter accused Beijing of reshaping globalization in such a fashion as to suit its own interests, such as "the reduction of surplus capacity, the creation of new export markets and safeguarding access to raw materials."[218] European countries have complained about a lack of transparency along the Silk Road. EU representatives, along with China, were meant to sign a declaration at the official launching of the Silk Road initiative, but the EU side asked that language be amended to call for transparency and "equal opportunities for all investors in transport infrastructure."[219] Beijing, however, refused to amend the document and it was not signed.

The US$40 billion Silk Road Fund, established in 2014, is another area which lacks transparency. To date, no specific guidelines have been published to explain who might qualify for help. According to research by the German government's foreign trade and investment marketing agency and the Association of German Chambers of Commerce and Industry, roughly "80% of projects funded by Chinese state banks had gone to Chinese companies."[220]

In addition to facing criticism, the BRI seems to be suffering from a financial crunch. Li Ruogu, the former president of China's Exim Bank, pointed out that most of the countries along the BRI were already suffering under heavy debt-to-GDP ratios and could not afford infrastructure development.[221] China has stated that it would be open to including private financing in the BRI, but the lack of creditworthiness of the borrowers would frighten off most investors. Additionally, BRI investments offer low profitability ratios, and a host of other problems.[222]

CHAPTER 11:

CHINA-US ECONOMIC RELATIONS

China is the largest trading partner of the US, and the US is China's largest trade partner. The US absorbs roughly 18% of China's exports, and the volume of trade is increasing almost every year. The US runs a trade deficit with China; in 2015 Chinese exports to the US totaled US$481.9 billion, while US exports to China were only US$116.2 billion.[1]

Quantifying China-US economic relations

Before the year 2000, Chinese investments in the United States were nearly non-existent.[2] By 2014, however, China's total outbound direct investment (ODI) had reached US$120 billion,[3] with the US being one of the largest recipients. Annual investment by Chinese companies in the US now exceeds American investment in China.[4] As of 2015, the Chinese had bought or created 1,583 US companies, employing 80,600 workers, for a total investment of US$50 billion.[5] In 2015, Chinese companies were involved in 26 mergers and acquisitions in the US totaling US$2.5 billion.[6] This trend has increased dramatically over the last five years. During this period, California has been the primary US recipient of Chinese investment with US$5.9 billion invested in 370 businesses.[7]

The two countries are also connected by debt. In October 2016, China slipped from the no. 1 to the no. 2 largest foreign holder of US debt, with holdings of US$1.115 trillion.[8] Those who ask why China has become a US creditor should understand it is normal for governments to carry some debt. Particularly during a recession, the government may need to increase government spending in order to stimulate the economy, while avoiding tax increases that could slow down the economy. The US debt is equal to 106% of its GDP.[9] In fact, all of the world's top four economies – the US, China, Japan, and Germany – carry large debt-to-GDP ratios. Japan's debt to GDP ratio is 250.20%, and Germany's is 68.3% of GDP.[10] Officially, China's government debt is only 43.9% of GDP.[11]

China's low debt-to-GDP ratio is a special case, however, as debt owed by Chinese SOEs is listed as corporate debt, although ultimately the government is responsible for the money.[12] When SOE debt is taken into account, China's total debt equals 237% of GDP.[13] Therefore, China is similar to the US in terms of maintaining large public debts. At the same time, China's economy is closely linked to the US economy through China's carriage of US federal debt.

US foreign debt is a much-discussed topic, but foreign debt is actually just a small piece of the puzzle. About two thirds of US debt is held by domestic investors, social security, military-personnel retirement plans, government agencies, corporations, and individual investors. The rest, about one third or US$14.1 trillion, is held by foreign countries and foreign investors. Japan was for a long time the no. 1 foreign holder of US debt, but in 2015 China overtook Japan to become the largest foreign holder of US debt. In 2016, Japan moved back to first place with a US$1.31 trillion as China's total dropped to US$1.115 trillion.[14] In 2017, China regained its no. 1 position, holding US$1.145 trillion of US debt.[15]

China holds US currency, often in the form of US government bonds, in order to help regulate the value of the yuan. While the yuan is allowed to fluctuate within a narrow band set by Beijing, China's currency is more or less pegged to the US dollar. Through the purchase or sale of US debt, Beijing can raise or lower the value of the yuan. The exchange rate influences the US-China trade deficit, as when Chinese products are cheaper for Americans, Americans buy more of them. Likewise, when American products are more expensive for Chinese consumers, so they buy them in smaller quantities.

At the time of writing, June 2018, there are 6.54 yuan to the US dollar. Not long ago, the yuan was as low as 6.8, making Chinese products cheaper on the world market as well as within the US. Another reason that Chinese products are cheaper than American products is because of the lower wages paid in China compared to the US. The average factory worker in the US earns US$11.93/hour or US$1,908/month. His Chinese counterpart only earns around 3,000 yuan per month (US$458).[16]

Many economists feel that China's wages are too low, considering that China is the world's second largest economy. Annual per capita GDP (used as average income) in the US is US$56,115, while in China it is only US$7,925.[17] In fact, China's per capita GDP is well below that of other, less developed nations, such as Malaysia with a per capita GDP of US$9,766, and Gabon with a per capita GDP of US$10,966.[18] Even Greece, which has perhaps the worst economy in Western Europe, has a per capita GDP of US$18,036.[19]

US President Donald Trump has repeatedly accused China of currency manipulation. At the time of his election, the People's Bank of China was holding US$3.121 trillion of

197

foreign reserves, mostly in the form of US dollars.[20] Macroeconomic theory says: If Beijing spent this money, it would increase the number of US dollars on the world markets, thereby decreasing the value of US dollars. At the same time, the number of yuan on the world markets would fall, so the yuan would rise in value.

Over the past two years, China has had three major selloffs of US debt. In August 2015, they sold US$94 billion.[21] In December 2015, China sold US$18 billion of US Treasury debt. In October 2016, the offshore yuan sank to more than 6.92 to the US dollar. In December of that year, the government dumped US$41.3 billion in US debt. Despite these selloffs in December, the yuan dropped to 6.94. In January 2017, it was reported that China's foreign currency reserves had slipped to US$2.998 trillion after the third straight month of declines.[22] Yet, as of November 2016 the yuan was still at 6.87. Beijing, as well as many China watchers, has rejected accusations of treasury manipulation. Even the US Treasury has refused to label China a currency manipulator.[23] Tim Worstall of *Forbes* published a tongue-in-cheek article confirming that China was a currency manipulator, but that China was doing everything it could to prop up the yuan.[24] Those who disagree with Trump's claims of currency manipulation believe that market factors are driving down the price of the yuan and that Beijing is not to blame.

During his election campaign, Trump repeatedly threatened to raise tariffs against China and withdraw the US from the Trans-Pacific Partnership (TPP), a 12-nation free trade agreement which included Australia, Brunei, Canada, Chile, Japan, Malaysia, Mexico, New Zealand, Peru, Singapore, United States, and Vietnam (but not China). On his first day in office, he made good on his promise to removed the US from the TPP, and the China tariffs materialized roughly a year later.

Opponents of the TPP cited a number of reasons for leaving. The US runs a trade deficit with nearly every TPP member country. Most TPP members charged higher tariffs on US exports than the US charged on their imports. Many TPP countries have barriers preventing US companies from investing in certain sectors. TPP partners have state-owned banks, and grant unfair trade subsidies to their state-run companies. Many political theorists believe that the US leaving the TPP may create an opportunity for China, whether to fill the vacant seat in the TPP, or by promoting the China-led Regional Comprehensive Economic Partnership (RECP).

Chinese outbound direct investment in the US

Austerity measures taken by China's government to curb infrastructure expenditure have pushed major SOEs – particularly those in the construction sector – to seek projects overseas.[25] This trend of increased foreign investment is also in keeping with the Chinese government's "going out" strategy, whereby President Xi Jinping has encouraged domestic companies to expand into foreign markets.[26] The US is the world's largest recipient of FDI, as well as a major destination for Chinese foreign investment.[27]

What the Chinese are buying

In 2015, Chinese citizens became the largest foreign purchasers of US homes, spending US$22 billion on residential real estate from April 2013 to March 2014. According to the National Association of Realtors, about 51% of reported purchases were in California, Washington, and

New York.[28] The recent trend of investments is not limited to Chinese real-estate companies buying US real estate. Chinese real-estate giant Dalian Wanda Group – which has an estimated US$86 billion of assets – purchased the Ironman Triathlon.[29] Wanda paid US$650 million for the World Triathlon Corporation, making it both the first Chinese company to invest in sports entertainment in the US, as well as one of the largest sports entertainment companies in the world.[30] Wanda has also bought a major stake in Hollywood filmmaker Legendary Entertainment.[31]

The list of deals and major purchases by Chinese companies in the US is staggering, both in number and in size. Chinese internet company Tencent Holdings Ltd. paid US$250 million for a controlling interest in the Los Angeles-based online game company Riot Games, which employs 1,000 people.[32] Tencent also bought a significant stake in San Francisco game-developer Glu Mobile Inc.[33] Alibaba Group opened a US based online retailer called 11 Main Inc; they also invested US$15 million in the US ecommerce site 1stdibs and US$200 million in Shoprunner.[34] Tsinghua Holdings announced its intention to buy Micron Technology Inc.[35] Far from the excitement of ecommerce, triathlons, and hotels, China's Shandong Tranlin Paper Co. bought into a fertilizer plant in Virginia.[36] Chinese investment in the US runs the full gamut of companies and industries.

In the first six months of 2015 Chinese companies completed 88 investment transactions in the US, totaling US$6.4 billion, almost half of which were in California. Virginia and New York were two other popular locations.[37] Of the 88 transactions, 53 were acquisitions, while the rest were new company launches.[38] The largest sectors were real estate and hospitality, followed closely by financial services and insurance, IT, and technology such as microchips makers.[39] The automotive industry was also favored by Chinese investment, as Chinese companies endeavor to acquire advanced manufacturing assets.[40] Chinese companies are increasingly interested in electric cars with Fisker Automotive, a subsidiary of Wanxiang, planning to compete in the US auto market directly by setting up a manufacturing facility in Moreno Valley, California. This will be the second Chinese automaker in the US, alongside the bus assembly plant owned by BYD in Lancaster, California. Additionally, Beijing Automobile Industry Holding (BAIC), a SOE, has already bought a significant stake in US electric car maker Lucid (formerly known as Atieva).[41]

The Chinese real-estate boom in the US

"This year, Chinese families represented the largest group of overseas home buyers in the United States."[42] According to the National Association of Realtors, in 2014 Chinese buyers spent US$22 billion on US real estate, a 70% increase over the previous year.[43]

A Beijing businessman and real-estate developer, Zhang Long, purchased 108 acres in Canyon Lake Ranch, 35 miles north of Dallas.[44] The Chinese boom in the US began with Chinese investors buying high-end apartments in big coastal cities, such as New York City, Los Angeles, and San Francisco, as well as in trendy areas like Silicon Valley.[45] The trend has now spread across the country to include inland areas where prices are much lower, but the houses and accompanying land are larger.[46] Some 80% of all homes purchased in the PRC are apartments,[47] so American homes – especially those with large lots outside of major urban areas – are tremendously attractive to Chinese buyers.

Chinese real estate investors pay a premium for their US

properties. This helps prop up the economies of some more remote communities, but also have drives apartment prices in places like New York out of the range of affordability for locals. Chinese investors comprise a very small percentage of the overall US real-estate market, but they are disproportionately represented in the luxury property segment. Of homes sold to Chinese buyers, "one in 14 homes sold for more than US$1 million."[48] According to a National Association of Realtors survey, the average price Chinese pay for a home in the US is US$831,800, over three times the average house purchase by Americans.[49] Another striking feature of these Chinese real estate investments is that 76% of them are in cash.[50]

Experts believe the trend will continue in spite of bumps in the Chinese economy. In fact, uncertainty in domestic markets is one of factor driving Chinese to invest abroad as they are looking for safe havens for their money.[51]

Economic factors driving outbound real-estate investment

A number of economic factors have encouraged Chinese investors to buy real estate in the US. One is that in China, even citizens cannot actually buy land; they only have property lease rights for 70 years.[52] In the US, even non-citizens are permitted to buy property.[53] Buying a US property, in addition to providing a Chinese investor with an ownership opportunity, also creates a storage of wealth, allowing them to build an inheritance that they can leave to their children.[54]

Although PRC law blocks people from buying land, they can buy apartments, houses, and other buildings. However, many investors – even those who have earned a fortune in Chinese real estate – are now wary that the market may collapse. Andrew Garthwaite, an analyst at Credit Suisse, has described China's economy as a triple bubble, with both over-inflated credit and investment, and "the second-biggest real estate bubble" of all time.[55] One of the reasons why real-estate prices rose so dramatically in China was the country's very high savings ratio (about 30% for many people) in conjunction with few alternative ways for people to invest their savings. The law has been very strict about the amount of money PRC citizens are allowed to send out of the country; the stock market is a fairly new concept and there were also tight regulations on stock investing. This left the average investor with only one choice: depositing the money in a state-owned bank, where it would earn a tiny amount of interest. When the government changed the law in 1990 and allowed people to purchase a 70-year lease on land for residential purposes,[56] there was an instant real-estate explosion as decades of savings were sunk into real-estate investments. The price of real estate soared with the average apartment in Shanghai costing at least 45 times the average salary.[57] Fearing a real-estate crash at home, Chinese investors want to invest overseas.

Other economic factors include the worsening state of China's economy. Economic growth has slowed, and both the stock market and the value of the Chinese currency have fallen sharply. According to Credit Suisse's Garthwaite, the domestic economy is plagued by "near record producer price deflation, near record low growth in bank deposits (the main source of internal liquidity), foreign exchange (FX) outflows (the main source of external liquidity), and falling house prices."[58]

In August 2015, Beijing suddenly devalued the yuan, decreasing the buying and investment power of Chinese citizens. Fearing further devaluations, many Chinese moved their assets to foreign currencies or began looking to move their money abroad.[59] Around the same time, China's stock markets crashed, with the Shanghai Composite Index declining 8.5%. "Many companies, including some large state-owned firms, fell by the maximum daily limit of 10%."[60] Within a short time, the index had dropped a total of 38%.[61]

Economists called the economic situation a "major slowdown," reporting that Beijing insiders were suggesting that GDP growth, which normally exceeds 6%, may slow to 2%. Investor sentiment – rather than real economic data – drives investor behavior.[62] Whether the actual growth is 2% or 20%, people will react to the number they believe in.[63] Historically, Chinese investors move their money abroad when they are nervous.[64] They fear that if they leave their money in China it will simply depreciate, particularly if the currency drops further.[65] Asia is full of cautionary tales: Taiwan, South Korea, Japan, and other economies grew at incredible rates then stopped, causing investors to lose faith in both the currency and the stock market and driving values down.[66] Understandably, people want to move their money before the crash comes.

Non-economic factors driving foreign real-estate investment

Many Chinese send their children abroad, particularly to the US, for education. According to a report by the Institute of International Education, 274,000 Chinese students were studying for bachelor's degrees in US universities in 2014.[67] Students' parents often make real-estate investments in the US to provide a home for their children living in the country.[68]

Immigrating is another reason for Chinese to invest in real estate abroad. Foreign investors can qualify under a US visa program called EB-5, if they have US$500,000 to invest and if they can prove the origin of the money. Around 80% of investors under the plan are Chinese.[69] "In 2013, three-quarters of US investment immigration visas were issued to Chinese nationals, with 6,124 Chinese receiving US green cards through the scheme."[70]

Another factor is China's ever-changing regulations. In the US, Chinese investors know the government is stable and the rules will not change overnight.[71] People are afraid that if they do not sell their Chinese properties now, they may not be permitted to later. Alternatively, they worry that if they do not move cash out now, they may not be able to in the future. A further concern is that unless they buy overseas real estate now, maybe they will not be permitted to in the future. As *International Business Times* put it in 2015, "in China you never know whether they'll change the regulations, change the taxes."[72] Investing in Africa or Latin America is an option, but there is always the possibility that the properties might suddenly be seized by the government. Chinese feel confident that confiscation will not happen in the US,[73] and a lot of Chinese investors have a fundamental faith in the US economy.[74]

Why Chinese companies are expanding in the US

Some Chinese companies invest in the US in order to obtain advanced manufacturing know-how. Push factors include higher costs in China for land and labor, as well as tariffs and trade barriers.[75] Trade barriers in the US such as "buy local" provisions can be overcome by Chinese companies acquiring US companies.[76] Vertical integration is another reason to buy up foreign companies, Chinese manufacturers wanting to invest in the raw materials which their factories back in China require.[77] Another factor driving China's overseas expansion is the slowing PRC economy. Political reasons for ODI include President Xi Jinping's strategy of "going out" or "going global."

Many of the companies going abroad are SOEs, such as Ambang Insurance Group which purchased New York's Waldorf Astoria Hotel.[78] Since 2010, total investment by SOEs in the US has been about US$17 billion, 34% of China's total investment in the US.[79] Making these large purchases abroad is also in keeping with another of China's official strategies, "grasping the big and letting go of the small."[80] While smaller SOEs are being sold off or privatized, the biggest SOEs are being encouraged to get bigger, both through domestic mergers and through overseas acquisitions.

The Trump-China economic dynamic

During his campaign, Donald Trump accused China of being a currency manipulator, a trade cheat, and a job thief. In a YouTube video which subsequently went viral, he said "China" 234 times. Trump's posturing on China has threatened the China-US economic relationship, the most important in the world. In addition to President Trump's harsh rhetoric against China, he has also packed his cabinet with advisors who are pro-Taiwan and anti-China. Trump's "anti-China triumvirate" includes Robert Lighthizer (US trade representative), Wilbur Ross (secretary of commerce), and Dr. Peter Navarro (head of the newly created White House National Trade Council and author of the book *Death by China*). All three have publicly stated their willingness to support Trump's "America First" policies, including shifting trade policy to a more protectionist stance.

Trump's proposed tariffs on Chinese goods

During the presidential campaign and during the first year of his presidency, Trump repeatedly threatened to levy a 45% tariff on Chinese goods. Some argued that this tariff would violate WTO agreements; Trump's counter argument is that China's unfair trade practices are already a violation of WTO treaties. Economists think Trump's approach may cause a destructive trade war.[81] Proponents of the tariff, including the president himself, claim that because the US runs a trade deficit with China, a trade war would hurt China worse.[82] Opponents of the tariff suggest that while a trade war would most likely hurt China more because it runs a surplus, it would also hurt the US. China could retaliate by hiking tariffs against US products, harming US airplane manufacturers, automakers and makers of farm machinery, as well as soybean exporters. US consumer goods manufacturers, such as Nike or Apple, could simply relocate their China-based manufacturing facilities to Indonesia or Vietnam. But even if they relocate, most of the jobs will not return to the US. In addition, these US companies could lose their China markets.[83]

The possibility that extra tariffs could be applied to Chinese imports has been compared to US President Herbert Hoover increasing tariffs in 1929 under the Smoot-Hawley Act, which experts feel drove the US and the world deeper into the Great Depression. Proponents of Trump's protectionism point out, however, that at the time of the Smoot-Hawley Act, the US was a net exporter. As the US is now a net importer, a trade war would not hurt the economy the way it did in the 1930s. Michael Schuman reporting for Bloomberg opposed higher tariffs, and suggested that Trump's best China strategy would be to arrange a free-trade agreement. China has a tremendous population with an economy growing at the rate of around 6%

per year. China now represents an extremely attractive market of more than 1.3 billion consumers with a per capita GDP of over US$7,000 per year. The Office of the United States Trade Representative (USTR) expects US exports to China to top US$161 billion in 2016,[84] but if a trade war breaks out, growth in US exports to China would halt. However, with a free trade agreement, the overall value of trade could increase.[85]

Opponents of Trump's proposed 45% tariff against China said that it would be illegal for the US president to levy such a high tariff without approval. While this is generally true, there are several loopholes to the tariff rules. Under US law, the president may levy a tariff without the permission of congress under the following conditions: 1. Unlimited tariffs 'during a time of war' – the president has the right to limit all trade war. The war need not be with China; having US troops in Syria may qualify. 2. Unlimited tariffs during 'a national emergency' – Under the International Emergency Economic Powers Act of 1977, the president can declare a national emergency, on almost any grounds, including severe unemployment. This legislation allows him to not only raise tariffs but also seize assets. 3. The president can also impose a 15% tariff without war or other justification for 150 days, either across the board or targeting a specific industry or product. 4. The Trade Expansion Act of 1962 – under this act, the president can raise tariffs on specific industries.[86]

Amid mounting trade tensions between China and the US, a positive development in the relationship came when President Trump finally acknowledged the "One China Policy" in a phone conversation with President Xi Jinping.[87] The general tone of the phone conversation was reported by both sides to have been very positive, serving to mend some of the damage done to US-China relations since the campaign began.

Just after the phone call between the two leaders, then US Secretary of State Rex Tillerson met with his opposite number, PRC Minister of Foreign Affairs Wang Yi, during the first major official state visit from the US to China since the election. Tillerson asked for China's cooperation in limiting North Korea's nuclear program. One sticking point, however, was that Tillerson reiterated the US commitment to disputed islands in the South China Sea.[88]

Another positive step in the US-China dynamic came when PRC courts ruled in favor of Trump in his long-running lawsuit to copyright the Trump name in China. Critics have shouted "conflict of interest" and "quid pro quo," even though the lawsuit predated his presidential campaign by many years.[89]

China at Davos

While the most capitalist nation on Earth was busy creating trade barriers, the world's largest communist nation was championing the cause of free trade at the 2017 World Economic Forum at Davos, Switzerland.[90] President Xi was the star of the forum, pushing Beijing's global initiatives, including the Asia Infrastructure Investment Bank and the Belt and Road Initiative.[91] Xi argued that globalization has made the world richer. Globalization has certainly made China richer through its broad range of investments and acquisitions across the globe.

Trump did not attend Davos because it coincided with his inauguration. Instead, US interests were represented by the president's chosen advisor, former hedge fund boss Anthony Scaramucci. Given the current global dynamic, it was no wonder that Xi, the first PRC president to attend Davos, was at center stage and that the US-China dynamic was the primary topic of discussion. His entourage was the largest Chinese delegation in history, and involved prominent millionaires including Alibaba founder Jack Ma and property magnate Wang Jianlin of Dalian Wanda. Xi pledged to lead a return to free trade.[92]

According to Reuters research, the most common concerns among global economists were a US-China trade war, as well as economic tensions caused by an adversarial Trump administration.[93] Davos attendees shared worries about a more protectionist US policy generated by Trump's advisory team, particularly Dr. Peter Navarro, who has been calling for increased barriers against China for years.

Who is more open to free trade, China or the US?

Whether the US is actually protectionist or China is supporting free trade is not a simple question. The US runs a trade deficit with China and most of its other trading partners, which would suggest that the US is open to trade. The Chinese currency is in steady decline, and China levies tariffs against US products which are a multiple of the tariffs the US levies against Chinese goods. This suggests China is more protectionist than the US. US markets are still essentially open, with Chinese companies free to invest in nearly any sector and to own 100% of their US subsidiaries. The reverse is not true, however, as countless rules in the PRC restrict American or other foreign enterprises as to where, how, and how much they can invest.

For example, foreign companies cannot own land in China, but Chinese companies can own land in the US. On the Chinese side, there is a list of strategic sectors, including entertainment and the construction of villas, which foreign companies are prohibited from investing in, while the US maintains no such list. Chinese SOEs are effectively subsidized by China's state-owned banks, making it nearly impossible for US companies to compete in open markets. And, of course, one of the terms of doing business in China is that US companies must agree to transfer technology to their hosts. Once again, mandatory technology transfer is not one of the terms of doing business in the United States.

Trump believes the US could win a trade war with China because the US runs a trade deficit with China. The US is one of the least trade dependent countries in the world—the implication being that if a trade war erupted, the US would be able to function. In 2015, only 12.6% of the US GDP derived from exports.[94] China's exports, on the other hand, accounted for 18% of GDP.[95] Trump has more or less stated that China needs the US more than the US needs China.

Many pro-Trump voices claim that the president is not actually against trade, but just against existing trade deals, and that much of his blustering, particularly against China, is a means of signaling a return to the negotiation table. In April 2017, the strategy appeared to have worked, when Xi and Trump met at Trump's Mar-a-Lago resort to negotiate a new trade deal.

China-US trade rebalancing in the new trade deal

In May 2017, the US and China reached a landmark ten-point trade deal which would open up certain sectors of the Chinese economy, such as credit card provision, to US firms while allowing additional Chinese products, such as cooked poultry, to enter the US.[96] The PRC would also lift its ban on liquefied natural gas (LNG) imports from the US. In return, Chinese banks would be permitted to enter the US market.[97] This new China-US trade deal was set to be implemented in

July 2017,[98] as part of a 100-day action plan of the US-China Comprehensive Economic Dialogue, a one-year initiative to increase US-China economic cooperation.[99]

US agriculture stood to gain as a result of the new deal, as now US beef producers would be permitted to export both processed beef and livestock to China. Chinese cooked poultry exports would also benefit US companies in China which produce cooked poultry, as they would now be able to export this product to the US. A further benefit to the US is that GM seeds from the US could now enter the Chinese market. US biotech companies such as Monsanto, DuPont, and Dow Chemical would now have their chance.[100]

The US financial sector was also going to benefit from the new arrangements. Under the deal, US credit-rating agencies and credit card companies would be allowed to operate as wholly-owned foreign entities in China.[101] Previously, credit-ratings companies such as Moody's and Standard & Poor's were only permitted to act in the form of joint ventures. This new development would not only boost their business, but improve their risk-management capabilities. Furthermore, China has promised to grant full market access to US electronic payment providers. Chinese banks will now be permitted to issue dual-branded cards, for example Industrial and Commercial Bank of China (ICBC) may choose to issue an ICBC MasterCard. This is expected to give a tremendous boost to American brands. Credit-card provision was the subject of an Obama-lead complaint to the WTO in 2012; however, under Trump's new trade agreement, Beijing is going to allow US credit-card providers such as Visa, MasterCard, and American Express a larger share of the Chinese market. Another improvement in the financial sector is that both bond underwriting and settlement licensing will be granted to US firms. US financial firms JPMorgan Chase and Citibank have both been granted licenses to operate in the PRC.[102]

US Secretary of Commerce Wilbur Ross praised the new trade agreement, stating that it should help to reduce the US trade deficit with China by the end of 2017.[103] The deal is significant as it represents a less confrontational approach; it may also pave the way for more American firms to tap into China's growing middle class. In return, China's banks, which are the largest in the world, will gain access to the much coveted US market. With the signing of the deal, Beijing also wins a soft-power victory by improving its image in the US and to the world.

Further proof of a shifting US attitude toward China was Trump's decision to send US representation to the Belt and Road Initiative Forum held in Beijing on May 15–16, 2017. The US president had originally said the US would not participate, but with an agreement from Beijing regarding a shift in trade policy, the US appears more willing to at least engage with China's massive global connectivity project.[104]

Ross called this deal, "The first real breakthrough we have had with China in decades."[105] He attributes this sudden progress to "the personal chemistry between President Xi Jinping and President Donald Trump." As evidence, he pointed out that the deal came just a month after the two met at Trump's Mar-a-Lago resort. Ross stated that the US had never had trade agreements with China before "with this precision to solve long standing trade problems."[106] He also marveled at how quickly the deal was not only agreed upon, but how soon it will go into effect. These types of trade deals typically take months or years to draft and implement, rather than weeks.

Larry Kudlow, a former Ronald Reagan adviser, heralded the trade agreement as great news, saying that both Trump and Ross had softened their China stance, averting a trade war. Kudlow went on to say that the deal will create jobs at home while helping both economies. In an interview he also stated, "I really like the China situation, both economically and strategically."[107]

Belpoint Chief Strategist David Nelson echoed Kudlow's sentiments, saying the deal was excellent news because beef and LNG would amount to billions of dollars of trade. He also saw the deal as the first step in a long-term strategy which will eventually open markets for US industries, and that by establishing these friendlier trade ties now, the stage will be set for better negotiations on serious issues later. He told Newsmax, "Trade can be a very effective foreign policy tool."[108]

While many saw the deal as an advance, some Americans criticized it, saying China stands to gain more than the US. Robert Atkinson of the Information Technology and Innovation Foundation said that China had outmaneuvered the US once again as the new deal opened Chinese markets to only a few US industries, while giving China the opportunity to buy up US businesses.[109] Representative Brad Sherman agreed: "This is a complete capitulation to China. Trump has betrayed working families."[110] Sherman expressed his belief that US beef going to China will help reduce the trade deficit, but he was very upset about accepting pre-cooked Chinese chicken as the US would not be able to regulate it and it would be difficult to monitor food safety.[111]

Even those who support the new trade deal do not see it as a panacea. Most experts think the agreement will help cut to the trade deficit with China, but is unlikely to result in the creation of jobs in the US.[112] Representative Keith Rofthus took a more balanced approach in his assessment, saying the deal would probably help agriculture in his state,

Pennsylvania, while stressing issues which still need to be addressed, such as anti-dumping and other policies. He went on to say that much work would be necessary before trade with China could be called fair.[113] While a number of markets have been opened to US companies, a number of key issues have yet to be addressed, such as US firms being subjected to mandatory technology transfer.[114]

Brad Blakeman, a former advisor to President George W. Bush, called the trade deal "a good first step,"[115] but only a first step. He also said it was good that the US is going slowly with deals, as a deal is only as good as the ability to enforce it.[116] Pushing too hard or moving too fast could cause a backlash and shut the dialogue down completely. In the same interview, *Wall Street Journal* assistant editor James Freeman said that the trade deal was a great success and if Trump can continue in this way, he could keep opening the Chinese market, and perhaps eventually get the Chinese to stop demanding joint ventures and stop stealing intellectual property. Blakeman went on to say that he believed that as a result of the deal, the US would have greater engagement with China, hopefully improving relations between the two countries.[117]

US-China relations in the wake of the US Section 301 IP investigation

In August 2017, President Trump asked US Trade Representative Robert Lighthizer to officially initiate an investigation of the PRC regarding intellectual property rights (IPR) and technology transfer, under Section 301 of the Trade Act of 1974.[118] Section 301 gives the president the authority to order the US Trade Representative to take any necessary measures to stop any foreign government from actions which violate international trade agreements or restrict US commerce.[119] While this move by the US is in their national interest, it undermines the emerging collaboration in US-China relations.

Past administrations have not used the act liberally for fear of retaliatory reactions against US trade. Industry magazine *Technology, Manufacturing, and Transportation Insider* (TMTI) reports that numerous US companies have filed complaints relating to China's insistence on technology transfers and alleged violations of IPR. In light of the new investigation, TMTI expects that US companies will have the opportunity to present evidence of these allegations, and that the president will enter into negotiations with China to remedy these grievances.[120] Should negotiations fail, the president has the power to impose tariffs or quotas against China within 30 days of receiving the results of the investigation. The results of an investigation under Section 301 generally have to be filed within 12 months of the start of the investigation. According to the statute, the recommended tariffs or other sanctions will be active for four years.[121]

The investigation has understandably caused upset in Beijing, which feels that the US should have used WTO mechanisms to resolve any disputes, rather than their own legislation.[122] The PRC issued strong condemnations: China's Ministry of Commerce (MOC) expressed "strong dissatisfaction" with the investigation.[123] Beijing sees the launch of the investigation as a regression in globalization and US-China relations. This move comes shortly after the US and China entered into the China Comprehensive Economic Dialogue (also known as the 100-Day Plan), a trade agreement which resulted from the very successful and productive meeting between Donald Trump and Xi Jinping in Florida. The plan allowed for US beef to enter the Chinese market and for US financial and banking institutions to take a more active role in the Chinese economy. The fact that the MOC mentioned the investigation within the context of the agreement may mean that, in retaliation, China may cancel some aspects of the agreement.[124]

In an official press release, the MOC said: "We urge the US to act prudently and respect the facts, the strong cooperation will of industries from both countries, and multilateral trade rules."[125] In the statement, the MOC suggested that the US should adhere to international trade agreements, and indicated that the US should take the dispute to the WTO rather than to launch an investigation based on US laws. The ministry went on to say that they believed the move would be condemned by the international community.[126]

A somewhat softer dismissal of the investigation came from the government's English-language *Beijing Review*; it pointed out that rising wages and regulatory issues in the PRC have already made the country a less desirable place for manufacturers, thus reducing opportunities for the theft of intellectual property. Banking and finance are the main industries the US wants to invest in; however, because these are protected sectors, investment has been slow and difficult. *Beijing Review*'s stance was that trade could be a basis for US-China relations and that the IPR issue should be dealt with through the WTO.[127]

Washington's view on the WTO handling this matter is the opposite. Commerce Secretary Ross has already criticized the WTO for not being tough enough in China, and has called China "protectionists dressed in free-market clothing."[128] Trump has expressed the view that he sees the WTO as infringing on US sovereignty.[129] A report by the American Enterprise Institute (AEI) called the most recent Section 301 investigation a good first step toward reforming US trade policy, but suggested that the investigation should go further to explore how China's special economic zones contribute to IP theft. AEI alleges that Chinese firms in special economic zones pilfer American technology and crowd out US firms.[130]

Official accusations against China began long before this most recent investigation. The last time an official Section 301 investigation was launched was in 2010 against China's energy industry.[131] A significant difference between previous 301 claims and the most recent one is that, in the past, the investigations were sought by industry associations. This time, by contrast, the federal government initiated the investigation. In April 2017, Trade Representative Lighthizer issued a Section 301 report specifically naming China as a country of concern regarding IPR, and for engaging in "coercive technology transfer."[132]

Earlier this year, President Trump announced that he was considering restricting China from trading in steel with the US under Section 232 of the 1962 Trade Act, which empowers the president to restrict trade on the grounds of national defense. He has since stated that he is postponing his final ruling on the steel issue.[133] Shortly after launching the investigation into steel, Trump launched a similar investigation into aluminum.[134] If these investigations indicate that Chinese steel and aluminum imports are compromising national security, then tariffs may be imposed.[135] Trump could also block China trade by evoking the International Emergency Economic Powers Act of 1977, as previous administrations have done against other countries. Historically, the Act has never been opposed by Congress.[136]

Regarding the current investigation of IPR issues, most believe that while China is guilty, Trump's protectionist stance could severely damage the world economy. Brian O'Shaughnessy, an IP attorney at Dinsmore & Shohl LLP and president and chair of the Board of the Licensing Executives Society (an organization for IP professionals), confirmed that most economists around the world are in agreement that China has problems with IP theft.[137] Tim Worstall of *Forbes* had a unique take on the investigation. While he generally believes that China or companies in China are stealing US IP, he believes the US should simply look the other way. First, ignoring the issue can help to avoid a costly trade war. Second, the wealth of the US is based on its ability to create IP. As a result, the US will continue to develop new IP and remain wealthy while China will only be able to copy IP and remain middle income.[138]

Business Insider more or less condemned the Section 301 investigation, calling it "the first shot in a trade war with China."[139] According to *Business Insider*, Beijing interprets actions under Section 301 as an act of aggression because it permits the US president to act without first consulting the WTO.[140]

Responding to allegations it does not enforce protection of intellectual property, Beijing pointed to the Thirteenth Five-Year Plan which includes provisions for increased IPR enforcement. According to the official news agency Xinhua, the plan called for an improvement of "the rules and regulations related to intellectual property rights in newly-emerged fields including Internet Plus, e-commerce, and big data."[141] However, the US-China Business Council and the American Chamber of Commerce in China report that while there have been some judicial improvements in cases of companies suing for IP violations, they specifically cited technology-transfer rules as being the real issue.[142] PRC law forces foreign firms to agree to transfer technology to their Chinese JV partners as a condition for gaining access to Chinese markets.[143] This technology transfer represents a

219

tremendous leakage of US intellectual property into China.

A China-US trade war could have detrimental effects for both economies as both are key receivers of exported goods. Some warn that protectionist measures by the US may hurt the Chinese economy, setback US-China relations and possibly even start a trade war. The US accounts for up to 20% of China's total exports and a trade war could have a significant impact on the Chinese economy. However, losing China as a trading partner would also cause the US economy to take a hit. In 2016, China accounted for 62% of US soybean exports, 25% of US aviation exports, 14% of US cotton exports, 17% of US automobile exports, and 15% of semiconductor exports.[144] *China Daily* reported that "A full-blown trade war between China and the US still doesn't seem inevitable, but that shouldn't prevent Beijing from taking measures to cope with the US trade protectionist weapon: Section 301."[145] According to the Brookings Institution, historically, when China is challenged on trade violations, they retaliate.[146]

Retaliation may already have begun. In mid-August, the Chinese government launched an anti-dumping investigation into hydrogenated butyl rubber from the US, the EU, and Singapore. At a press conference, the Ministry of Commerce spokesperson said that this investigation was simply routine and not related to any other case.[147]

Since 1974, Section 301 investigations have been enacted 120 times, although most have not resulted in sanctions. In fact, the 2010 investigation against China's renewable energy sector did not result in sanctions being taken.[148] Some believe Trump's initiation of the 301 investigation is simply a means to some other end.

Some journalists believe that Trump's threats under Section 301 might be a case of using trade as a bargaining chip in dealing with the North Korea situation.[149] Another theory is that Trump is using the investigation to gain Chinese concessions for the US steel industry.[150] Yet another theory is that the US is looking for concessions in light of China's cyber-security law, which requires US companies to store their data in China. As the law was enacted under the guise of national defense, it is non-negotiable. Therefore, it is possible that Trump is trying to use the 301 investigation to negotiate some other trade-related issues as compensation for forced compliance with the cyber-security law.[151]

A game of back and forth with no end

As the US tightens its sanctions on North Korea, it was imposing secondary sanctions on countries which continue to support the North Korean economy. The US Department of the Treasury's Office of Foreign Assets Control added ten companies to its sanction list, five of which were Chinese. These sanctions are imposed on countries purchasing coal and oil from North Korea, and China represents 90% of North Korea's total trade.[152] China opposed the US sanctions as being extraterritorial legal restrictions that bypass the UN and other international bodies. Meanwhile, China has increased tariffs on semiconductors which the US claims violates WTO agreements.[153]

The same US-China Economic and Security Review Commission which reported that Trump had launched a Section 301 investigation against China also stated that the US trade deficit with China had increased by 10% since the previous year due to growing US imports. US oil exports to China have also increased.[154] Therefore, it seems for every action there is a similar reaction. The Section 301 and 2015 US 232 investigation into the Chinese steel industry,[155] and the isolated tariffs and restrictions on various products from both sides, simply represent the ups and downs in a complicated relationship between the world's two largest powers. The global media often predicts some cataclysmic event, dramatically and permanently changing US-China economic relations, but what seems more likely is that the relationship will continue as it is now, plagued by suspicion, marred by distrust, and even occasionally heating up or flaring into legal action. However, at the end of the day, nothing will have changed. The Section 301 investigation will eventually be negotiated away and simply become one more bump on an already rocky road.

There is no doubt that China has a history of weak IPR protection and that mandatory technology transfer has been a component of many JVs in China. It is also true that when challenged, China lashes out. Therefore, confronting China on IP issues at this exact moment in time, while justified, will undoubtedly damage US-China trade relations. This is particularly disappointing coming on the wake of the 100-Day Action Plan, which represented the largest positive step in US-China trade relations in decades. As always, a trade war between the US and China is extremely unlikely; however, this dispute may undo the progress made earlier this year.

China-Trump trade policy review at the close of 2017

The central story for the world's economy in 2017 had been the relationship between the US and China. However, while the volume of trade and investment passing between the world's two largest trading partners are significant to the global financial system, it is the shifting alliances of the rest of the world that possibly has greater implications in the long term. The erratic and often abrasive behavior of US President Trump seems to be driving US allies and enemies alike into the Chinese sphere of influence.

Shifts in US policy under Trump have given China the opportunity to court traditional US allies. The US withdrawal from the Paris Climate Accords has given China an opportunity to move closer to Europe through cooperation on environmental issues.[156] Trump's enmity with Chancellor Angela Merkel has reminded Germany that China represents a tremendous market for Volkswagens.[157] Accusations from the US that Pakistan is harboring terrorists are also helping to move Pakistan firmly into the Chinese camp.[158] Panama, a country which uses the US dollar as its currency and owes its independence to a US invasion of Colombia, has decided to rescind its recognition of US ally Taiwan and recognize the PRC, a move which many see as a move away from Washington.[159] Elsewhere in Latin America, China and Argentina signed a nuclear cooperation agreement whereby China is providing Argentina with two nuclear reactors worth US$1.5 billion, and providing 85% of the financing.[160] There is even speculation that China may build a naval base in Argentina. Australia, a country which has been called "the most China dependent economy in the developed world" is moving to strengthen its bilateral China trade, which is already worth over US$124 billion.[161]

Chinese foreign policy also indicates a desire to draw in traditional rivals of the US. China recently held joint naval exercises with Russia, and by virtue of US-led international sanctions, Iran has no other option but to accept Chinese loans and investments, the most recent round of which total US$15 billion and US$10 billion, respectively.[162,163]

Any discussion of the effectiveness of Trump's China policy so far would have to see this realignment of global allegiances as a direct result of his overall foreign policy, and as having a significant impact on China. One could argue that Trump's foreign policy has given China a better position in the world. In general, Trump has been disengaging with the rest of the world. The US withdrawal from the Trans Pacific Partnership (TPP) on the first day of the Trump presidency was a concrete step toward a retraction from the current world order. Shortly afterwards, at the World Economic Forum in Davos, PRC President Xi Jinping promised to lead the world's globalization initiatives.[164] For each step the US takes toward isolation, China appears to be taking a step toward engagement.

Since taking office, Trump had signaled that he and many of his supporters are displeased with Washington's role since World War II as the underwriter and leader of most global initiatives, including the UN and the World Bank.[165] Xi, on the other hand, has personally offered to lead the globalization of trade through such initiatives as China's Belt and Road, and in the reduction of greenhouse gases through the Paris Climate Accords. Most recently, through the G20, Xi has proposed that China participate with the world's most developed countries to manage global energy issues.[166]

During his presidential campaign, Trump threatened heavy tariffs and restrictions on trade with China. Although he has not taken such extreme steps, he has begun restricting some trade with China. Trump blocked China-backed Canyon Bridge Capital Partners' attempt to buy the US company Lattice Semiconductor on the grounds of national security.[167] This blockade prompted Beijing's top advisory board to warn Trump that closing doors could be damaging for the US.[168]

Halting the Lattice deal was not a unilateral move by Trump; it had some cross-party support in the form of a bipartisan group of 22 House of Representatives members who also opposed the acquisition.[169] The Committee on Foreign Investment in the United States (CFIUS), which operates under Section 721 of the Defense Production Act of 1950,[170] also expressed opposition to the deal. Secretary of the Treasury Steven Mnuchin is chairman of CFIUS, an inter-agency body which investigates the implications of foreign investment in the US. Before he left the White House, Trump advisor Steve Bannon called for a strengthening of CFIUS, an idea backed by Senate Majority Whip John Cornyn of Texas and Representative Robert Pittenger (Republican, North Carolina).[171] As a result of increased scrutiny by CFIUS, Chinese investment in the US in 2017 was down 70% by value compared to the previous year.[172]

Other voices in Washington are also advising restrictions on China. Many in the US government see China as an adversary because of China's aggressive economic expansion beyond its own borders, its military buildup, and its claims on the South China Sea.[173] Trade Representative Lighthizer said that China's economic strategy is a major threat to world trade, citing the sheer scale of the Chinese economy, as well as China's strategies of coordinated economic development, subsidies to SOEs, forced technology transfer, and the creation of national champions.[174] Some believe that the departure of Steve Bannon, who *New York Times* called "the man who all but declared economic war with China,"[175] might signal a softer stance toward China. However, Lighthizer appears to be continuing in a similar fashion.[176]

Trump is using the various legal tools at his disposal to place restrictions on imports from China. In August 2017, he ordered the Office of the USTR to launch an investigation into alleged IP theft and technology transfer by China. Under Section 301 of the Trade Act of 1974, the president has broad powers to restrict trade or impose tariffs against trade which he feels represents a threat to national security.[177] In addition, Trump has already raised tariffs on Chinese aluminum-foil imports on the grounds that China's aluminum industry is heavily subsidized. Tariffs of up to 81% were enacted by Washington under Section 232 of Trade Expansion Act of 1962, which empowers the president to levy tariffs if a US industry is threatened.[178] The US Department of Justice has also filed a complaint against PRC-backed Zhongwang US, accusing its affiliate Perfectus Aluminum of illegally importing aluminum into the US, evading billions of dollars' worth of import duties.[178]

Trump's actions, however, do not necessarily signal a coordinated anti-China shift in US trade policy. He has enacted a number of tariffs against Chinese imports and prevented some Chinese acquisitions, but these actions seem to be occurring in isolation. *New York Times* recognized that while Trump has acknowledged the importance of the US-China relationship, he has yet to formulate a coherent China policy.[180]

Despite these complications in Sino-US relations, some positive movements have come from the American side. Trump and Xi had what the former called a "good conversation" about North Korea and about Trump's then-upcoming visit to China. Xi stressed to China's state media the importance of this visit, which will occur in November.[181] Xi and Trump also agreed to take a coordinated and stronger stance against North Korea. However, Beijing will most likely be careful not to take steps which might topple the regime for fear of unleashing a humanitarian crisis just across the border.[182] In August, PRC and US military leaders signed an agreement increasing communication.[183] As of July, China allowed US imports of rice for the first time.[184] In late

September, Bloomberg announced that Beijing may be preparing to loosen restrictions on US access to China's automotive market, as well as allowing foreign companies to own controlling interests in JVs in the financial industry.[185]

In conclusion, while certain of Washington's and Beijing's policy aims may appear to be at odds, the two countries can find areas where their interests overlap, such as North Korea and mutually beneficial trade. Additionally, neither country actually wants a trade war. Although trade with China represents a relatively small amount of US total exports, losing any exports would be bad for the economy. Furthermore, in the absence of a clear China policy, the two presidents could take issues on a case-by-case basis, and agree or disagree in isolation without a single issue threatening to wreck the entire relationship.

At the end of the day, both presidents want their respective countries to make money, and for their citizens to have the fairest trade deals possible. It seems this goal is most likely to be achieved through repeated dialogue and step-by-step agreements. On the other hand, both countries also appear to want to be the world's leader, and there can only be one leader; it seems that no matter how much negotiation and tit-for-tat the countries engage in, they will eventually hit a wall which diplomacy cannot dissolve.

Trump's China tariffs reactions and possible outcomes

Trump has announced that he has instructed Trade Representative Lighthizer to raise at least US$50 billion in tariffs on imports from China. Among these tariffs will be a 25% duty on certain PRC products such as aerospace, information and communication technology, and machinery. The president has said that additional tariffs will be coming, and that when all is said and done, the tariffs may reach as high as US$60 billion.[186] A new list of tariffs is expected to be released by the Lighthizer's office within 15 days. Experts believe the next round of tariffs will be applied to robotics, hi-tech trains, and aerospace.[187] Trump said the US was in positive negotiations with world leaders. He also stated that, "This is the first of many" tariffs and actions.[188]

Beijing's immediate response was that China does not fear a trade war with the US and that China would retaliate with US$3 billion of tariffs on imports from the US, including pork, recycled aluminum, steel pipes, fruit, and wine. China has also stated that they will pursue legal action against the US at the WTO.[189] Li Yong, senior fellow of China Association of International Trade, has called Trump's move the start of a trade war.[190]

Further US actions

This latest round of tariffs is in addition to tariffs raised earlier on steel and aluminum. The president has also directed US Treasury Secretary Steven Mnuchin to restrict PRC investment in certain strategic sectors on grounds of national security. Meanwhile, the Trump administration is moving forward with a complaint against China at the WTO related to discriminatory licensing practices.[191]

Further sanctions are planned, associated with the US Section 301 IPR investigation against China, led by the Office of the USTR.[192] Lighthizer told the press that the investigation had determined that China does have a policy of forced technology transfer, requiring licensing at less than economic value, the use of state capitalism to purchase technology, and of cyber theft.[193] According to *Los Angeles Times*, "The investigation found that the Chinese government has hacked US computer systems to benefit Chinese companies, routinely pressured US companies to enter into JVs with Chinese partners that required sharing valuable technology, and used state funds to purchase US companies to get their patents and other intellectual property."[194] Consequently, tariffs will be placed on certain products. Restrictions will be placed on Chinese investment in certain sectors of the US economy, and a WTO case will be filed.[195]

Reactions outside China

In Europe, the initial reaction to the tariffs was generally negative. Leaders in Europe and other countries are complaining that US tariffs against China could harm the global economy. The Bank of England warned that US protectionism could potentially damage the entire world. Within 24 hours of announcing the tariffs, however, President Trump announced that the tariffs would not apply to imports from EU, Australia, Argentina, Brazil, Canada, Mexico and South Korea.[196] After this second announcement, Europe watered down its criticism of the tariffs. Trump was quick to point out that the EU imposes heavy duties on imports from the US, and that he has asked the EU – in light of not being subjected to new tariffs – to re-evaluate the duties they charge on US products. The EU response to the tariffs is already on the agenda for the next EU leaders' meeting.[197]

The Dow plummeted 724 points on news of the tariffs.[199] By the next day, however, it had almost fully recovered.[200] MSNBC reported that Americans and American companies are concerned that the tariffs will cause a downturn in the US economy, as well as an increase in the cost of consumer goods.[201] Similar warnings, about higher consumer prices, came from US companies such as Walmart Inc. and Amazon.com Inc.; 49 major retailers sent a letter to the president, warning that the tariffs would hurt working families.[202] A similar letter was drafted by companies in the US apparel and footwear industry. The US Chamber of Commerce also spoke out against the tariffs. The Information Technology Industry Council and 44 other trade associations drafted a letter, voicing their opposition to the tariffs.[203]

Wall Street Journal has criticized Trump's tariffs. "Mr. Trump will pay a political price for his rotten policy, and he should. But far worse is the arbitrary damage to businesses and workers like Mark Foster (a worker displaced because an increase in steel costs) who are being punished not by competition but by their own government."[204]

Farmers have expressed concerns that their produce will now be banned in China. Retaliation by China is expected to hurt US agricultural exports particularly soy beans and pork. Other US companies dependent on China trade are Apple, Ford and Boeing.[205]

Not everyone in the US is against the tariffs, however. National Economic Council Director Larry Kudlow stated "China has earned a tough response." He went on to say, "A thought that I have is the United States could lead a coalition of large trading partners and allies against China, or to let China know that they're breaking the rules left and right."[206]

White House trade advisor Peter Navarro, author of *Death by China*, heralded the decision, saying it was part of a dramatic shift in the US-China economic order. "China seeks, 'domination of the industries of the future' and has used 'discriminatory, unreasonable practices' to force US companies to help it achieve that goal."[207] Navarro went on to say that through these tariffs the US was "strategically defending itself [from] … economic aggression."[208]

Certain industries are supportive of the tariffs. Over the last several weeks, an advert from US steel manufacturers has been running on American television, reminding the president that during his campaign, he promised to raise tariffs against China to protect American steel.[209] Commerce Secretary Ross also recommended that Trump levy tariffs on steel imports.[210] A representative of the US aerospace industry spoke out in favor of Trump's actions as protecting the IPR which are important for the country's future economic development.[211] *Los Angeles Times* reported: "US politicians of both parties have grown increasingly worried about Chinese efforts to get hold of American technology — by forcing US companies to share innovations as a price of doing business in China or, in many cases, by industrial espionage, cyber attacks and other crimes."[212]

Senator Charles E. Schumer (Democrat, New York) praised the president for taking steps to protect US interests. House Ways and Means Committee chair Kevin Brady (Republican, Texas) also supported the president's actions, but qualified his praise by saying that the president should find a way to punish China without hurting American interests.[213]

The White House's way forward

Far from taking an adversarial stance, President Trump has repeatedly stated that he respects President Xi and considers him a friend. Ross has predicted that the response from China will not be devastating,[214] going on to say that, in his opinion, Washington and Beijing will wind up negotiating rather than fighting.[215]

Ross has suggested that all China has to do to decrease the trade deficit would be to buy more American liquid natural gas (LNG).[216] The PRC is the world's no. 3 importer of LNG, and since Xi and Trump signed the New China Trade Deal last summer, Beijing now allows imports of LNG from the US. China does not use enough LNG to completely eradicate the trade deficit, but importing more LNG from the US would be a step in the right direction, rather than a tit-for-tat response which could escalate into a trade war.

This China-economist's opinion

Since President Donald Trump took office in 2017, the media has been hypothesizing the destructive effects of a global trade war. Similar stories have come back in vogue since US tariffs against Chinese imports were announced in March 2018. And while the various scenarios and doomsday prophecies may follow mathematical logic, the point everyone seems to be missing is that there is no trade war. The US did not declare a trade war. Washington exercised its right to levy tariffs against Chinese products, just as China does against US products, just as all sovereign nations do against products from other nations. More importantly, China's reaction was not to create a trade war. The country's first reaction was to levy US$3 billion worth of tariffs against the US$50 billion of tariffs. Even if both sides carried out these threats, this would not constitute a trade war. Neither would it signal a collapse of the global economy. US$3 billion in tariffs would not automatically equal US$3 billion in lost revenue for the US, just as US$50 billion in tariffs would not equal US$50 billion in lost revenue for China.

The US imports more steel from Canada than it does from China. If the US blocked all Chinese steel imports – which has not even been suggested – the Americans would either produce more steel themselves or buy from Canada. Steel produced locally would create jobs, which would be a win for the US. If the US imported from Canada, global GDP would not change; Canadian exports would increase, while China's would fall. If China were to block 100% of US pork imports (again, this has not been suggested), they might be hard pressed to find another country that could produce the same quantity of pork, but they would not starve, and neither would the US. Exports represent less than 12% of US GDP, and of them a mere 8% goes to China.[217] And of this 8% of 12%, pork represents only a fraction. Even in a worst case scenario, Chinese tariffs against the US would not drive US exports to China down to zero. Neither would US tariffs against the PRC end China's exports to the US. At present, neither country is even hinting at breaking trading relations with the other.

China runs a tremendous trade surplus with the US. All China needs do to appease Trump would be to increase imports from the US. Trump was not even asking for balance, simply a reduction in the size of the surplus. Roughly 20% of China's GDP comes from exports and roughly 20% of that number goes to the US, meaning the US accounts for about 4% of the Chinese GDP. It would not be logical for China to stop selling to the US. In fact, while leaders in Beijing have repeatedly criticized Trump's protectionist stance, almost none of them have expressed any interest in engaging in a trade war. Trump was not calling for a trade war. He was calling for a change in the status quo.

Critics around the globe find Trump's blustering inappropriate for a world leader. And while this may or may not be true, the current reality is that Trump is the leader, and it would be more constructive to try and interpret his blustering than to reject it outright. He has clearly stated exactly what he wants, time and time again. He wants a reduction of the US trade deficit with China. He has also stated that he is willing to sit down and negotiate. The recent round of tariffs and restrictions on trade are "a shot across the bow" – a sudden and aggressive action designed to shock the opposition and brings them to the negotiating table.

Commerce Secretary Ross has already suggested a move that China could take as a show of good faith, simply buying more LNG from the US. Beijing could also buy more soybeans or pork or open some restricted sectors to US trade. If China made these adjustments, the US would most likely be willing to drop some of the tariffs and investigations. When announcing these tariffs, Trump repeatedly used the word "reciprocal." By definition, this means that if China cuts duties and restrictions on some US products, the US would decrease duties and restrictions on some Chinese products.

The president was not calling for a trade war, nor was he calling for a halt to China's exports to the US. He asked for reciprocal trade agreements which would help to decrease China's trade surplus with the US.

One month after Trump's China tariff announcement

The current round of tariffs by President Trump against China are just the latest actions in a long series of trade disputes between the US and China.

In April 2017, Trump launched an investigation into steel imports. In August 2017, he commissioned a Section 301 investigation into possible Chinese IPR violations. In January 2018, he levied a 30% tariff on imported solar panels as well as a 20% tax on large residential washing machines. In February 2018, the Commerce Department proposed a 24% tariff on steel and 7.7% on aluminum. On March 9, 2018, Trump proposed a 25% tariff on steel and 10% on aluminum imports.[218] The US is not the only country to have charged

China with violating anti-dumping laws. For steel and aluminum, supply exceeds demand in China, and trading partners such as the EU have similarly complained that China is exporting at sub-market prices, making it difficult for foreign firms to compete.[219]

In response to the Trump tariffs, on April 2, 2018, China levied US$3 billion of tariffs on US imports. As a result of the findings of the Section 301 investigation on IPR violations, the Office of the USTR proposed a 25% tax on nearly 1,300 Chinese goods. In retaliation, on April 4, 2018, China threatened an additional US$50 billion of tariffs on American goods. The next day, President Trump called for another US$100 billion in tariffs on Chinese imports. To this end, he asked Trade Representative Lighthizer to determine which Chinese products could be hit with tariffs to reach the target of US$100 billion.[220] By April 9, Beijing had already proposed US$50 billion worth of tariffs on American goods, while threatening further punitive actions.[221]

Protesting the US tariffs, China has filed a complaint at the WTO. "China claims the duties of 25% and 10% on imports of steel and aluminum products respectively are inconsistent with provisions of the WTO's General Agreement on Tariffs and Trade (GATT) 1994 and of the Agreement on Safeguards."[222] Beijing has requested 60 days of consultations with Washington regarding the tariffs.[223]

In the midst of the US-China trade dispute, the annual Boao Forum – China's version of the World Economic Forum at Davos – was held from April 8–11 on Hainan Island. The theme of the forum was "An Open and Innovative Asia for a World of Greater Prosperity."

In his keynote address at the forum, President Xi Jinping presented China as the defender of free and open trade and the US as the protectionist, anti-globalist who was going to be left behind. His central message was that "China was a safe and reliable partner while the United States was not."[224] He repeatedly stressed that China was now open. "China's door of opening up will not be closed…Human society is facing a major choice to open or close, to go forward or backwards." He also warned against revisiting Cold War thinking, "cooperation is moving forward and a Cold War mentality and zero-sum game thinking is outdated."[225] Xi specifically used Chinese terms translated as "zero sum game" (a concept often attributed to Trump), as a way of referencing Trump without actually saying his name. A friend to the world, China sent the message, "We must [always] refrain from seeking dominance [by rejecting] power politics."[226]

Xi renounced trade barriers and pledged, once again, to lower tariffs on imported cars and to further open China's financial and insurance industries.[227] Once again, he was speaking to the Americans, although no one from Trump's administration was in attendance. US automakers have repeatedly complained that the high tariffs they face in China are unfair. China charges a 25% tariff on American cars, while the US only charges a 2.5% tariff on Chinese cars.[228]

Despite the higher prices, Chinese consumers still prefer American cars, and in the auto sector the US actually runs a trade surplus with China. Last year, the US imported 58,000 passenger cars from China, but China imported 267,000 cars from the US. If Xi moves forward with his promise to cut tariffs on American cars, that surplus could increase further, and bring down the overall US-China trade deficit.[229]

Chinese tariffs not only hamper US exports to China, but also have a secondary effect of fueling technology transfer. High tariffs are an incentive for US auto manufacturers to set up inside of China, to avoid import duties. China requires US auto makers to establish JVs with local companies, giving local Chinese partners access to US technology and intellectual property.[230]

Trump also finds the closed nature of China's financial sector unfair. In China, financial services and banking is a restricted sector which is very difficult for foreign firms to enter. In the US, financial services and banking carry few specific restrictions on foreign investment.

Trump has repeatedly complained about China's trade surplus with the US, but Xi assured attendees that "China does not seek a trade surplus. We have a genuine desire to increase imports and achieve a greater balance of international payments under the current account."[231] Historically, however, increasing imports has meant a concerted effort by PRC companies to find markets overseas. Meanwhile, Foreign firms complain that it is becoming increasingly difficult to sell to customers in China.[232]

Xi addressed these concerns, saying that he would improve "the investment environment for international companies, and reduce duties on consumer products."[233] He said China would further open its economy to the world, promising that Beijing would relax its restrictions on foreign shareholding and on foreign investment in the automobile industry.[234] In return, he said that he hoped developed countries would stop imposing restrictions on trade in high-tech.[235] Xi made other statements regarding the importance of technological exchange with other countries, but within the framework of protecting IPR. These proclamations are familiar to China watchers; Beijing has made these promises in the past, and yet failed to follow through. Last year, the EU Chamber of Commerce in China coined a new phrase to describe their feelings about China trade: "promise fatigue."[236]

There is an often-repeated pattern each time China is about to move into a Western market. Beijing promises a reduction in tariffs or a liberalization of investment rules which never materializes.[237] In 2001, when China joined the WTO, it was expected that China would bring about democratic reforms and move toward market capitalism. But this has not happened.[238] CNN journalist Stephen Moore reported that there has been no increase in democracy, and that SOEs were growing not shrinking.[239] China has implemented laws that mirror those of other WTO members, but *Forbes* felt that China had not been enforcing those rules.[240] Due to the government's involvement in industry and the accusations of intellectual property theft, China is not considered a market economy by the WTO.[241]

As recently as November, Chinese regulators announced that they would reduce tariffs on auto imports.[242] PRC Premier Li Keqiang also pledged to give American firms greater access to China, stating, "China would treat foreign and domestic firms equally."[243] However, these reforms have not yet materialized.[244] Typically, with the latest promises he made at Boao, "Xi gave no details on how those conditions might change."[245] According to CNN Money: "China often says it will cooperate on trade. And then doesn't."[246]

One difference between the promises made at the Boao Forum and previous promises is that for almost the first time, Beijing set a time frame for certain reforms. People's Bank of China Governor Yi Gang announced that, as of May 1, "the daily Shanghai-Hong Kong stock connect quota will quadruple to 52 billion yuan (US$8.3 billion)" He went on to say that further opening of the financial sector was planned by June 30, including easing the limits on foreign insurers and foreign-ownership caps on securities companies.[247] Additional reforms included allowing foreign banks to set up branches and subsidiaries, as well as allowing foreigners to own 51% of a brokerage or futures firm, investment fund, or life insurance company. Yi also said that there would be "a stock trading tie-up between Shanghai and London later this year."[248]

One glaring omission at Boao, however, was any discussion of how US tariffs could impact China's economy, only that "the United States would be left behind."[249] People's Daily reported afterwards that China's proposed lowering of auto tariffs and opening more of the economy was not in response to the trade dispute with the US.[250] Trump, for his part, was apparently aware of what was being said at the forum and via Twitter thanked Xi for saying that he may reduce tariffs. Trump concluded, "We will make great progress together!"[251]

The irony is, for all of the talk of China's openness, Boao delegates were unable to read Trump's tweets as Twitter, Facebook, and Google are all blocked in China.[252] In fact, across China, the champion of the open door, approximately six million websites are blocked, including WhatsApp, YouTube, Gmail, Yahoo Taiwan and Yahoo Hong Kong, Chinese Wikipedia, and Instagram. Many news sites are also blocked, such as *New York Times*, Bloomberg, *Wall Street Journal*, Reuters, *The Economist*, *Time*, *Le Monde*, Nikkei Japan, and the BBC. Promises of economic openness do not apply to the free flow of information, it appears. In this respect, the Boao Forum was under the same restrictions as the rest of China.

Reactions to the tariffs

The day after the tariffs were announced, US stock markets took a dive. They recovered within 24 hours however, as cooler heads prevailed, taking a wait-and-see approach. When Xi made his speech at the Boao Forum, pledging to reduce tariffs and open China's economy, the markets reacted with a temporary surge, the S&P 500 gaining 1.77%, and the Dow Jones Industrial Average and NASDAQ gaining 1.89% and 2.00%, respectively.[253]

Shortly after the tariffs were announced, South Korea committed to reducing its trade barriers against US products, agreeing to purchase more Ford and GM cars and trucks.[254] EU and NAFTA, however, agreed to meet for negotiations, but made no concrete changes to their trading relationships with the US. Manufacturers in the EU are complaining that many of the products China exports to the US contain components manufactured in the EU, and that the tariffs will reduce demand and hurt European workers.[255] Another way of interpreting this situation would be that US allies have been using China as a backdoor to profit from unbalanced US trade.

China had begun publishing a list of US products which will be subject to tariffs, including a number of food stuffs and US movies. China also began giving tax incentives to certain industries which fall within their "Made in China 2025" plan.[256] "Made in China 2025" aims to help China move up the value chain by supporting the development of "information technology, high-end machinery and robotics, aerospace, marine equipment and ships, advanced rail transport, new-energy vehicles, electric power, agricultural machinery, new materials and bio-medical."[257] Although Beijing had not said that these incentives were specifically being given to industries hit by US tariffs, the list mirrors the list of industries (mostly connected to high-tech manufacturing) associated with Trump's tariffs.[258] This may mean that, in spite of the tariffs, Beijing will continue to ship these goods to the US, and tax incentives will be a way for these industries to lower the cost of their goods. It may also mean that the tax incentives will compensate for lost revenue until these companies can find other markets beyond the US.

The US asked China to stop subsidizing companies associated with "Made in China 2025," but according to Liu He, a vice premier overseeing economics and finance, Beijing has rejected these requests.[259]

Voices in the US in favor of restricting China trade

Visiting Beijing, Senator Elizabeth Warren (Democrat, Massachusetts) spoke out in favor of the tariffs, saying that US-China trade relations were experiencing a long-needed recalibration. "Warren said the US government was waking up to Chinese demands for US companies to give up their know-how in exchange for access to its market, after years of assuming economic engagement would lead to a more open China."[260]

US Federal Communications Commission Chairman Ajit Pai proposed a rule that would prohibit local US communities from using FCC money to purchase telecommunications equipment from China, which the FCC feels poses a threat to national security. Two Chinese firms with close ties to the government were specifically named, Huawei and ZTE. The fear raised by the FCC and others is that telecommunications equipment is particularly vulnerable to spying. This move came in response to a congressional inquiry led by senators Tom Cotton (Republican, Arkansas) and Marco Rubio (Republican, Florida), who have already launched separate legislation to prohibit any US government funds from being used to purchase equipment from Huawei and ZTE.[261] Senator Cotton stated, "Huawei is effectively an arm of the Chinese government, and it's more than capable of stealing information from US officials by hacking its devices." On a similar note, Senator Rubio cited Huawei's direct relationship to the Chinese Communist Party. He referred to China as a "foreign adversary" and warned about national security issues associated with embedding Chinese technology "in US government systems or critical infrastructure."[262]

Cotton was quoted as saying, "Companies like Huawei and other telecom firms are essentially arms of the Chinese Communist Party and are subject to doing its political bidding."[263] FBI Director Christopher A. Wray has officially registered his concerns about allowing companies associated with foreign governments to gain access to US telecommunications infrastructure.[264]

The Committee on Foreign Investment in US, which has the ability to block deals which it deems to endanger national security, has stopped deals from other countries as well. They recently halted the purchase of US telecom company Qualcomm by Singaporean firm Broadcom. Other US government departments are now looking more closely at foreign investment deals. The Department of Defense is currently investigating America's security vulnerability within its industrial base. The National Security Council is focusing its attention on protecting the US semiconductor industry. And, of course, President Trump has spoken out against forced technology transfer in China.[265]

Another point of contention between Washington and Beijing has been China's national champions, companies which receive preferential treatment and unfair advantages from the government such as subsidies, soft loans, and preferential access to markets as well as raw materials. According to *Washington Post*, a high ranking member of the Trump administration has stated "if Chinese 'national champion' companies are allowed to unfairly take over the industries of the future, both our economic and national security will be gravely damaged."[266] A Democratic member

242

of the US-China Economic and Security Review Commission, Michael Wessel, co-chaired a hearing on the "Chinese government's attempts to use its technology firms to bolster its internal control and export its repression beyond its borders."[267]

CNN's Stephen Moore said, that with the "Made in China 2025" initiative, China was aggressively seeking economic superiority over the US. He credited Trump for recognizing that "China poses a clear and present danger to the United States," accusing Beijing of blatantly cheating and stealing intellectual property, costing the US billions. Moore additionally said that the PRC is building up its military and expanding its empire by laying claim to islands and waters in the South China Sea.[268] Moore called China "the 21st century version of the Soviet Union" and an enemy to the US.[269]

Michael Stumo reported in *The Hill* that Trump should be praised for fighting back, as the US had already become "a natural resource colony for China as well as a quaint tourist destination."[270] Larry Kudlow, director of the White House's National Economic Council, told CNBC, "we have to say to China: You're no longer a developing nation, act like it."[271] Kudlow went on to say that Trump sent the tariffs as a warning, after decades of abuse.[272]

What about a trade war?

Bloomberg felt that China's promises would not be enough to appease the US and avert a further escalation of trade tensions. "The US side will likely want to see deeds, not just words, before it considers softening its protectionist stance."[273]

Larry Kudlow downplayed any fears of a trade war on the grounds that the US has a very strong economy, no tariffs have actually been enacted yet, and because negotiations were underway. He went on to reiterate that there is no trade war and that this is the first step in a process.[274]

US Treasury Secretary Steven Mnuchin said that he did not expect a trade war and that no matter what happens between the US and China, trade with China is a very small percentage of the US economy. Therefore, he does not expect this to negatively impact the US economy. Additionally, he referred to a possible rebalancing of US-China trade as one of the "single biggest opportunities for US companies long term."[275] Similarly, "Commerce Secretary Wilbur Ross said last week that China's new tariffs on 106 products do not represent a threat to the United States."[276]

As of mid-2018, despite blustering on both sides, China seems to be keeping a cool head, and Trump has not stated that he would retaliate against China's tariffs, escalating the situation.

Some Chinese-language articles about the tariffs have been surprisingly moderate, as this translation shows: "The fundamental reason for the huge trade gap is that China and the United States are in different economic stages... In this case, the US needs a large amount of industrial products from China, while the US mainly produces agricultural products, chemical products, and large aircraft. There is a certain demand for high-tech products, and the resulting poor trade is difficult to avoid. The data show that since 2000, the Sino-US trade surplus has experienced a rapid growth, and the issue of trade balance has continued to be a hot topic in the economic and trade fields of both sides."[277]

Next, the article takes a more antagonistic stance, reflecting a widely held belief in China that the US is trying to prevent China from developing: "But why are trade frictions appearing in such a fierce form at this time? In addition to Trump's voters' base and ruling style, the United States began to worry about the development of China's knowledge, culture, information, and finance and other soft industries. This is one of the important reasons. The outbreak of this trade friction was caused to a large extent by the concerns of the United States caused by China's industrial upgrading."[278]

Another article gave a very balanced take on the trade dispute and suggested ways of reducing the US-China trade deficit by having China move up the value chain, and depending less on high-volume, low-end exports to the US. "Wang Yong, a professor at the Institute of International Relations at Peking University, believes that it is in China's own interests to expand the import of clean energy such as agricultural products and natural gas from the United States. He believes that during the transition period between the old and new kinetic energy, China's expansion of imports of energy and agricultural products from the United States will better meet the people's growing good living needs, and promote the economy's shift towards high quality development. It will also help the US to reduce the trade deficit."[279]

The same article references Song Guoyou, deputy director of the Center for American Studies at Fudan University, who "believes it is very important to resolve the US-China trade deficit and strengthen communication. The United States should look more comprehensively and historically at the background causes of the trade imbalance between China and the United States and the joint efforts of both sides to reduce trade imbalances. While China is expanding imports, the US should also relax its export control with more confidence and create more favorable conditions for mutual investment and market access."[280] While this article is encouraging, in that it recognizes the need to reduce the trade imbalance, it is also worrying that Song believes the best way to do this is for the

US to decrease trade restrictions.

Other articles were far more antagonistic. "Obviously, Trump's trade friction with China is downright unilateralism," goes one. From the fact that the US initiated a US$50 billion US tariff levy in China, the 301 investigation on which it was based was not in accordance with the rules of the WTO itself, but in accordance with Article 301 of the US Trade Act 1974. It is not difficult to see that the Trump administration's introduction of tariff lists based on the results of the 301 investigation is not justified..."[281]

The article adds: "The recent statement made by the US Department of Commerce, the United States ... ignores the essence of the mutually beneficial and win-win development of Sino-US economic and trade cooperation ... and is not conducive to the national interests of the United States and is not conducive to the Chinese nation. Interests are also not conducive to global economic interests."[282]

"In order to defend China's legitimate rights and interests in violation of international obligations caused by the United States, the Chinese government will respond according to the laws and regulations of the PRC Foreign Trade Law and the basic principles of international law..." Just like Xi Jinping at Davos, the official line in China is that Beijing favor's free trade, in order to help the world, but the US is selfishly protectionist. Additionally, China operates within the established framework of the WTO and other bodies of international law, whereas the US does not, it claimed.

Next, the article sees the trade restrictions as a direct attack on "Made in China 2025." "The US side also made it clear that the US initiated the 301 investigation ... aimed at 'Made in China 2025'."[283] The article demonstrates a strong understanding of the US electoral process as it predicts a Chinese ban on US soybean imports would reduce the GDP of ten US states, eight of which backed Trump in 2016. The article states that Trump supporters in these states "will be disappointed with Trump's policies, naturally from the inside, and apply pressure on Trump."[284]

The article recognizes that many of the imports which will bear US tariffs are manufactured by US companies in China, and the writer likens the US taxing these products to "taking a rock and hitting your own feet."[285]

Another report saw Trump's tariff threats as a warning, designed to bring China to the negotiating table. Li Wei of the National Academy of Development and Strategy, Renmin University of China, opined that "in fact, the initial purpose of the United States was not to really fight a trade war with China, but rather to force Beijing to help it reverse trade imbalances by transmitting threat signals or pushing the limits."[286] He follows this by toting the party line. "However, instead of intimidating China, the big stick of trade has caused China's unprecedented counterattack."[287]

Next, he evokes Xi Jinping's claims of openness, whereby China is opening and the US is closing itself off from the world. "While countering the United States, China has released a strong signal to the world to further expand its opening to the outside world."[288] He references the Boao Forum, stating that Xi "announced a series of new major initiatives to open wider to the outside world to provide new opportunities for China in the shadow of the US trade."[289] When restating Xi's position of China opening to the world, he goes on to say that this will provide more opportunities for China. This differs from the more common party line which says that China is creating opportunities for the world. He concludes the article by saying: "China's response to the Trump administration has made it clear that sitting down to talk about it is the best way to solve the problem."[290]

These and other Chinese-language reports show that China is aware of the US-China trade deficit and of Washington's desire to narrow that deficit. China does not want to be pushed around or seen to lose face. China is always walking a tightrope in its dealings with the US. As the ultimate example of a capitalist country, the US should be the enemy. But in many ways, the US is the model for Chinese economic development. China can vilify the US, but only to a certain point. In the world, China wants to project itself as the savior of free trade, a safe haven for those fleeing American economic oppression. Meanwhile, China wants and needs to win the most favorable trade conditions to support its own interests. Further complicating things is that China is dependent on doing business with the US. And in spite of all of the friction, China seems to be moving forward with its bid for business in the US.

According to a spokesperson for the Alaska Gasline Development Corp., in spite of the tariffs, Bank of China is moving forward with its joint financing of a LNG pipeline project in Alaska.[291] This willingness on the part of China to continue to invest in the US is a good sign that an escalation of tensions is not inevitable. If both sides remain calm, this could wind up being a simple rebalancing of trade agreements, with both sides walking away saving face and feeling that they have reached an acceptable resolution.

If the situation should escalate, Xi has certain advantages over Trump. First, as all media in China is state-run in China, Xi will not have to deal with any media criticism. Neither will he have to deal with public outrage or protests. Internationally, China can play the victim of unfair tariffs and US bullying.[292] Since the World Economic Forum in Davos last year, Xi has presented China to the world as a champion of free trade and openness, a friendly alternative to a protectionist US which is becoming increasingly nationalist and less global. Working against China, however, is that trade with the US accounts for much of China's GDP growth. A trade war or a further escalation of tensions could negatively impact China's economy. The US, on the other hand, has the advantages of a strong economy, low dependence on exports, a stated goal of reducing the trade deficit, and possible support from other countries who would also push for China to further open its economy to foreign firms and to resolve the IPR issue.

NOTES

Chapter 1

1. Huang, Y., "China's Economy Is Not Normal. It Doesn't Have to Be," March 13, 2018, *New York Times*, https://www.nytimes.com/2018/03/13/opinion/china-economy-corruption.html
2. Eckart, J., "8 things you need to know about China's economy," WEForum, June 23, 2016 https://www.weforum.org/agenda/2016/06/8-facts-about-chinas-economy/
3. Ibid.
4. Shane, D., "China's economy hit the ground running in 2018," April 17, 2018, CNN, http://money.cnn.com/2018/04/16/news/economy/china-first-quarter-gdp-2018/index.html
5. Statista, "China: Urbanization from 2006 to 2016," https://www.statista.com/statistics/455793/urbanization-in-china/
6. Trading Economics, "China Average Yearly Wages 1952-2018," https://tradingeconomics.com/china/wages
7. Skidmore, D., "Understanding Chinese President Xi's anti-corruption campaign," October 27, 2017, The Conversation, https://theconversation.com/understanding-chinese-president-xis-anti-corruption-campaign-86396
8. Huang, Y., "China's Economy Is Not Normal. It Doesn't Have to Be."
9. Statista, "The 20 countries with the largest gross domestic product (GDP) in 2017," https://www.statista.com/statistics/268173/countries-

with-the-largest-gross-domestic-product-gdp/

10. Duncan, H. and D. Martisko, "America usurped: China becomes world's largest economy - putting USA in second place for the first time in 142 years, October 9, 2014, *Daily Mail*, http://www.dailymail.co.uk/news/article-2785905/China-overtakes-U-S-world-s-largest-economy-IMF-says-economy-worth-17-6trillion-America-falls-second-place-time-1872.html#ixzz3xUxtzpOj

11. Barboza, D., "China Passes Japan as Second-Largest Economy," August 10, 2010, *New York Times*, http://www.nytimes.com/2010/08/16/business/global/16yuan.html?pagewanted=all&_r=0

12. Huang, Z., "Your guide to understanding OBOR, China's new Silk Road plan," May 15, 2017, Quartz, https://qz.com/983460/obor-an-extremely-simple-guide-to-understanding-chinas-one-belt-one-road-forum-for-its-new-silk-road/

13. Searcey, D. and K. Bradsher, "Chinese Cash Floods US Real Estate Market," November 28, 2015, *New York Times*, https://www.nytimes.com/2015/11/29/business/international/chinese-cash-floods-us-real-estate-market.html

14. National Association of Realtors Research Department, "2016 Profile of International Investor Activity in US Residential Real Estate," 2016, https://www.nar.realtor/sites/default/files/reports/2016/2016-profile-of-international-home-buying-activity-06-06-2016.pdf

15. Agarwal, S., "Global 2000: China's Largest Companies 2016," May 25, 2016, *Forbes*, https://www.forbes.com/sites/shreyaagarwal/2016/05/25/global-2000-chinas-largest-companies-

2016/#11744e302b29

16. Schaefer, S., "The World's Largest Companies 2016," May 25, 2016, *Forbes*, https://www.forbes.com/sites/steveschaefer/2016/05/25/the-worlds-largest-companies-2016/#4bc4e02345a6

17. Tyler, P., "Deng Xiaoping: A Political Wizard Who Put China on the Capitalist Road," February 20, 1997, *New York Times*, https://archive.nytimes.com/www.nytimes.com/learning/general/onthisday/bday/0822.html

18. Ibid.

19. Vogel, E. "China under Deng Xiaoping's leadership," September 27, 2011, East Asia Forum, http://www.eastasiaforum.org/2011/09/27/china-under-deng-xiaopings-leadership/

20. Yardley, J., "China Enacts Major Land-Use Reform," October 19, 2008, *New York Times*, https://www.nytimes.com/2008/10/20/world/asia/20china.html

21. BBC, "Quick guide: China's economic reform," November 3, 2006, http://news.bbc.co.uk/2/hi/asia-pacific/5237748.stm

22. Zweig, D., "Chinese Politics Part 1 – China and Political Science," The Hong Kong University of Science and Technology. Lecture.

23. Fewsmith, J., "Studying the Three Represents," *China Leadership Monitor*, http://www.hoover.org/sites/default/files/uploads/documents/clm8_jf.pdf

24. Zweig, D., "Chinese Politics Part 1 – China and Political Science."

25. *The Economist*, "We are the champions," March 18, 2004, http://www.economist.com/node/2495172

26. Leutert, W., "Challenges Ahead in China's Reform of State-Owned Enterprises," January 2016, *Asia Policy* no. 21, 83–99.

27. Orlik, T., "Charting China's Economy: 10 Years Under Hu," November 16, 2012, *Wall Street Journal*, http://blogs.wsj.com/chinarealtime/2012/11/16/charting-chinas-economy-10-years-under-hu-jintao/

28. *The Economist*, "We are the champions."

29. Ibid.

30. Bloomberg News, "China Tells Foreign Firms to Brace for Bigger Competitors," March 16, 2016, https://www.bloomberg.com/news/articles/2016-03-15/china-congress-to-foreign-firms-brace-for-bigger-competitors

31. Levesque, G., "China's Evolving Economic Statecraft," April 12, 2017, *The Diplomat*, http://thediplomat.com/2017/04/chinas-evolving-economic-statecraft/

32. Hemphill, T.A. and G.O. White III, "China's National Champions: The Evolution of a National Industrial Policy – Or a New Era of Economic Protectionism?" 2013, Wiley Online Library, Wiley Periodicals, Inc., DOI: 10.1002/tie.21535 (p. 199)

33. Greene, J. and R. Cheng, "Inside Huawei, the Chinese tech giant that's rattling nerves in DC," August 27, 2012, CNET, https://www.cnet.com/news/inside-huawei-the-chinese-tech-giant-thats-rattling-nerves-in-dc/

34. Buckley, C., "Xi Jinping's Remedy for China's Economic Gloom Has Echoes of Reaganomics," March 3, 2016, *New York Times*, https://www.nytimes.com/2016/03/04/world/asia/xi-jinping-china-economic-policy.html

35. Fan, G. and N. Hope, "Chapter 16: The Role of State-

Owned Enterprises in the Chinese Economy,"
https://www.chinausfocus.com/2022/wp-
content/uploads/Part+02-Chapter+16.pdf

36. Zhang, D. and O. Freestone, "China's Unfinished State-
Owned Enterprise Reforms," Economic Roundup Issue
2, 2013 (Australian Government, The Treasury),
https://treasury.gov.au/publication/economic-roundup-
issue-2-2013-2/economic-roundup-issue-2-2013/chinas-
unfinished-state-owned-enterprise-reforms/

37. Zweig, D., "Chinese Politics Part 1 – China and Political
Science."

38. Skidmore, D., "Understanding Chinese President Xi's
anti-corruption campaign."

39. Kroeber, A., "Xi Jinping's Reform Express Gathers
Steam," December 15, 2014, Brookings,
http://www.brookings.edu/research/opinions/2014/12/15
-xi-jinpin-reform-kroeber

40. Ibid.

41. Ibid.

42. Hewitt, D., "China Relaxes Rules To Let Foreigners
Purchase More Real Estate, In Attempt To Boost
Slowing Economy, August 28, 2015, *International
Business Times*, http://www.ibtimes.com/china-relaxes-
rules-let-foreigners-purchase-more-real-estate-attempt-
boost-slowing-2072571

43. Kroeber, A., "Xi Jinping's Reform Express Gathers
Steam."

44. Ibid.

45. Ibid.

46. APCO Worldwide, "China's 2015 National People's
Congress: The Xi-Li Administration Seeks Alignment to
Push Through Reforms," 2015, APCO,
http://www.apcoworldwide.com/docs/default-

source/default-document-library/Thought-
Leadership/apco_china_analysis-of-
npc_2015.pdf?sfvrsn=2

47. Tejada, C., "China Places Cap on Local Government
Debt," August 15, 2015, *Wall Street Journal*,
http://www.wsj.com/articles/china-places-cap-on-local-
government-debt-1440928627

48. Kroeber, A., "Xi Jinping's Reform Express Gathers
Steam."

49. APCO Worldwide, "China's 2015 National People's
Congress: The Xi-Li Administration Seeks Alignment to
Push Through Reforms."

50. Ibid.

51. Harris, D., "China WFOE Formation And Minimum
Capital Requirements," November 8, 2014, China Law
Blog, http://www.chinalawblog.com/2014/11/china-
wfoe-formation-and-minimum-capital-
requirements.html

52. APCO Worldwide, "China's 2015 National People's
Congress: The Xi-Li Administration Seeks Alignment to
Push Through Reforms."

53. Ibid.

54. Reuters, "China steps up banking reforms, lets broader
ownership at Bank of Communications," June 17, 2015,
https://www.reuters.com/article/china-bank-of-
communications-financial-r/china-steps-up-banking-
reforms-lets-broader-ownership-at-bank-of-
communications-idUSL3N0Z318B20150617

55. Schmidt, M., "A Look At Fiscal And Monetary Policy,"
May 27, 2018, Investopedia,
http://www.investopedia.com/articles/economics/12/fisc
al-or-monetary-policy.asp

56. Wildau, G. and T. Mitchell, "China economy steadies on

stimulus boost," July 15, 2015, *Financial Times*.

57. Egan, M., "China is dumping US debt," September 11, 2015, CNN Money, http://money.cnn.com/2015/09/10/investing/china-dumping-us-debt/index.html

58. Wildau, G. and T. Mitchell, "China economy steadies on stimulus boost."

59. Burkitt, L., "China's Working-Age Population Sees Biggest-Ever Decline," January 22, 2016, *Wall Street Journal*, http://blogs.wsj.com/chinarealtime/2016/01/22/chinas-working-age-population-sees-biggest-ever-decline/

60. Ibid.

61. Ibid.

62. Frett, L., "The End of China's One-Child Policy Isn't Enough," November 9, 2015, *Time*, http://time.com/4098745/china-one-child-policy-rights/

63. Bier, D., "End of China's One-Child Rule: Too Little, Too Late,' November 2, 2015, *Newsweek*, http://www.newsweek.com/end-chinas-one-child-rule-too-little-too-late-389560

64. Joseph, N., "Despite China's modernization, the hukou system remains," February 2010, Perspectives Newsletter, University of Washington, https://artsci.washington.edu/news/2010-02/despite-chinas-modernization-hukou-system-remains

65. Yang, J., "Why living in Hong Kong as mainland Chinese is no piece of cake," May 21, 2013, *South China Morning Post*, http://www.scmp.com/comment/insight-opinion/article/1242671/living-hong-kong-mainlander-no-piece-cake?page=all

66. Chan, K. and W. Buckingham, "Is China Abolishing the Hukou System?" September 1, 2008, The China

Quarterly Volume 195, 582–583.

67. Phillips, T., "China's villages vanish amid rush for the cities," November 23, 2013, *The Daily Telegraph*, http://www.telegraph.co.uk/news/worldnews/asia/china/10470077/Chinas-villages-vanish-amid-rush-for-the-cities.html

68. Joseph, N., "Despite China's modernization, the hukou system remains."

69. Marshall, J. "China: Urbanization and Hukou Reform," October 11, 2013, *The Diplomat*, http://thediplomat.com/2013/10/china-urbanization-and-hukou-reform/

70. Congressional-Executive Commission on China, "Special Topic Paper: China's Household Registration System: Sustained Reform Needed to Protect China's Rural Migrants, http://www.cecc.gov/publications/issue-papers/cecc-special-topic-paper-chinas-household-registration-system-sustained

71. Joseph, N., "Despite China's modernization, the hukou system remains."

72. Beller, P., and M. Maiello, "Pimco's New Normal," January 21, 2010, *Forbes*, http://www.forbes.com/forbes/2010/0208/investing-mutual-funds-stocks-pimco-new-normal.html

73. Angang, H., "Embracing China's 'New Normal'," May 2015, *Foreign Affairs*, https://www.foreignaffairs.com/articles/china/2015-04-20/embracing-chinas-new-normal

74. Peston, R., "What is China's 'new normal'?" September 24, 2015, BBC, https://www.bbc.com/news/business-34344926

Chapter 2

1. Cheremukhin, A. et al, *The Economy of People's Republic of China from 1953*, July 2015, NBER Working Paper No. 21397, National Bureau of Economic Research, http://www.nber.org/papers/w21397.pdf

2. Rutland, P., "Post-socialist states and the evolution of a new development model: Russia and China compared," June 2009, *Polis* (Moscow), no. 376, http://prutland.faculty.wesleyan.edu/files/2015/07/Rutland-China-Russia-Compared.pdf

3. World Bank, "GDP (current US$)," https://data.worldbank.org/indicator/NY.GDP.MKTP.CD

4. Inflation.eu, 2016, "Historic inflation Russia – CPI inflation," http://www.inflation.eu/inflation-rates/russia/historic-inflation/cpi-inflation-russia.aspx

5. Numbeo, 2016, "Crime Index for country," https://www.numbeo.com/crime/rankings_by_country.jsp

6. Andvig, J. C., "Corruption in China and Russia Compared," 2005, Norwegian Institute of International Affairs, https://www.files.ethz.ch/isn/27336/679.pdf

7. Rutland, P., "Post-socialist states and the evolution of a new development model: Russia and China compared."

8. Ibid.

9. Ibid.

10. Ibid.

11. Cheremukhin, A. et al, "Six questions about China's rise from 1953," September 2, 2015, VOX, http://voxeu.org/article/six-questions-about-china-s-rise-1953

12. Brandt, L., and T.G. Rawski, *China's Great Economic*

Transformation, 2008, Cambridge University Press.

13. Cheremukhin, A. et al, *The Economy of People's Republic of China from 1953*.

14. Cheremukhin, A. et al, "Six questions about China's rise from 1953."

15. Brandt, L., and T.G. Rawski, *China's Great Economic Transformation*.

16. Ibid.

17. Johnson, D., "These Are the Most Productive Countries in the World," January 4, 2017, *Time*, http://time.com/4621185/worker-productivity-countries/

18. Brandt, L., and T.G. Rawski, *China's Great Economic Transformation*.

19. Ibid.

20. Ibid.

21. Ibid.

22. Ibid.

23. Gao, S., "A Study on the Productivity and Efficiency Effects of Enterprise Reforms in China," 2010, PhD diss., Western Michigan University.

24. Prokopenko, J., "Privatization: Lessons from Russia and China," January 24, 2000, Enterprise and Management Development Working Paper EMD/24/E, https://sites.ualberta.ca/~smartynk/Resources/Social%20 Studies/Social%2020%20-- %20Interesting%20Sources/Lessons%20from%20Russia %20and%20China/Lessons%20from%20Russia%20and% 20China%20-%20Employment%20Sector.html

25. Brandt, L., and T.G. Rawski, *China's Great Economic Transformation*.

26. Ibid.

27. Prokopenko, J., "Privatization: Lessons from Russia and China."

28. Santander Trade Portal, "China: Foreign Investment," May 2018, https://en.portal.santandertrade.com/establish-overseas/china/foreign-investment

29. Xinhua, "China becomes world's largest FDI recipient amid mixed global outlook," June 25, 2015, http://www.xinhuanet.com/english/2015-06/25/c_134353221.htm

30. Dumon, M., "Top 6 Factors That Drive Investment In China," Investopedia, http://www.investopedia.com/articles/economics/09/factors-drive-investment-in-china.asp

31. OECD, "Main Determinants and Impacts of Foreign Direct Investment on China's Economy," December 2000, OECD Working Papers on International Investment, http://dx.doi.org/10.1787/321677880185

32. World Bank, "Exports of goods and services (% of GDP)," http://data.worldbank.org/indicator/NE.EXP.GNFS.ZS

33. Prokopenko, J., "Privatization: Lessons from Russia and China."

34. Koopman, R. and W. Zhi, "How Much of China's Exports is Really Made in China? Estimating Domestic Content in Exports When Processing Trade is Pervasive," March 2008, US International Trade Commission Office of Economics Working Paper, https://www.usitc.gov/publications/332/ec200803b_revised.pdf

35. Trading Economics, "China GDP Annual Growth Rate 1989–2018," https://tradingeconomics.com/china/gdp-growth-annual

36. Fan, A., "China's labor force shrinking," January 22, 2015, China.org.cn, http://www.china.org.cn/china/2015-

01/22/content_34625754.htm

37. Center for Strategic and International Studies, "Does China have an aging problem?" February 15, 2016, http://chinapower.csis.org/aging-problem

38. Hu, V., "The Chinese Economic Reform and Chinese Entrepreneurship," May 2005, *X Jornada d'Economia de Caixa Manresa*, http://www.uoc.edu/symposia/caixamanresa/jornadaeco nomia/2005/eng/vicky_hu.pdf

39. Wildau, G., "China deploys state enterprises to economic stimulus effort," 2016, *Financial Times*, https://www.ft.com/content/3d10e5cc-3754-11e6-a780-b48ed7b6126f

40. Reuters, "China's non-performing loans hit 11-year high," May 12, 2016, http://www.reuters.com/article/china-economy-loans-idUSL3N18935N

41. Wildau, G., "China deploys state enterprises to economic stimulus effort."

42. Agence France-Presse, "China's debt is 250% of GDP and 'could be fatal', says government expert," June 16, 2016, *The Guardian*, https://www.theguardian.com/business/2016/jun/16/chi nas-debt-is-250-of-gdp-and-could-be-fatal-says-government-expert

43. Kroeber, A., "China's Future: Neither Boom Nor Bust," April 19, 2016, Bloomberg, https://www.bloomberg.com/view/articles/2016-04-18/china-s-economy-may-be-headed-for-a-japan-style-slump

44. Ibid.

Chapter 3

1. *The Economist*, "From SOE to GLC," November 23, 2013,
    https://www.economist.com/finance-and-
    economics/2013/11/23/from-soe-to-glc

2. Curran, E. "State Companies: Back on China's To-Do
    List," July 31, 2015, Bloomberg,
    https://www.bloomberg.com/news/articles/2015-07-
    30/china-s-state-owned-companies-may-face-reform

3. Zhang, D. and O. Freestone, "China's Unfinished State-
    Owned Enterprise Reforms."

4. Aivazian, V.A. et al, "Can Corporatization Improve The
    Performance Of State-Owned Enterprises Even Without
    Privatization?" *Journal of Corporate Finance* 11 (2005) 791–
    808,
    http://citeseerx.ist.psu.edu/viewdoc/download?doi=10.1.
    1.454.2242&rep=rep1&type=pdf

5. Cooke, F.L., "Acquisitions Of Chinese State-Owned
    Enterprises By Multinational Corporations: Driving
    Forces, Barriers And Implications For HRM," *British
    Journal of Management* 17.S1 (2006): S105-S121,
    https://onlinelibrary.wiley.com/doi/full/10.1111/j.1467-
    8551.2006.00481.x

6. Wu, Y., "Redundancy and Firm Characteristics in
    Chinese State-Owned Enterprises," The University of
    Western Australia Discussion Paper,
    https://ecompapers.biz.uwa.edu.au/paper/PDF%20of%2
    0Discussion%20Papers/1998/98-18.pdf

7. Zhang, D. and O. Freestone, "China's Unfinished State-
    Owned Enterprise Reforms."

8. Aivazian, V.A. et al, "Can Corporatization Improve The
    Performance Of State-Owned Enterprises Even Without
    Privatization?"

9.   Chen, H. and J. Whalley, "The State-Owned Enterprises Issue in China's Prospective Trade Negotiations," October 2014, Center for International Governance Innovation, https://www.files.ethz.ch/isn/185024/no.48.pdf

10. Aivazian, V.A. et al, "Can Corporatization Improve The Performance Of State-Owned Enterprises Even Without Privatization?"

11. Ibid.

12. Zhang, D. and O. Freestone, "China's Unfinished State-Owned Enterprise Reforms."

13. Forrester and Porter, 1999; Scot, 2002 cited in Bai and Bennington, see note 15 below.

14. Zhang, D. and O. Freestone, "China's Unfinished State-Owned Enterprise Reforms."

15. Bai, X. and L. Bennington, "Steering and Rowing in Chinese SOEs: the Modern Enterprise System in China," 2005, Proceedings of the 15th Annual Conference of the Association for Chinese Economics Studies Australia.

16. Lee, J., "The Real Picture On China's State-owned Enterprises," December 12, 2014, *The Australian*, https://www.theaustralian.com.au/business/business-spectator/the-real-picture-on-chinas-stateowned-enterprises/news-story/a468612a4cc1ee271ed4da7a749a8265

17. Skadden Arps Slate Meagher & Flom LLP, "China M&A: reform plan promotes mixed ownership of State-Owned Enterprises," January 28, 2015, Lexology, https://www.lexology.com/library/detail.aspx?g=26c80c48-6d8f-4ccd-839a-af3ad9c7d1ba

18. Bland, B., "China Plans Shake-Up Of State-Owned Enterprises To Boost Growth," September 13, 2015, *Financial Times*, https://www.ft.com/content/aff90924-

5a01-11e5-9846-de406ccb37f2

19. Ibid.

20. Cendrowski, S., "China's Global 500 Companies Are Bigger Than Ever – And Mostly State-Owned," *Fortune*, July 22, 2015, http://fortune.com/2015/07/22/china-global-500-government-owned/

21. Zhang, J., "Big State-Owned Enterprises Pillar Of Economy In China," September 13, 2015, CCTV News (English).

22. Ibid.

23. Wang, Y., "Report: China Announces Timeline For Reforming State-Owned Enterprises," August 28, 2014, Forbes, https://www.forbes.com/sites/ywang/2014/08/28/report-china-announces-timeline-of-reforming-state-owned-enterprises/#49bf767f6534

24. Cendrowski, S., "China's Global 500 Companies Are Bigger Than Ever – And Mostly State-Owned."

25. Kong, X. et al, "Technical Efficiency, Technological Change And Total Factor Productivity Growth In Chinese State-Owned Enterprises In The Early 1990s," *Asian Economic Journal* 1998, Vol. 12 No. 3, 267–281, https://pdfs.semanticscholar.org/ccb8/98c2c8f4535a7bc52402a70fd8bca2922a0d.pdf

26. Tian, L. and S. Estrin, "Retained State Shareholding In Chinese PLCs: Does Government Ownership Reduce Corporate Value?" December 2007, *Journal of Comparative Economics* 36 (2008) 74–89, http://personal.lse.ac.uk/estrin/Publication%20PDF%27s/Retained%20state%20shareholding%20in%20Chinese%20PLCs.pdf

27. Dong, X. and L. Putterman, "Investigating The Rise Of Labor Redundancy In China's State Industry," *China*

Economic Quarterly 2002-01,
http://en.cnki.com.cn/Article_en/CJFDTOTAL-
JJXU200201008.htm

28. Bajona, C. and T. Chu, "Reforming State Owned
Enterprises in China: Effects of WTO Accession," *Review
of Economic Dynamics* Vol. 13 (4), 2010.

29. Tian, L. and S. Estrin, "Retained State Shareholding In
Chinese PLCs: Does Government Ownership Reduce
Corporate Value?"

30. Das, A., "Warren Buffett Is Winning Fans In China,"
June 9, 2015, *Wall Street Journal*,
https://www.wsj.com/articles/warren-buffett-is-
winning-fans-in-china-1433875091

31. Tian, L. and S. Estrin, "Retained State Shareholding In
Chinese PLCs: Does Government Ownership Reduce
Corporate Value?"

32. Bajona, C. and T. Chu, "Reforming State Owned
Enterprises in China: Effects of WTO Accession."

33. Wang, Y., "Report: China Announces Timeline For
Reforming State-Owned Enterprises," August 28, 2014,
Forbes,
https://www.forbes.com/sites/ywang/2014/08/28/report-
china-announces-timeline-of-reforming-state-owned-
enterprises/#2ff6163d6534

34. Curran, E., "State Companies: Back On China's To-Do
List," July 31, 2015, Bloomberg,
https://www.bloomberg.com/news/articles/2015-07-
30/china-s-state-owned-companies-may-face-reform

35. Canadian Trade Commissioner Service, "Working with
state-owned enterprises in China," August 16, 2016,
http://tradecommissioner.gc.ca/canadexport/140205.asp
x?lang=eng

36. Ibid.

37. Mobius, M., "The Reform Of China's State-Owned Enterprises," June 9, 2015, Investment Adventures in Emerging Markets, http://emergingmarkets.blog.franklintempleton.com/201 5/06/09/developments-in-the-reform-of-chinas-state-owned-enterprises/

38. Gong, Y. et al, "Employment Effects Of Privatisation And Foreign Acquisition Of Chinese State-Owned Enterprises," *International Journal of the Economics of Business* Vol 14 No. 2, 2007.

39. Ralston, D. et al, "Today's state-owned enterprises of China: Are they dying dinosaurs or dynamic dynamos?" *Strategic Management Journal* Vol 27 No 9, September 2006.

40. Ibid.

41. Tian, L. and S. Estrin, "Retained State Shareholding In Chinese PLCs: Does Government Ownership Reduce Corporate Value?"

42. State-owned Assets Supervision and Administration Commission of the State Council, "Main Functions," http://en.sasac.gov.cn/n1408028/n1408521/index.html

43. Szamosszegi, A. and C. Kyle, "An Analysis Of State-Owned Enterprises And State Capitalism In China," October 26, 2011, US-China Economic and Security Review Commission, https://www.uscc.gov/sites/default/files/Research/10_26 _11_CapitalTradeSOEStudy.pdf

44. Fu, J., "Reforming Management Of State-Owned Assets In Enterprises: Towards A Chinese Version Of The Temasek Model?" 2014, University of Canberra.

45. Ibid.

46. Mattlin, M., "The Chinese Government's New Approach To Ownership And Financial Control Of

Strategic State-Owned Enterprises," BOFIT Discussion Papers 10 (2007), Bank of Finland Institute for Economies in Transition, http://citeseerx.ist.psu.edu/viewdoc/download?doi=10.1.1.121.6319&rep=rep1&type=pdf

47. Ibid.

48. Fidelity Worldwide Investment, "Reform Of China's SOEs," August 2014, http://www.fidelity.com.cn/zh-cn/data/MarketCommentary/PDF/MC-english/ReformofChinaSOEs.pdf

49. Ibid.

50. Qiu, Z. "The Impact Of SOE Reform On Chinese Overseas Investment," January 23, 2015, The Jamestown Foundation, https://jamestown.org/program/the-impact-of-soe-reform-on-chinese-overseas-investment/

51. He, H. et al, "Breaking The 'Iron Rice Bowl' And Precautionary Savings: Evidence From Chinese State-Owned Enterprises Reform," Federal Reserve Bank of San Francisco Working Paper 2014-04 (2014), https://www.frbsf.org/economic-research/files/wp2014-04.pdf.

52. O'Connor, N. et al, "The Adoption Of 'Western' Management Accounting/Controls In China's State-Owned Enterprises During Economic Transition," *Accounting, Organizations and Society* 29 (2004).

53. Ibid.

54. Bai, X. and L. Bennington, "Steering and Rowing in Chinese SOEs: the Modern Enterprise System in China."

55. O'Connor, N. et al, "The Adoption Of 'Western' Management Accounting/Controls In China's State-Owned Enterprises During Economic Transition."

56. Freeman, R. and X. Li, "Has China's new labour contract law worked?" December 22, 2013, CEPR Policy Portal,

https://voxeu.org/article/has-china-s-new-labour-contract-law-worked

57. Li, K., "Practice And Problems: The Fixed-Term Employment Contract In China," 1997, Anhui University

58. Ibid.

59. Orr, G., "China Announces State-Owned Enterprise Reform…Again," September 16, 2015, McKinsey China, http://mckinseychina.com/china-announces-state-owned-enterprise-reformagain/

60. Li, K., "Practice And Problems: The Fixed-Term Employment Contract In China."

61. Hassard et al. (1999) cited in O'Connor, N. et al, "Political constraints, organization design and performance measurement in China's state-owned enterprises," *Accounting, Organizations and Society*, 2006, Vol 31, (2), 157-177

62. O'Connor, N. et al, "Political constraints, organization design and performance measurement in China's state-owned enterprises."

63. Tan, L. and J. Wang, "Modelling An Effective Corporate Governance System For China's Listed State-Owned Enterprises: Issues And Challenges In A Transitional Economy," *Journal of Corporate Law Studies* 7(1), August 2007

64. Ibid.

65. Ralston, D., et al. "Today's State-Owned Enterprises Of China: Are They Dying Dinosaurs Or Dynamic Dynamos?" *Strategic Management Journal* 27.9 (2006): 825-843.

66. Tan, L. and J. Wang, "Modelling An Effective Corporate Governance System For China's Listed State-Owned Enterprises: Issues And Challenges In A Transitional Economy."

67. Ibid.
68. Song, L. et al, "State-Owned Enterprises' Outward Investment And The Structural Reform In China," *China & World Economy* 19.4 (July-August 2011): 38-53
69. Ibid.
70. Lok, P., "The Economic Performance of Chinese State-Owned Enterprises After Denationalization," 1998, University of Hong Kong
71. Ibid.
72. Fan, J. et al, "Institutions And Organizational Structure: The Case Of State-Owned Corporate Pyramids," *Journal of Law, Economics, and Organization* 29.6 (2012), http://www.cuhk.edu.hk/ief/josephfan/doc/research_pu blished_paper/20.pdf
73. Ibid.
74. Tan, L. and J. Wang, "Modelling An Effective Corporate Governance System For China's Listed State-Owned Enterprises: Issues And Challenges In A Transitional Economy."
75. O'Connor, N. et al, "The Adoption Of 'Western' Management Accounting/Controls In China's State-Owned Enterprises During Economic Transition."
76. Tan, L. and J. Wang, "Modelling An Effective Corporate Governance System For China's Listed State-Owned Enterprises: Issues And Challenges In A Transitional Economy."
77. Ibid.
78. Sipf.com.cn, "False Statement Yinguangxia's Civil Compensation Case Concerning False Statement - SIPF," 2011
79. Tan, L. and J. Wang, "Modelling An Effective Corporate Governance System For China's Listed State-Owned Enterprises: Issues And Challenges In A Transitional

Economy."

80. Ibid.

81. Green, S. and J. Ho, "Old Stocks, New Owners: Two Cases Of Ownership Change In China's Stock Market," *Journal of Chinese Economic and Business Studies* 2.3 (2004): 267-280.

82. Fu, J., "Reforming Management Of State-Owned Assets In Enterprises: Towards A Chinese Version Of The Temasek Model?" 2014, University of Canberra

83. Anderlini, J., "China Corruption Purge Snares 115 SOE 'Tigers'," May 18, 2015, *Financial Times*, https://www.ft.com/content/ad997d5c-fd3c-11e4-9e96-00144feabdc0

84. Qiu, Z. "The Impact Of SOE Reform On Chinese Overseas Investment."

85. Fan, J. et al, "Institutions And Organizational Structure: The Case Of State-Owned Corporate Pyramids."

86. Ibid.

87. Fu, J., "Reforming Management Of State-Owned Assets In Enterprises: Towards A Chinese Version Of The Temasek Model?"

88. Song, L. et al, "State-Owned Enterprises' Outward Investment And The Structural Reform In China."

89. Ibid.

90. SOASAC, 2010, cited in Song, L. et al, "State-Owned Enterprises' Outward Investment And The Structural Reform In China."

91. Song, L. et al, "State-Owned Enterprises' Outward Investment And The Structural Reform In China."

92. Ibid.

93. Cendrowski, S., "China's Global 500 Companies Are Bigger Than Ever—And Mostly State-Owned," July 22, 2015, *Fortune*, http://fortune.com/2015/07/22/china-

global-500-government-owned/

94. Dobson, W., "China's State-Owned Enterprises And Canada's FDI Policy," March 2014, School Of Public Policy SPP Research Papers Vol 7 Issue 10, https://www.policyschool.ca/wp-content/uploads/2016/03/chinas-soes-dobson.pdf

95. Szamosszegi, A. and C. Kyle, "An Analysis Of State-Owned Enterprises And State Capitalism In China."

96. Ibid.

97. Canadian Trade Commissioner Service, "Working with state-owned enterprises in China."

98. Tan-Mullins, M., "The Environmental Implications Of Chinese State-Owned Enterprises (CSOEs) Investment In Africa's Energy Sector," *International Journal of Energy Security and Environmental Research*, Vol. 1 No. 2, 43-58

99. Hackley, R. and L. Westhuizen, "African Energy's New Friends In China," September 9, 2011, Bloomberg, https://www.bloomberg.com/news/articles/2011-09-08/african-energy-s-new-friends-in-china

100. The Jakarta Post, "China's State-Owned Companies To Invest In West Sumatra," July 30, 2015, http://www.thejakartapost.com/news/2015/07/30/chinas-state-owned-companies-invest-west-sumatra.html

101. Chen, A. "China State Firms To Start Pumping New Oil In Iran," July 31, 2015, Reuters, https://www.reuters.com/article/china-iran-oil-idUSL3N10B29620150731

102. Dobson, W., "China's State-Owned Enterprises And Canada's FDI Policy."

103. Qiu, Z. "The Impact Of SOE Reform On Chinese Overseas Investment."

104. Dobson, W., "China's State-Owned Enterprises And Canada's FDI Policy."

105. Areddy, J., "Rio Tinto China Employees Get Prison Terms," March 30, 2010, *Wall Street Journal*, https://www.wsj.com/articles/SB10001424052702304370304575151032293098898

106. Silk, M. and J. Ashley, "Understanding China's State Secrets Laws," January 1, 2011, China Business Review, https://www.chinabusinessreview.com/understanding-chinas-state-secrets-laws/

107. Ibid.

108. Dobson, W., "China's State-Owned Enterprises And Canada's FDI Policy."

109. Brødsgaard, K., "Can China Keep Controlling Its SOEs?" March 5, 2018, *The Diplomat*, https://thediplomat.com/2018/03/can-china-keep-controlling-its-soes/

110. Ibid.

111. Asia Society Policy Institute, "State-Owned Enterprise Policy Reform," Winter 2018, https://chinadashboard.asiasociety.org/winter-2018/page/state-owned-enterprise

112. Ibid.

113. Ibid.

114. Wang, X., "China's Railways: A Cautionary Tale for SOE Reform," January 31, 2018, The Diplomat, https://thediplomat.com/2018/01/chinas-railways-a-cautionary-tale-for-soe-reform/

115. Asia Society Policy Institute, "State-Owned Enterprise Policy Reform."

116. Wang, X., "China's Railways: A Cautionary Tale for SOE Reform."

117. Asia Society Policy Institute, "State-Owned Enterprise Policy Reform."

118. Ibid.

Chapter 4

1. *The Economist*, "Why China's five-year plans are so important," October 26, 2015, https://www.economist.com/the-economist-explains/2015/10/26/why-chinas-five-year-plans-are-so-important

2. MacFarquhar, R., "Mao's Failure, Deng's Success," June 24, 2010, Asia Society, http://chinaboom.asiasociety.org./essays/detail/209

3. Chen, F. and T. Orlik, "China's Five Year Plans: A Brief History," November 11, 2015, Bloomberg, https://www.bloomberg.com/news/articles/2015-11-10/china-s-five-year-plans-a-brief-history

4. Cairns, R., "The First Five-Year Plan," 2015, Alpha History, http://alphahistory.com/chineserevolution/first-five-year-plan/

5. Trueman, C., "China and the First Five-Year Plan," 26 May 2015, The History Learning Site, https://www.historylearningsite.co.uk/modern-world-history-1918-to-1980/china-1900-to-1976/china-and-the-first-five-year-plan/

6. Chen, F. and T. Orlik, "China's Five Year Plans: A Brief History."

7. MacFarquhar, R., "Mao's Failure, Deng's Success."

8. Trueman, C., "China and the First Five-Year Plan."

9. Chen, F. and T. Orlik, "China's Five Year Plans: A Brief History."

10. Cairns, R., "The First Five-Year Plan."

11. Ibid.

12. Cheremukhin, A. et al, *The Economy of People's Republic of China from 1953.*

13. Cairns, R., "The First Five-Year Plan."

14. Ibid.
15. Jacob, E., "Mao and the Great Leap Forward," 2013, Newark College of Arts and Sciences Rutgers, https://www.ncas.rutgers.edu/mao-and-great-leap-forward
16. Cheremukhin, A. et al, *The Economy of People's Republic of China from 1953.*
17. MacFarquhar, R., "Mao's Failure, Deng's Success."
18. Cheremukhin, A. et al, *The Economy of People's Republic of China from 1953.*
19. Jacob, E., "Mao and the Great Leap Forward."
20. Manning, S., "The Causes of Starvation During the Great Leap Forward," March 25, 2009, Historian on the Warpath, https://scottmanning.com/content/the-causes-of-starvation-during-the-great-leap-forward/
21. Watkins, T., "The Great Leap Forward Period in China, 1958–1960," San José State University Department of Economics, http://www.sjsu.edu/faculty/watkins/greatleap.htm
22. Dikotter, F., "Mao's Great Leap to Famine," December 15, 2010, *New York Times*, https://www.nytimes.com/2010/12/16/opinion/16iht-eddikotter16.html
23. Branigan, T., "China's Great Famine: the true story," January 1, 2013, *The Guardian*, https://www.theguardian.com/world/2013/jan/01/china-great-famine-book-tombstone
24. Qian, Y., "The Process of China's Market Transition (1978–98): The Evolutionary, Historical, And Comparative Perspectives," April 1999, *Journal of Institutional and Theoretical Economics* symposium on "Big-Bang Transformation of Economic Systems as a Challenge to New Institutional Economics,"

http://citeseerx.ist.psu.edu/viewdoc/download?doi=10.1.1.198.5013&rep=rep1&type=pdf

25. Galloway, T., "Chinese Five Year Plans: An Economic Catalyst?" 2011, Center for Strategic Leadership, US Army War College Vol 11.11, https://csl.armywarcollege.edu/usacsl/publications/IP11_11.pdf

26. Ibid.

27. Naughton, B., "The New Common Economic Program: China's Eleventh Five Year Plan and What it Means," October 30, 2005, China Leadership Monitor, No. 16, https://www.hoover.org/research/new-common-economic-program-chinas-11th-five-year-plan-and-what-it-means

28. KPMG Advisory China Limited, "China's Twelfth Five-Year Plan Overview," 2011, 1.

29. Ibid.

30. Ibid.

31. Galloway, T., "Chinese Five Year Plans: An Economic Catalyst?"

32. Institute for Industrial Productivity, "Energy Intensity Target of the 11th Five Year Plan," Industrial Efficiency Policy Database, http://iepd.iipnetwork.org/policy/energy-intensity-target-11th-five-year-plan

33. Hatton, C., "Taking stock of China's five year economic model," October 30, 2015, BBC, https://www.bbc.com/news/blogs-china-blog-34674395

34. Ibid.

35. Ibid.

36. Moody, A., "Dissecting China's five-year plan," November 23, 2015, *Daily Telegraph*, https://www.telegraph.co.uk/news/world/china-

watch/politics/chinas-five-year-plan/

37. Melton, O., "China's Five-Year Planning System: Implications For The Reform Agenda," April 22, 2015, US-China Economic and Security Review Commission, https://www.uscc.gov/sites/default/files/Melton%20-%20Written%20Testimony.pdf

38. Cendrowski, S., "China's New 5-Year Plan Is About Growth," October 30, 2015, *Fortune*, http://fortune.com/2015/10/30/chinas-new-5-year-plan-is-about-growth/

39. Feldstein, M., "China's Latest Five-Year Plan," November 28, 2015, Project Syndicate, https://www.project-syndicate.org/commentary/china-new-five-year-plan-by-martin-feldstein-2015-11?barrier=accesspaylog

40. Wong, E., "China Aims For 6.5% Economic Growth Over Next 5 Years, Xi Says," November 4, 2015, *New York Times*, https://www.nytimes.com/2015/11/04/world/asia/china-economic-growth-xi.html

41. Cendrowski, S., "China's New 5-Year Plan Is About Growth."

42. Moody, A., "Dissecting China's five-year plan."

43. Cendrowski, S., "China's New 5-Year Plan Is About Growth."

44. Hsu, S., "China's Next Five-Year Plan: Realistic Objectives?" November 7, 2015, The Diplomat, https://thediplomat.com/2015/11/chinas-next-five-year-plan-realistic-objectives/

45. Galloway, T., "Chinese Five Year Plans: An Economic Catalyst?"

46. Cendrowski, S., "China's New 5-Year Plan Is About Growth."

47. Li, L., "China's 7 million recent graduates compete in toughest job market ever," November 3, 2015, NBC, https://www.nbcnews.com/news/world/chinas-7-million-recent-graduates-compete-toughest-job-market-ever-flna8C11161546

48. Hsu, S., "China's Next Five-Year Plan: Realistic Objectives?"

49. Moody, A., "Dissecting China's five-year plan."

50. Feldstein, M., "China's Latest Five-Year Plan."

51. Moody, A., "Dissecting China's five-year plan."

52. China Labor Bulletin, "Reform of State-owned enterprises in China," December 19, 2007, http://www.clb.org.hk/en/content/reform-state-owned-enterprises-china

53. Moody, A., "Dissecting China's five-year plan."

54. Hsu, S., "China's Next Five-Year Plan: Realistic Objectives?"

55. Ibid.

56. Cendrowski, S., "China's New 5-Year Plan Is About Growth."

57. Hsu, S., "China's Next Five-Year Plan: Realistic Objectives?"

58. Cendrowski, S., "China's New 5-Year Plan Is About Growth."

59. Moody, A., "Dissecting China's five-year plan."

60. Ibid.

61. Feldstein, M., "China's Latest Five-Year Plan."

62. Moody, A., "Dissecting China's five-year plan."

63. Ibid.

64. Feldstein, M., "China's Latest Five-Year Plan."

65. Cendrowski, S., "China's New 5-Year Plan Is About Growth."

66. Matthews, C., "The Real Ticking Time Bomb In China's

Economy," September 9, 2015, *Fortune,*
http://fortune.com/2015/09/09/china-economy-trouble/

67. Pilling, D., "China's economic facts and fakes can be hard to tell apart," September 16, 2015, *Financial Times,* https://www.ft.com/content/fa48bdc2-5b8b-11e5-9846-de406ccb37f2

68. Ibid.

69. Ibid.

70. Cendrowski, S., "China's New 5-Year Plan Is About Growth."

71. Pilling, D., "China's economic facts and fakes can be hard to tell apart."

72. Ibid.

73. Cendrowski, S., "China's New 5-Year Plan Is About Growth."

74. Bloomberg, "China's Leaders Shift From Short-Term Stimulus to Five-Year Plan," October 26, 2015, https://www.bloomberg.com/news/articles/2015-10-25/china-s-leaders-add-stimulus-dose-as-5-year-prescription-mulled

75. *The Guardian,* "China GDP: how it has changed since 1980," https://www.theguardian.com/news/datablog/2012/mar/23/china-gdp-since-1980

Chapter 5

1. Clark, S. et al, "The Trouble With Sovereign-Wealth Funds," December 22, 2015, *Wall Street Journal,* https://www.wsj.com/articles/the-trouble-with-sovereign-wealth-funds-1450836278

2. Zhu, R., "Report on the Outline of the Tenth Five-Year Plan for National Economic and Social Development

(2001)," Delivered at the Fourth Session of the Ninth National People's Congress on March 5, 2001, http://www.gov.cn/english/official/2005-07/29/content_18334.htm

3. Koch-Weser, I. and O. Haacke, "China Investment Corporation: Recent Developments in Performance, Strategy, and Governance," June 13, 2013, US-China Economic and Security Review Commission, https://www.uscc.gov/sites/default/files/Research/China%20Investment%20Corporation_Staff%20Report_0.pdf

4. Clark, S. et al, "The Trouble With Sovereign-Wealth Funds."

5. Koch-Weser, I. and O. Haacke, "China Investment Corporation: Recent Developments in Performance, Strategy, and Governance."

6. Ibid.

7. Rocha, E., "China's sovereign wealth fund to open first US office," December 15, 2015, Reuters, https://www.reuters.com/article/us-cn-invst-new-york-idUSKBN0TX22120151214

8. BBC, "China fund buys 10% stake in London's Heathrow airport," November 1, 2012, https://www.bbc.com/news/business-20163907

9. Reuters, "China 'to move £500bn sovereign wealth fund to New York'," December 14, 2015, *Daily Telegraph*, https://www.telegraph.co.uk/finance/china-business/12050244/China-to-move-500bn-sovereign-wealth-fund-to-New-York.html

10. Cao, B., "CIC buys stake in New York tower in US property push," January 5, 2011, *China Daily*, http://www.chinadaily.com.cn/bizchina/2011-01/05/content_11798373.htm

11. Wei, L. and J. Dean, "CIC Looks to Pile Cash Into US

Real Estate," September 9, 2009, *Wall Street Journal*, http://www.wsj.com/articles/SB125243309793493085

12. Koch-Weser, I. and O. Haacke, "China Investment Corporation: Recent Developments in Performance, Strategy, and Governance."

13. McMahon, D., "CIC Offers a Glimpse Into US Holdings," February 9, 2010, *Wall Street Journal*, http://www.wsj.com/articles/SB100014240527487034277 04575052303975503216

14. Bloomberg, "China Wealth Fund CIC Posts 10.6% Return as Equity Rally," July 27, 2013, http://www.bloomberg.com/news/articles/2013-07-26/china-wealth-fund-reports-10-6-return-amid-global-equity-rally

15. Reuters, "China to Move Wealth Fund HQ to NY, Signaling Increased Focus on US," December 15, 2015, http://www.nbcnews.com/business/business-news/china-move-wealth-fund-hq-n-y-signaling-increased-focus-n479906

16. Rocha, E., "China's sovereign wealth fund to open first US office."

17. Welitzkin, P., "Sovereign wealth fund opens NY office," December 18, 2015, *China Daily*, http://usa.chinadaily.com.cn/us/2015-12/18/content_22747713.htm

18. Koch-Weser, I. and O. Haacke, "China Investment Corporation: Recent Developments in Performance, Strategy, and Governance."

19. McMahon, D., "CIC Offers a Glimpse Into US Holdings."

20. Wei, L. and J. Dean, "CIC Looks to Pile Cash Into US Real Estate."

21. Koven, P. and C. Cattaneo, "Fortune Lost: The short,

brutal and costly ride of China Investment Corp. in Canada," June 1, 2015, *Financial Post*, http://business.financialpost.com/commodities/energy/fortune-lost-the-short-brutal-and-costly-ride-of-china-investment-corp-in-canada

22. Nguyen, D., "China FDI in Vietnam after Twenty Years," 2015, Vietnam Social Sciences, No.6 (170), http://www.vjol.info/index.php/VSS/article/viewFile/22914/19583

23. Ibid, and Amer, R. "Vietnam's Relations with China – A Multifaceted Partnership," March 17, 2014, Asia Dialogue, http://theasiadialogue.com/2014/03/17/vietnams-relations-with-china-a-multifaceted-partnership/

24. Nguyen T. et al, "Interview: More Chinese investment boosts China-Vietnam trade ties," Xinhua English News, http://news.xinhuanet.com/english/indepth/2014-01/16/c_133050466.htm

25. Ibid.

26. Nguyen, D., "China FDI in Vietnam after Twenty Years."

27. Lotova, E., "Laying Foundations for Growth: The Future of Vietnamese Infrastructure," August 21, 2017, Vietnam Briefing, http://www.vietnam-briefing.com/news/infrastructure-vietnam.html/

28. Xinhua, "Bank of China ready to finance Vietnam's infrastructure," November 3, 2015, *China Daily*, http://www.chinadaily.com.cn/business/2015-11/03/content_22360436.htm

29. Vietnam.net, "Chinese investment in Vietnam soars," April 20, 2014, http://english.vietnamnet.vn/fms/business/100245/chinese-investment-in-vietnam-soars.html

30. *Hanoi Times*, "Chinese investment in Vietnam is accelerating," March 24, 2016, http://www.hanoitimes.com.vn/investment/opportunities/2016/03/81E0A0EE/chinese-investment-in-vietnam-is-accelerating/

31. Ibid.

32. Ibid.

33. GAN Business Portal, "Vietnam Corruption Report," September 2017, http://www.business-anti-corruption.com/country-profiles/vietnam

34. GlobalSecurity.org, "Vietnam – Corruption," January 30, 2016, http://www.globalsecurity.org/military/world/vietnam/corruption.htm

35. Clark, H., "China–Vietnam relations: past sovereignty and sea," October 7, 2016, The Strategist – The Australian Strategic Policy Institute Blog, http://www.aspistrategist.org.au/china-vietnam-relations-past-sovereignty-sea/

36. *Hanoi Times*, "Chinese investment in Vietnam is accelerating," March 24, 2016, http://www.hanoitimes.com.vn/investment/opportunities/2016/03/81E0A0EE/chinese-investment-in-vietnam-is-accelerating/

37. Vietnam.net, "Chinese investment in Vietnam soars," April 20, 2014, http://english.vietnamnet.vn/fms/business/100245/chinese-investment-in-vietnam-soars.html

38. Clark, H., "China–Vietnam relations: past sovereignty and sea."

39. Boudreau, J., "The Biggest Winner From TPP Trade Deal May Be Vietnam," October 9, 2015, Bloomberg, http://www.bloomberg.com/news/articles/2015-10-

08/more-shoes-and-shrimp-less-china-reliance-for-vietnam-in-tpp

40. Clark, H., "China–Vietnam relations: past sovereignty and sea."

41. Ibid.

42. Ho, T. and K. Sothear, "Cambodia-China Trade to Top $5 Billion by 2017," June 23, 2015, *Cambodia Daily*, https://www.cambodiadaily.com/business/cambodia-china-trade-to-top-5-billion-by-2017-86222/

43. Sophavy, S., "Chinese Companies Invest a Total of US$10.1 Billion in Cambodia," September 21, 2015, Agence Kampuchea Presse, http://www.akp.gov.kh/?p=69060

44. Cheong, D., "Cambodians flock to learn Mandarin," March 1, 2013, *Phnom Penh Post*, http://www.phnompenhpost.com/national/cambodians-flock-learn-mandarin

45. Heng, P., "Cambodia–China Relations: A Positive-Sum Game?" *Journal of Current Southeast Asian Affairs*, 31, 2, 57-85, https://journals.sub.uni-hamburg.de/giga/jsaa/article/view/545/543

46. Morm, K. and M. Thong, "The 21st Century Chinese Maritime Silk Road: Impacts on Cambodia," IS 409: Foreign Policy II (Cambodia Focus), Royal University of Phnom Penh, Institute of Foreign Languages Department of International Studies

47. Sotharith, C., "Trade, FDI, and ODA between Cambodia and China/Japan/Korea," in *Economic Relations of China, Japan, and Korea, and the Mekong River Basin Countries*, BRC (Bangkok Research Center) Research Report No.3.

48. Kunmakara, M. "Derivatives trading inches closer to reality," December 26, 2014, *Phnom Penh Post*, http://www.phnompenhpost.com/derivatives-trading-

inches-closer-reality

49. Heng, P., "Cambodia–China Relations: A Positive-Sum Game?"

50. Ibid.

51. Realestate.com.kh, "Chinese Property Investment in Cambodia, with Kim Heang on Realestate.com.khTV," February 16, 2017, http://realestate.com.kh/news/chinese-property-investment-in-cambodia-with-kim-heang-on-realestate-com-khtv/

52. Phnom Penh Post, "Mixed blessing from China's stock market crash," August 27, 2015, http://www.phnompenhpost.com/real-estate/mixed-blessing-chinas-stock-market-crash

53. Heng, P., "Cambodia–China Relations: A Positive-Sum Game?"

54. Ibid.

55. Kurlantzick, J., "China's Charm Offensive in Southeast Asia," Carnegie Endowment, https://carnegieendowment.org/files/Kurlantzick_SoutheastAsia_China.pdf

56. Realestate.com.kh, "How China influences the Cambodian Real Estate Market," February 16, 2017, http://realestate.com.kh/news/how-china-influences-the-cambodian-real-estate-market/

57. Boyle, D., "Foreign Investors Surge into Cambodian Condo Market," April 8, 2016, VOA News, http://www.voanews.com/a/foreign-investors-surge-cambodia-condo-market/3277029.html

58. Pheap, A., "Cambodia to Invest US$62M in China's Asia Bank," October 12, 2015, *Cambodia Daily*, https://www.cambodiadaily.com/news/cambodia-to-invest-62m-in-chinas-asia-bank-97098/

59. Soeung, S., "Chinese Bank an Opportunity for Aid Reform, Fulbright Scholar Says," March 24, 2015, VOA Khmer, http://www.voacambodia.com/a/chinese-bank-an-opportunity-for-aid-reform-scholar-says/2686898.html

60. Xinhua, "First Chinese commercial bank to open branch in Cambodia," June 11, 2010, http://www.asean-china-center.org/english/2010-06/11/c_13382151.htm

61. Xinhua, "Forum on RMB internationalization held in Phnom Penh, Cambodia," November 5, 2015, http://www.xinhuanet.com/english/photo/2015-11/05/c_134786843.htm

62. Yao, K., "China-Arab States Cooperation Forum in the Last Decade," 2014, *Journal of Middle Eastern and Islamic Studies (in Asia)* Vol. 8, No. 4

63. Ibid.

64. Ibid.

65. Alterman, J., "China's Balancing Act in the Gulf," August 21, 2013, Middle East Program, Center for Strategic and International Studies, https://www.csis.org/analysis/chinas-balancing-act-gulf

66. Aronson, G., "China's vision of the Middle East," January 21, 2016, Al Jazeera, http://www.aljazeera.com/indepth/opinion/2016/01/china-vision-middle-east-160121052018955.html

67. Liu, T., "China's economic engagement in the Middle East and North Africa," January 2014, FRIDE Policy Brief, http://fride.org/descarga/PB_173_China_economic_engagement_in_MENA.pdf

68. Ibid.

69. Ministry of Foreign Affairs and Ministry of Commerce of the PRC, "Vision and Actions on Jointly Building Silk

Road Economic Belt and 21st-Century Maritime Silk Road," March 28, 2015, http://www.fmprc.gov.cn/mfa_eng/zxxx_662805/t124961 8.shtml

70. China's Arab Policy Paper, January 2016, Xinhua, http://www.xinhuanet.com/english/china/2016-01/13/c_135006619.htm

71. Yao, K., "China-Arab States Cooperation Forum in the Last Decade."

72. Chen, D., "Study and Revelation on China-Arab States Economic and Trade Relationship — A Discussion," 2011, China-Arab States Economic and Trade Forum

73. Zhao, M., "China's Middle East Opportunity," February 3, 2016, China & US Focus, http://www.chinausfocus.com/foreign-policy/chinas-middle-east-opportunity/

74. Feng, C., "Embracing Interdependence: The Dynamics of China and the Middle East," April 28, 2015, Brookings Institution, https://www.brookings.edu/research/embracing-interdependence-the-dynamics-of-china-and-the-middle-east/

75. Liu, T., "China's economic engagement in the Middle East and North Africa."

76. Zha, D. and M. Meidan, "China and the Middle East in a New Energy Landscape," October 2015, Chatham House Asia Programme, https://www.chathamhouse.org/sites/default/files/public ations/research/20151021ChinaMiddleEastEnergyDaojio ngMeidan.pdf

77. Chen, D., "Study and Revelation on China-Arab States Economic and Trade Relationship — A Discussion."

78. Ibid.

79. Liu, T., "China's economic engagement in the Middle East and North Africa."

80. Alterman, J., "China's Balancing Act in the Gulf."

81. Mackenzie, P., "A Closer Look at China-Iran Relations," September 2010, CNA Analysis and Solutions, https://www.cna.org/CNA_files/PDF/D0023622.A3.pdf

82. Ibid.

83. Alterman, J., "China's Balancing Act in the Gulf."

84. Singh, M., "China's Middle East Tour, Beijing's Post-Sanctions Ambitions," January 24, 2016, Foreign Affairs, https://www.foreignaffairs.com/articles/china/2016-01-24/chinas-middle-east-tour

85. McGiffert, C., "Chinese Soft Power and Its Implications for the United States: Competition and Cooperation in the Developing World," March 10, 2009, Center for Strategic and International Studies

86. Mackenzie, P., "A Closer Look at China-Iran Relations."

87. Ibid.

88. Alterman, J., "China's Balancing Act in the Gulf."

89. Pigato, M. and W. Tang, "China and Africa: Expanding Economic Ties in an Evolving Global Context," March 1, 2015, World Bank, http://documents.worldbank.org/curated/en/241321468024314010/China-and-Africa-expanding-economic-ties-in-an-evolving-global-context

90. Wharton School of the University of Pennsylvania, "China's Investments in Africa: What's the Real Story?" January 19, 2016, http://knowledge.wharton.upenn.edu/article/chinas-investments-in-africa-whats-the-real-story/ and: Robertson, W. and L. Benabdallah, "China pledged to invest US$60 billion in Africa. Here's what that means," January 7, 2016, *Washington Post*,

https://www.washingtonpost.com/news/monkey-cage/wp/2016/01/07/china-pledged-to-invest-60-billion-in-africa-heres-what-that-means/

91. 91.University of Aberdeen, "Different development partners," Africa Sustainable Development for All? (course)

92. Chen, W. et al, "China's direct investment in Africa: Reality versus myth," September 3, 2015, Brookings Institution, https://www.brookings.edu/blog/africa-in-focus/2015/09/03/chinas-direct-investment-in-africa-reality-versus-myth/

93. University of Aberdeen, "Different development partners."

94. Pigato, M. and W. Tang, "China and Africa: Expanding Economic Ties in an Evolving Global Context."

95. Chen, W. et al, "China's direct investment in Africa: Reality versus myth."

96. Maverick, J., "The 3 Reasons Why Chinese Invest in Africa," Investopedia, http://www.investopedia.com/articles/active-trading/081315/3-reasons-why-chinese-invest-africa.asp

97. Chen, W. et al, "China's direct investment in Africa: Reality versus myth."

98. Shinn, D., "China's Investments in Africa," November 20, 2012, Woodrow Wilson International Center for Scholars, https://africaupclose.wilsoncenter.org/chinas-investments-in-africa/

99. Ibid.

100. England, A., "ICBC buys stake in Standard Bank's UK business," February 2, 2015, *Financial Times*, https://www.ft.com/content/b4c8903c-aade-11e4-91d2-00144feab7de

101. Dollar, D. et al, "Why is China investing in Africa?

Evidence from the firm level," August 12, 2015, Brookings Institution, http://www.brookings.edu/research/papers/2015/08/wh y-is-china-investing-in-africa and: Wharton School of the University of Pennsylvania, "China's Investments in Africa: What's the Real Story?"

102. Robertson, W. and L. Benabdallah, "China pledged to invest US$60 billion in Africa. Here's what that means."

103. *The Economist*, "Not as easy as it looks," November 21, 2015 https://www.economist.com/news/middle-east-and-africa/21678777-western-worries-about-chinas-burgeoning-influence-africa-may-be-overblown-not

104. Wharton School of the University of Pennsylvania, "China's Investments in Africa: What's the Real Story?"

105. Robertson, W. and L. Benabdallah, "China pledged to invest US$60 billion in Africa. Here's what that means."

106. Chen, W. et al, "China's direct investment in Africa: Reality versus myth."

107. Robertson, W. and L. Benabdallah, "China pledged to invest US$60 billion in Africa. Here's what that means."

108. Meyer, R. et. al., "Chinese Financial Institutions and Africa," November 2011, China in Africa Project, Occasional Paper No. 103, https://www.saiia.org.za/occasional-papers/44-chinese-financial-institutions-and-africa/file

109. Wharton School of the University of Pennsylvania, "China's Investments in Africa: What's the Real Story?"

110. Chen, W. et al, "China's direct investment in Africa: Reality versus myth."

111. Meyer, R. et. al., "Chinese Financial Institutions and Africa."

112. Ibid.

113. Zadek, S., "How China is rewriting the rules of

investment in Africa," December 4, 2013, China Dialogue,
https://www.chinadialogue.net/article/show/single/en/5
896-How-China-is-rewriting-the-rules-of-investment-in-Africa

114. Middlehurst, C., "Chinese loans to Africa could trigger another debt crisis," December 12, 2015, China Dialogue, https://www.chinadialogue.net/article/show/single/en/8 470-Chinese-loans-to-Africa-could-trigger-another-debt-crisis

115. Bosshard, P., "Chinese loans could fuel regional conflict in East Africa," January 14, 2013, China Dialogue, https://www.chinadialogue.net/article/show/single/en/5 601-Chinese-loans-could-fuel-regional-conflict-in-East-Africa

116. Meyer, R. et. al., "Chinese Financial Institutions and Africa."

117. Ventures Africa, "Africa: CAD Fund Set to Boost Agricultural Investment," May 22, 2012, http://venturesafrica.com/africa-cad-fund-set-to-boost-agriculture-investment/

118. Meyer, R. et. al., "Chinese Financial Institutions and Africa."

119. Ibid.

120. Ibid.

121. Ibid.

122. Peters, E., "China's Evolving Role in Latin America: Can It Be a Win-Win?" September 2015, Atlantic Council Adrienne Arsht Latin America Center, http://publications.atlanticcouncil.org/chinalatam//

123. Gillespie, P., "China's big bet on Latin America is going bust," February 16, 2016, CNN Money, http://money.cnn.com/2016/02/16/news/economy/china-

latin-america-projects-fail/
124. Peters, E., "China's Evolving Role in Latin America: Can It Be a Win-Win?"
125. Gillespie, P., "China's big bet on Latin America is going bust."
126. Pineo, R., "China and Latin America: What You Need To Know," July 29, 2015, http://www.coha.org/china-and-latin-america-what-you-need-to-know/
127. Weich, R, "China Looks to Expand Investment in Latin America, Eyes Raw Materials," February 12, 2016, Latin Post, http://www.latinpost.com/articles/114867/20160212/china-looks-to-expand-investment-in-latin-america-eyes-raw-materials.htm
128. Gillespie, P., "Latin America: China's power play right under the US," February 11, 2016, CNN Money, http://money.cnn.com/2016/02/11/news/economy/china-latin-america-billions-of-dollars-loans-investments/
129. Ibid.
130. Peters, E., "China's Evolving Role in Latin America: Can It Be a Win-Win?"
131. Gillespie, P., "China's big bet on Latin America is going bust."
132. Kaplan, S., "Why China is investing US$250 billion in Latin America," January 24, 2015, *Washington Post*, https://www.washingtonpost.com/blogs/monkey-cage/wp/2015/02/04/why-china-is-investing-250-billion-in-latin-america/
133. Pacific Basin Research Center, "The Opportunities and Challenges of Growing East Asian-Latin American Economic Relations," August 19, 2015, http://www.pbrc.soka.edu/pacific_basin_news/2015/08/taskforce-report.pdf

134. Ibid.

135. Ibid.

136. Ibid.

137. Ibid.

138. Peters, E., "China's Evolving Role in Latin America: Can It Be a Win-Win?"

139. Pacific Basin Research Center, "The Opportunities and Challenges of Growing East Asian-Latin American Economic Relations."

140. Peters, E., "China's Evolving Role in Latin America: Can It Be a Win-Win?"

141. Xinhua, "China, CELAC to map out cooperation plan over next five years: Xi," January 8, 2015, http://news.xinhuanet.com/english/china/2015-01/08/c_133905137.htm

142. Peters, E., "China's Evolving Role in Latin America: Can It Be a Win-Win?"

143. Myers, M., "China & LAC: Doing the Math," July 20, 2015, The Dialogue, http://www.thedialogue.org/blogs/2015/07/china-lac-doing-the-math/

144. Xinhua, "China, CELAC to map out cooperation plan over next five years: Xi."

145. Myers, M., "China & LAC: Doing the Math."

146. Ibid.

147. Peters, E., "China's Evolving Role in Latin America: Can It Be a Win-Win?"

148. Ray, R. et. al, "China in Latin America: Lessons for South-South Cooperation and Sustainable Development," 2015, Boston University, Global Economic Governance Initiative, https://www.bu.edu/pardeeschool/files/2014/12/Working-Group-Final-Report.pdf

149. Pacific Basin Research Center, "The Opportunities and Challenges of Growing East Asian-Latin American Economic Relations."

150. Coyer, P., "Undermining America While Washington Sleeps: China In Latin America," January 31, 2016, *Forbes*, https://www.forbes.com/sites/paulcoyer/2016/01/31/und ermining-america-while-washington-sleeps-china-in-latin-america/

151. Gillespie, P., "Latin America: China's power play right under the US."

Chapter 6

1. Kochhar, R., "China's middle class surges, while India's lags behind," July 15, 2015, Pew Research, http://www.pewresearch.org/fact-tank/2015/07/15/china-india-middle-class/

2. Associated Press, "China's middle class grew by 203 million in 10 years," July 10, 2015, *South China Morning Post*, http://www.scmp.com/news/china/article/1835527/china s-middle-class-grew-203-million-10-years-report

3. He, A.,"Asia's middle class a trend for 2014," November 18, 2013, *China Daily USA*, http://usa.chinadaily.com.cn/epaper/2013-11/18/content_17112311.htm

4. Kharas, H., "The Emerging Middle Class in Developing Countries," January 31, 2010, Brookings Institution, https://www.brookings.edu/research/the-emerging-middle-class-in-developing-countries/

5. Censky, A. "China's middle class boom," June 26, 2012, CNN Money,

http://money.cnn.com/2012/06/26/news/economy/china-middle-class/index.htm

6. Kochhar, R., "China's middle class surges, while India's lags behind."

7. Ibid.

8. Sinha, K., "China's middle class 10 times larger than that in India," October 14, 2014, Times of India, http://timesofindia.indiatimes.com/world/china/Chinas-middle-class-10-times-larger-than-that-in-India/articleshow/44816063.cms

9. Jian, L. and Niu, X., "The New Middle Class in Peking, A Case Study," February 2003, *China Perspectives*, http://journals.openedition.org/chinaperspectives/228

10. Ibid.

11. Bian, Y., "Chinese Social Stratification and Social Mobility," August 2002, *Annual Review of Sociology*, Vol 28(1), 91-116.

12. Jian, L. and Niu, X., "The New Middle Class in Peking, A Case Study."

13. The Globalist, "6 Facts: China's Growing Middle Class," February 10, 2015, https://www.theglobalist.com/6-facts-chinas-growing-middle-class/

14. Goodman, D., "Why There is No New Middle Class," in *The New Rich in China: Future Rulers, Present Lives* ed D. Goodman (London: Routledge, 2008).

15. Elfick, J., "Class Formation and Consumption among Middle-Class Professionals in Shenzhen," 2011, *Journal of Current Chinese Affairs*, Vol. 40, No. 1, 187-211, https://journals.sub.uni-hamburg.de/giga/jcca/article/view/408/406

16. Goodman, D., "Why There is No New Middle Class."

17. Hays, J., "Middle class in China," July 2015, Facts And Details,

http://factsanddetails.com/china/cat11/sub70/item156.html

18. Zhang, Y. et al, "The Rise of the Middle Class in The People's Republic of China," February 2011, Asian Development Bank Working Paper Series, https://www.adb.org/sites/default/files/publication/28436/economics-wp247.pdf

19. Ibid.

20. Jian, L. and Niu, X., "The New Middle Class in Peking, A Case Study."

21. Ibid.

22. Zhang, Y. et al, "The Rise of the Middle Class in The People's Republic of China."

23. Ibid.

24. Sudworth, J., "Can China's middle class spend the world out of recession?" June 20, 2013, BBC, http://www.bbc.com/news/business-22949602

25. The Globalist, "6 Facts: China's Growing Middle Class."

26. Sudworth, J., "Can China's middle class spend the world out of recession?"

27. Chinanews.cn, "Parents Want Most to Give Their Children Best Education, Survey," May 17, 2007, China.org.cn, http://www.china.org.cn/english/education/211069.htm

28. The Globalist, "6 Facts: China's Growing Middle Class."

29. Rappler, "New concerns for China's rising middle class," May 24, 2014, http://www.rappler.com/business/29898-new-concerns-for-china-s-rising-middle-class

30. The Globalist, "6 Facts: China's Growing Middle Class."

31. Sudworth, J., "Can China's middle class spend the world out of recession?"

32. Hays, J., "Middle class in China."

33. Boulter, J., "China's Emerging Middle Class Challenges and Opportunities," February 28, 2013, Future Directions International, http://www.futuredirections.org.au/publication/china-s-emerging-middle-class-challenges-and-opportunities/

34. Ibid.

35. Hays, J., "Middle class in China."

36. Ibid.

37. Zhang, Y. et al, "The Rise of the Middle Class in The People's Republic of China."

38. Wang, H., "Get Ready For Coming Asian Consumer Boom: 3 Trends to Look For," January 13, 2015, *Forbes*, https://www.forbes.com/sites/helenwang/2015/01/13/coming-asian-consumer-boom-three-trends-to-look-for/#662aa2614777

39. Wang, H., *The Chinese Dream, The Rise of the World's Largest Middle Class and What it Means to You*, 2010, CreateSpace Independent Publishing Platform.

40. Zhou, X., "Chinese Middle Class: Reality or Illusion," 2008, Nanjing University, http://gpsw.doshisha.ac.jp/pdf/s_071109b.pdf

41. Ibid.

42. Ibid.

43. Ibid.

44. Ibid.

45. Elfick, J., "Class Formation and Consumption among Middle-Class Professionals in Shenzhen."

46. Ibid.

47. Barton, D. et al, "Mapping China's middle class, Generational change and the rising prosperity of inland cities will power consumption for years to come," June 2013, *McKinsey Quarterly*, https://www.mckinsey.com/industries/retail/our-

insights/mapping-chinas-middle-class

48. Elfick, J., "Class Formation and Consumption among Middle-Class Professionals in Shenzhen."

49. Ibid.

50. Ibid.

51. Sudworth, J., "Can China's middle class spend the world out of recession?"

52. Luhby, T., "China's growing middle class," April 26, 2012, CNN Money, https://money.cnn.com/2012/04/25/news/economy/china-middle-class/index.htm

53. Cotriss, D., "Singles Day supercharges China's new middle class consumers," August 4, 2013, CNBC, https://www.cnbc.com/id/100932791

54. Luhby, T., "China's growing middle class."

55. Carlson, B., "Who belongs to the Chinese middle class?" September 10, 2012, Global Post, https://www.pri.org/stories/2012-09-10/who-belongs-chinese-middle-class

56. Doctoroff, T., "China's New Middle Class: Constants and Variables," May 29, 2010, HuffPost, https://www.huffingtonpost.com/tom-doctoroff/chinas-new-middle-class-c_b_594579.html

57. Ibid.

58. Ibid.

59. Brown, M., "Will China's new middle class save it from disaster?" October 31, 2012, *Daily Telegraph*, https://www.telegraph.co.uk/news/worldnews/asia/china/9630307/Will-Chinas-new-middle-class-save-it-from-disaster.html

60. Doctoroff, T., "China's New Middle Class: Constants and Variables."

61. Song, K. and A. Cui, "Understanding China's Middle

Class," China Business Review, January 1, 2009, https://www.chinabusinessreview.com/understanding-chinas-middle-class/

62. Boulter, J., "China's Emerging Middle Class Challenges and Opportunities."

63. Doctoroff, T., "China's New Middle Class: Constants and Variables."

64. Sheehan, M. "Cirque Du Soleil Enters China With Big Bet On Rising Middle Class," June 16, 2015, HuffPost, https://www.huffingtonpost.com/2015/06/16/cirque-du-soleil-china-fosun_n_7595194.html

65. Barton, D. et al, "Mapping China's middle class, Generational change and the rising prosperity of inland cities will power consumption for years to come."

66. Moody, A. and L. Chang, "China's middle class emerges, to spend more," June 6, 2013, *China Daily*, http://en.people.cn/90778/8272768.html

67. Brown, M., "Will China's new middle class save it from disaster?"

68. Censky, A. "China's middle class boom."

69. Ibid.

70. Senauer, B. and L. Goetz, "The Growing Middle Class in Developing Countries and the Market for High-Value Food Products," February 2004, Working Paper 03-02, The Food Industry Center (University of Minnesota), http://www.researchgate.net/publication/5105128

71. Zhou, X., "Eat, drink, and sing, and be modern and global," in *Patterns of Middle Class Consumption in India and China* ed C. Jaffrelot and P. Van Der Veer (Thousand Oaks: Sage Publications, 2008) 157.

72. Halverson, N., "How will China feed its growing middle class?" September 13, 2014, PBS, https://www.pbs.org/newshour/show/feed-chinas-

middle-class-wants-eat-like-americans

73. Zhou, X., "Eat, drink, and sing, and be modern and global."

74. Chang, L., "Gilded Age, Gilded Cage," May 2008, *National Geographic*, 78.

75. Moody, A. and L. Chang, "China's middle class emerges, to spend more."

76. Ibid.

77. Ibid.

78. Hong, L. "Marketing to China's Middle Class," January 6, 2014, China Business Review, https://www.chinabusinessreview.com/marketing-to-chinas-middle-class/

79. Ibid.

80. Stalk, G. and D. Michael, "What the West Doesn't Get About China," June 2011, Harvard Business Review, https://hbr.org/2011/06/what-the-west-doesnt-get-about-china

81. Censky, A. "China's middle class boom."

82. Gertz, G. and H. Kharas, "The New Global Middle Class: A Cross-Over from West to East," March 22, 2010, Brookings Institution, https://www.brookings.edu/research/the-new-global-middle-class-a-cross-over-from-west-to-east/

83. Stalk, G. and D. Michael, "What the West Doesn't Get About China."

84. Hays, J., "Middle class in China."

85. Carlson, B., "Who belongs to the Chinese middle class?"

86. Hays, J., "Middle class in China."

87. Cai, Y., "China's Moderate Middle Class: The Case of Homeowners' Resistance," October 2005, *Asian Survey* 45(5): 777-799.

88. Barton, D. et al, "Mapping China's middle class,

Generational change and the rising prosperity of inland cities will power consumption for years to come."

89. Hays, J., "Middle class in China."

90. Brown, M., "Will China's new middle class save it from disaster?"

91. China.org.cn, "Who are China's middle class?" January 23, 2010, http://www.china.org.cn/china/2010-01/23/content_19293900.htm

92. Ibid.

93. Brown, M., "Will China's new middle class save it from disaster?"

94. Ibid.

95. Barton, D. et al, "Mapping China's middle class, Generational change and the rising prosperity of inland cities will power consumption for years to come."

96. Ibid.

97. Schwarz, B., "Open Lecture: Marketing to China's Generation Y," MBS China Centre News Release.

98. Waldmeir, P., "Office girls lead charge to boost spending," January 18, 2010, *Financial Times*, http://www.ft.com/cms/s/0/161f9330-038c-11df-a601-00144feabdc0.html#axzz42Uyd0FAd

99. Ibid.

100. Cotriss, D., "Singles Day supercharges China's new middle class consumers."

101. Monaghan, A. and J. Kaiman, "Why global recovery could depend on China's taste for luxury," May 11, 2014, *The Guardian*, https://www.theguardian.com/business/2014/may/11/why-global-recovery-china-luxury-western-export-middle-class-consumer

102. Gertz, G. and H. Kharas, "The New Global Middle Class: A Cross-Over from West to East."

103. Collier, R., "China's middle class in love with big cars," August 18, 2007, SFgate.com, http://www.sfgate.com/news/article/China-s-new-middle-class-in-love-with-cars-big-2546582.php

104. Scutt, D., "China's Rising Middle Class Will Create Opportunities The World Has Never Seen Before," May 14, 2015, *Business Insider UK*, http://uk.businessinsider.com/chinas-rising-middle-class-will-create-opportunities-the-world-has-never-seen-before-2015-5

105. Barton, D. et al, "Mapping China's middle class, Generational change and the rising prosperity of inland cities will power consumption for years to come."

106. Gertz, G. and H. Kharas, "The New Global Middle Class: A Cross-Over from West to East."

107. Wang, H., *The Chinese Dream, The Rise of the World's Largest Middle Class and What it Means to You.*

108. Gertz, G. and H. Kharas, "The New Global Middle Class: A Cross-Over from West to East."

109. Pezzini, M., "An emerging middle class," 2012, OECD Observer, http://www.oecdobserver.org/news/fullstory.php/aid/3681/An_emerging_middle_class.html#sthash.WWwN1CBM.dpuf

110. Farrell, D. et al, "The value of China's emerging middle class," June 2006, *McKinsey Quarterly*, https://www.mckinsey.com/featured-insights/china/the-value-of-emerging-middle-class-in-china

111. Boulter, J., "China's Emerging Middle Class Challenges and Opportunities."

112. Xin Z., "Dissecting China's 'middle class'," October 27, 2004, *China Daily*, http://www.chinadaily.com.cn/english/doc/2004-

10/27/content_386060.htm

113. Fewsmith, J., "The Political Implications of China's Growing Middle Class," *China Leadership Monitor*, http://media.hoover.org/sites/default/files/documents/CLM21JF.pdf

114. Ibid.

115. Yang, J., "Stumbling on the Rocky Road: Understanding China's Middle Class," October 2010, *International Journal of China Studies*.

116. Ibid.

117. Goodwin, D., "Why The Middle Class Support the Communist Party," October 22, 2013, *Christian Science Monitor*, https://www.csmonitor.com/Commentary/Global-Viewpoint/2013/1022/Why-China-s-middle-class-supports-the-Communist-Party

118. Ibid.

119. He, A.,"Asia's middle class a trend for 2014," November 18, 2013, *China Daily USA*, http://usa.chinadaily.com.cn/epaper/2013-11/18/content_17112311.htm

120. Xin Z., "Dissecting China's 'middle class.'"

121. Moody, A. and L. Chang, "China's middle class emerges, to spend more."

122. Luhby, T., "China's growing middle class."

123. Barton, D. et al, "Mapping China's middle class, Generational change and the rising prosperity of inland cities will power consumption for years to come."

124. *The Economist*, "Middle-class flight: Yearning to breathe free," April 26, 2014, https://www.economist.com/china/2014/04/26/yearning-to-breathe-free

125. Rappler, "New concerns for China's rising middle

class."

126. *The Economist*, "Middle-class flight: Yearning to breathe free."

127. Babones, S., "China's Middle Class Is Pulling Up the Ladder Behind Itself," February 1, 2018, *Foreign Policy*, http://foreignpolicy.com/2018/02/01/chinas-middle-class-is-pulling-up-the-ladder-behind-itself/

128. Bulloch, D., "Should China Worry About the Finances of its Rising Middle-Class?" April 2, 2018, CKGSB Knowledge, http://knowledge.ckgsb.edu.cn/2018/04/02/chinese-economy/concern-finances-china-middle-class/

129. Ibid.

130. Wen, P., "Beijing, Shanghai, Shenzhen: the cities where house prices rose by 30 to 40 per cent," October 7, 2016, *The Sydney Morning Herald*, https://www.smh.com.au/world/beijing-shanghai-shenzhen-the-cities-where-house-prices-rose-by-30-to-40-per-cent-20161003-grtwe6.html

131. Zimmer, A., "Average Home Prices in Brooklyn and Queens Hit Record Highs," July 9, 2015, DNAInfo, https://www.dnainfo.com/new-york/20150709/park-slope/average-home-prices-brooklyn-queens-hit-new-record-highs/

132. Zillow Home Value Index, "Manhattan Home Prices & Values," March 31, 2018, https://www.zillow.com/manhattan-new-york-ny/home-values

133. Bulloch, D., "Should China Worry About the Finances of its Rising Middle-Class?"

134. Beijing vs New York, NY Property Prices Comparison Between Beijing and New York: https://www.numbeo.com/property-

investment/compare_cities.jsp?country1=China&city1=B
eijing&country2=United+States&city2=New+York%2C+
NY

135. China.org.cn, "Chinese Families Spend Heavily on Children's Education," November 23, 2001, http://www.china.org.cn/english/2001/Nov/22548.htm

136. *China Daily*, "Parents spend extra to give kids an edge," October 30, 2017, http://www.chinadaily.com.cn/china/2017-10/30/content_33880964.htm

137. Sisci, F., "China's middle class and its growing dilemma," February 9, 2017, *Asia Times*, http://www.atimes.com/article/chinas-middle-class-growing-dilemma/

138. Ibid.

139. Bulloch, D., "Should China Worry About the Finances of its Rising Middle-Class?"

140. Worstall, T., "China's Now The World Number One Economy And It Doesn't Matter A Darn, December 7, 2014, *Forbes*, http://www.forbes.com/sites/timworstall/2014/12/07/chinas-now-the-world-number-one-economy-and-it-doesnt-matter-a-darn/#502c30a35cb4

141. Milanovic, B. "Winners of Globalization: The Rich and The Chinese Middle Class. Losers: The American Middle Class," January 21, 2014, HuffPost, https://www.huffingtonpost.com/branko-milanovic/winners-of-globalization-_b_4603454.html

Chapter 7

1. DeFotis, D., "IMF Adds Chinese Yuan To SDR Currency Basket," November 30, 2015, Barrons,

https://www.barrons.com/articles/imf-adds-chinese-yuan-to-sdr-currency-basket-1448905233

2. Ibid.
3. Cohen, B., "Bretton Woods System," in *Routledge Encyclopedia of International Political Economy.*
4. Stephey, M.J., "Bretton Woods System," October 21, 2008, Time, http://content.time.com/time/business/article/0,8599,1852254,00.html
5. Ibid.
6. Cohen, B., "Bretton Woods System."
7. Ibid.
8. Ibid.
9. Ibid.
10. International Monetary Fund, "The End Of The Bretton Woods System (1972–81)," https://www.imf.org/external/about/histend.htm
11. Cohen, B., "Bretton Woods System."
12. Stephey, M.J., "Bretton Woods System,"
13. International Monetary Fund, "The End Of The Bretton Woods System (1972–81)."
14. Bretton Woods Project, "The IMF's special drawing rights (SDRs)," April 1, 2009, http://www.brettonwoodsproject.org/2009/04/art-564135/
15. Ibid.
16. McDowell, D., "The IMF Just Approved The Chinese Yuan As A Major World Currency. What Comes Next Is Political," November 30, 2015, *Washington Post*, https://www.washingtonpost.com/news/monkey-cage/wp/2015/11/30/the-imf-just-approved-the-chinese-yuan-as-a-major-world-currency-what-comes-next-is-political/?noredirect=on&utm_term=.e6a9b4ea2135

17. China Economic Review, "IMF to add yuan to SDR reserve currency basket," December 1, 2015, https://chinaeconomicreview.com/imf-add-yuan-sdr-reserve-currency-basket/

18. Hughes, K., "IMF Gives China's Currency Prized Reserve Asset Status," December 1, 2015, Yahoo Finance, https://finance.yahoo.com/news/imf-approves-chinas-yuan-currency-172916699.html

19. Yan, S., "IMF Admits China's Yuan To Elite Currency Club," December 1, 2015, CNN Money, http://money.cnn.com/2015/11/30/investing/imf-yuan-reserve-currency/index.html

20. China Economic Review, "IMF to add yuan to SDR reserve currency basket."

21. DeFotis, D., "IMF Adds Chinese Yuan To SDR Currency Basket."

22. Yan, S., "IMF Admits China's Yuan To Elite Currency Club."

23. McDowell, D., "The IMF Just Approved The Chinese Yuan As A Major World Currency. What Comes Next Is Political."

24. Hughes, K., "IMF Gives China's Currency Prized Reserve Asset Status."

25. Chandran, N., "SDR inclusion to help China lure trillion-dollar inflows," November 30, 2015, CNBC, https://www.cnbc.com/2015/11/30/china-could-see-2-3-trillion-inflows-after-yuan-enters-imfs-currency-basket.html

26. Hughes, K., "IMF Gives China's Currency Prized Reserve Asset Status."

27. Investopedia, "Hard Currency," http://www.investopedia.com/terms/h/hardcurrency.asp#ixzz4aW7waQA6

28. Ibid.

29. Ibid.

30. Guilford, G., "The Chinese yuan won't become a global reserve currency any time soon," November 30, 2015, Quartz, https://qz.com/561635/the-chinese-yuan-wont-become-a-global-reserve-currency-any-time-soon/

31. Central Banking, "Renminbi as a reserve currency," August 11, 2014, http://www.centralbanking.com/central-banking-journal/advertisement/2357296/renminbi-as-a-reserve-currency

32. Kindergan, A., "Here's why central banks won't be loading up on China's currency right away," December 6, 2015, *Business Insider*, http://www.businessinsider.com/why-central-banks-wont-be-buying-yuan-yet-2015-12?pundits_only=0&get_all_comments=1&no_reply_filter=1

33. Mukeredzi, T., "Chinese yuan penetrates African markets," August 2014, Africa Renewal, http://www.un.org/africarenewal/magazine/august-2014/chinese-yuan-penetrates-african-markets

34. Hanke, S. and A. Kwok, "On the Measurement of Zimbabwe's Hyperinflation," Cato Journal, Vol. 29, No. 2 (Spring/Summer 2009), https://object.cato.org/sites/cato.org/files/serials/files/cato-journal/2009/5/cj29n2-8.pdf

35. Ibid.

36. Central Banking, "Renminbi as a reserve currency."

37. Chen, J., "It's time to free up the yuan," March 23, 2015, *China Daily*, http://www.chinadaily.com.cn/business/2015-03/23/content_19877793.htm

38. Yan, S., "IMF Admits China's Yuan To Elite Currency Club."

39. Chen, J., "It's time to free up the yuan."

40. Kuepper, J., "Chinese Currency – From Yuan To Renminbi," November 10, 2016, The Balance, https://www.thebalance.com/chinese-currency-from-yuan-to-renminbi-1978913

41. Hughes, K., "IMF Gives China's Currency Prized Reserve Asset Status."

42. Sweeney, P. and J. Lu, "China doubles yuan trading band, seen as sign of confidence," March 15, 2014, Reuters, https://www.reuters.com/article/us-china-yuanband/china-doubles-yuan-trading-band-seen-as-sign-of-confidence-idUSBREA2E07V20140315

43. Yan, S., "IMF Admits China's Yuan To Elite Currency Club."

44. Li, F., "China To Allow Direct Conversion Between Yuan And Swiss Franc," November 9, 2015, Bloomberg, https://www.bloomberg.com/news/articles/2015-11-09/china-to-allow-direct-conversion-between-yuan-and-swiss-franc

45. Allen, K., "Q&A: Chinese Yuan Set To Join IMF Currency Basket," November 30, 2015, *The Guardian*, https://www.theguardian.com/business/2015/nov/30/qa-chinese-yuan-set-to-join-imf-currency-basket

46. Yan, S., "IMF Admits China's Yuan To Elite Currency Club."

47. Wei, L., "China Moves To Devalue Yuan," August 11, 2015, *Wall Street Journal*, https://www.wsj.com/articles/china-moves-to-devalue-the-yuan-1439258401

48. Gough, N., and K. Bradsher, "China Devalues Its Currency As Worries Rise About Economic Slowdown,"

August 10, 2015, *New York Times,*
https://www.nytimes.com/2015/08/11/business/internati
onal/china-lowers-value-of-its-currency-as-economic-
slowdown-raises-concerns.html

49. Ibid.

50. Sweeney, P. and J. Lu, "China lets yuan fall further, fuels fears of 'currency war'," August 12, 2015, Reuters, https://www.reuters.com/article/us-china-markets-yuan/china-lets-yuan-fall-further-fuels-fears-of-currency-war-idUSKCN0QG04U20150812

51. Cendrowski, S., "Here's Why China Devalued Its Currency," August 11, 2015, *Fortune,* http://fortune.com/2015/08/11/why-china-devalued-yuan/

52. Bloomberg Intelligence, "China's RMB Devaluation: Economic And Industry Implications," September 2, 2015, Bloomberg Professional Services, https://www.bloomberg.com/professional/blog/chinas-rmb-devaluation-economic-and-industry-implications/

53. Evans, G., "Exchange Rates," March 14, 2014, http://pages.hmc.edu/evans/ExchangeRates.pdf

54. Ding, Y., "How Do Currency Pegs Work? How Does The Chinese Government Peg The Renminbi To The Dollar?" April 8, 2010, Quora, https://www.quora.com/How-do-currency-pegs-work-How-does-the-Chinese-Government-peg-the-Renminbi-to-the-dollar

55. Ibid.

56. Yeung, K. "PBoC adjusts formula for yuan fixing, sparking rise in currency," May 26, 2017, *South China Morning Post,* http://www.scmp.com/business/article/2095829/pboc-plans-adjust-yuan-fixing-methodology-fed-interest-rate-

rise-looms

57. Wei, L., "China Moves To Devalue Yuan."
58. Cendrowski, S., "Here's Why China Devalued Its Currency."
59. Yeung, K. "PBoC adjusts formula for yuan fixing, sparking rise in currency."
60. Wei, L., "China Moves To Devalue Yuan."
61. Inman, P. et al, "China Stuns Financial Markets By Devaluing Yuan For Second Day Running," August 12, 2015, *The Guardian*, https://www.theguardian.com/business/2015/aug/12/china-yuan-slips-again-after-devaluation
62. Gough, N., and K. Bradsher, "China Devalues Its Currency As Worries Rise About Economic Slowdown."
63. Cendrowski, S., "Here's Why China Devalued Its Currency."
64. Gough, N., and K. Bradsher, "China Devalues Its Currency As Worries Rise About Economic Slowdown."
65. Sweeney, P. and J. Lu, "China lets yuan fall further, fuels fears of 'currency war'."
66. Yeung, K. "PBoC adjusts formula for yuan fixing, sparking rise in currency."
67. Wildau, G., "Renminbi Devaluation Tests China's Commitment To Free Markets," August 13, 2015, *Financial Times*, https://www.ft.com/content/65d07e26-40d0-11e5-9abe-5b335da3a90e
68. Ibid.
69. Ibid.
70. Herman, S., "Asian Currencies, Stocks Drop On Yuan Devaluation," August 12, 2015, VOA, https://www.voanews.com/a/china-further-devalues-yuan-currency/2914660.html
71. Smith, P., "A Drop In The Value Of The Overpriced

Yuan Isn't Going To Spark A Currency War," 2015, *Business Insider*.

72. Herman, S., "Asian Currencies, Stocks Drop On Yuan Devaluation."

73. Yeung, K. "PBoC adjusts formula for yuan fixing, sparking rise in currency."

74. Mullaney, T., "5 reasons why China's woes are shaking the global markets," August 25, 2015, CNBC, https://www.cnbc.com/2015/08/25/5-reasons-why-chinas-woes-are-shaking-the-global-markets.html

75. Wei, L., "China Moves To Devalue Yuan."

76. Inman, P. et al, "China Stuns Financial Markets By Devaluing Yuan For Second Day Running."

77. Smith, P., "A Drop In The Value Of The Overpriced Yuan Isn't Going To Spark A Currency War."

78. Mullaney, T., "5 reasons why China's woes are shaking the global markets."

79. Euromoney, "China: Special Focus," January 15, 2018, https://www.euromoney.com/article/b12kl9r7s2mnhf/china-special-focus

80. Inman, P. et al, "China Stuns Financial Markets By Devaluing Yuan For Second Day Running."

81. Yan, S., "China's Stock Market Continues To Free Fall," July 28, 2015, CNN Money, http://money.cnn.com/2015/07/27/investing/china-stock-market/index.html

82. Hu, Z., "Q&A: China's Yuan And A Potential Global Currency War," August 13, 2015, Al Jazeera, https://www.aljazeera.com/news/2015/08/qa-china-yuan-potential-global-currency-war-150812140139263.html

83. Wei, L., "China Moves To Devalue Yuan."

84. Sender, H., "Capital flight now the big concern for

slowing China," September 6, 2015, CNBC, https://www.cnbc.com/2015/09/06/as-chinas-economy-slows-declining-foreign-reserves-are-a-concern.html

85. Wildau, G., "Renminbi Devaluation Tests China's Commitment To Free Markets."
86. Ibid.
87. Wei, L., "China Moves To Devalue Yuan."
88. Sweeney, P. and J. Lu, "China lets yuan fall further, fuels fears of 'currency war'."
89. Wei, L., "China Moves To Devalue Yuan."
90. Smith, P., "A Drop In The Value Of The Overpriced Yuan Isn't Going To Spark A Currency War."
91. Ibid.
92. Ibid.
93. Ibid.
94. Sweeney, P. and J. Lu, "China lets yuan fall further, fuels fears of 'currency war'."
95. Gough, N., and K. Bradsher, "China Devalues Its Currency As Worries Rise About Economic Slowdown."
96. Sweeney, P. and J. Lu, "China lets yuan fall further, fuels fears of 'currency war'."
97. Gough, N., and K. Bradsher, "China Devalues Its Currency As Worries Rise About Economic Slowdown."
98. Makinen, J. and S. Masunaga, "Why China's Devaluation Of The Yuan Matters So Much," August 12, 2015, *Los Angeles Times*, http://www.latimes.com/business/la-fi-china-devalues-yuan-20150811-htmlstory.html
99. Mullaney, T., "5 reasons why China's woes are shaking the global markets."
100. Inman, P. et al, "China Stuns Financial Markets By Devaluing Yuan For Second Day Running."
101. Mullaney, T., "5 reasons why China's woes are shaking

the global markets."

102. Ibid.
103. Bloomberg Intelligence, "China's RMB Devaluation: Economic And Industry Implications."
104. Ibid.
105. Wei, S. et al, "The China Money Puzzle: Will Devaluation Of The Yuan Help Or Hurt The Hong Kong Dollar?" *China Economic Review* 11.2 (2000): 171-188, https://schar.gmu.edu/sites/default/files/faculty-staff/cv/The_China_money_puzzle_will_devaluation_of _the_yuan_help_or_hurt_the_Hong_Kong_dollar_Zhi_ Wang.pdf
106. Li, S., "Retail Sector In Hong Kong To Suffer Most From Yuan Devaluation," August 14, 2015, *South China Morning Post*, http://www.scmp.com/business/companies/article/18493 68/hong-kong-retail-sector-suffer-most-yuan-devaluation
107. Wei G. and J. Steinberg, "Cash From China Is Boon For Hong Kong," September 1, 2015, Wall Street Journal, https://www.wsj.com/articles/lower-yuan-keeps-hong-kong-money-changers-busy-1441113850
108. Makinen, J. and S. Masunaga, "Why China's Devaluation Of The Yuan Matters So Much."
109. Ibid.
110. Hu, Z., "Q&A: China's Yuan And A Potential Global Currency War."
111. Inman, P. et al, "China Stuns Financial Markets By Devaluing Yuan For Second Day Running."
112. Spence, P. and S. Chan, "Why China Has Devalued The Renminbi And How It Will Affect The UK," August 12, 2015, *Daily Telegraph*, https://www.telegraph.co.uk/finance/china-

business/11795811/Chinas-renminbi-gambit-why-it-has-devalued-the-yuan.html

113. Ibid.

114. Kicklighter, J., "What Does Yuan's Devaluation Mean For Chinese And Global Markets?" August 12, 2015, DailyFX, https://www.dailyfx.com/forex/fundamental/article/special_report/2015/08/11/What-Does-Yuans-Devaluation-Mean-for-Chinese-and-Global-Markets.html

115. Powell, R., "Collateral Damage For Aussie As China Lets Yuan Slide," August 12, 2015, *Sydney Morning Herald*, https://www.smh.com.au/business/markets/australian-dollar-plummets-as-china-devalues-yuan-again-20150812-gix826.html

116. Ibid.

117. Ibid.

118. Ibid.

119. Mullaney, T., "5 reasons why China's woes are shaking the global markets."

120. Herman, S., "Asian Currencies, Stocks Drop On Yuan Devaluation."

121. Joiner, A., "Examining The Vietnamese Dong," August 2006, Economics@ANZ, http://www.anz.com/documents/economics/Vietnam_currency_update_Aug_2006.pdf

122. Herman, S., "Asian Currencies, Stocks Drop On Yuan Devaluation."

123. Hu, Z., "Q&A: China's Yuan And A Potential Global Currency War."

124. Herman, S., "Asian Currencies, Stocks Drop On Yuan Devaluation."

125. Makinen, J. and S. Masunaga, "Why China's

Devaluation Of The Yuan Matters So Much."

126. Bloomberg, "India rupee weakens to two-year low as stocks drop on yuan slump," August 12, 2015, *The Business Times*, https://www.businesstimes.com.sg/government-economy/india-rupee-weakens-to-two-year-low-as-stocks-drop-on-yuan-slump

127. Bhattacharya, S., "India And The Devalued Yuan: The Good, The Bad And The Ugly," August 17, 2015, Quartz, https://qz.com/480615/india-and-the-devalued-yuan-the-good-the-bad-and-the-ugly/

128. Ashworth, D., "How Did The Yuan's Devaluation Impact Indian Equities?" August 25, 2015, Market Realist, https://finance.yahoo.com/news/did-yuan-devaluation-impact-indian-184502518.html

129. Bhattacharya, S., "India And The Devalued Yuan: The Good, The Bad And The Ugly."

130. Ibid.

131. Ibid.

132. BBC, "What The Yuan Devaluation Means Around The World," August 12, 2015, https://www.bbc.com/news/world-asia-33881478

133. Ibid.

134. Ibid.

135. Ibid.

136. Ibid.

137. Ibid.

138. Ibid.

139. Ibid.

140. RT, "Death of US dollar? China launches petro-yuan to challenge greenback's dominance," March 26, 2018, https://www.rt.com/business/422314-petro-yuan-futures-dollar-death/

141. ZeroHedge, "China Prepares Death Blow To The Dollar," March 24, 2018, Oilprice.com, https://oilprice.com/Geopolitics/International/China-Prepares-Death-Blow-To-The-Dollar.html
142. Cunningham, N., "Washington My Be Speeding Up The Death Of The Dollar With Increased Sanctions On Iran," January 9, 2018, Ottawa Bullion, http://www.ottawabullion.com/washington-my-be-speeding-up-the-death-of-the-dollar-with-increased-sanctions-on-iran/
143. Investopedia, "Petrodollars," https://www.investopedia.com/terms/p/petrodollars.asp
144. Reuters, "UN to let Iraq sell oil for euros, not dollars," October 30, 2000, CNN, http://www.cnn.com/2000/WORLD/meast/10/30/iraq.un.euro.reut/
145. Ibid.
146. Escobar, P., "China plans to break petrodollar stranglehold," December 21, 2017, Asia Times, http://www.atimes.com/article/china-plans-break-petrodollar-stranglehold/
147. BBC, "China buying oil from Iran with yuan," May 8, 2012, http://www.bbc.com/news/business-17988142
148. Verma, N., "Iran wants euro payment for new and outstanding oil sales," February 6, 2016, Reuters, https://www.reuters.com/article/us-oil-iran-exclusive/exclusive-iran-wants-euro-payment-for-new-and-outstanding-oil-sales-source-idUSKCN0VE21S
149. Asia Times, "Growing bloc aims to dethrone US dollar," April 25, 2018, http://www.atimes.com/article/growing-bloc-aims-to-dethrone-us-dollar/?utm_source=The+Daily+Report&utm_campaign=c9afe59746-

EMAIL_CAMPAIGN_2018_04_25&utm_medium=email
&utm_term=0_1f8bca137f-c9afe59746-31520157

150. Steinbock, D., "The Rise of Petro Yuan," January 18, 2018, *Georgetown Journal of International Affairs*, https://www.georgetownjournalofinternationalaffairs.or g/online-edition/2018/1/18/the-rise-of-petroyuan

151. Reuters, "China establishes yuan-ruble payment system," October 12, 2017, https://www.reuters.com/article/us-china-yuan-rouble/china-establishes-yuan-ruble-payment-system-idUSKBN1CH0ML

152. Steinbock, D., "The Rise of Petro Yuan."

153. Mohammed, A. and J. Landay, "US suspends at least US$900 million in security aid to Pakistan," January 5, 2018, Reuters, https://www.reuters.com/article/us-usa-pakistan-aid/u-s-suspends-at-least-900-million-in-security-aid-to-pakistan-idUSKBN1ET2DX

154. The Economic Times, "Pakistan central bank allows yuan-based trade with China," January 3, 2018, https://economictimes.indiatimes.com/news/internation al/business/pakistan-central-bank-allows-yuan-based-trade-with-china/articleshow/62350266.cms

155. Investopedia, "Petrodollars."

156. Escobar, P., "China plans to break petrodollar stranglehold."

157. Ibid.

158. Asia Times, "Growing bloc aims to dethrone US dollar."

159. Jegarajah, S., "China has grand ambitions to dethrone the dollar," October 24, 2017, CNBC, https://www.cnbc.com/2017/10/24/petro-yuan-china-wants-to-dethrone-dollar-rmb-denominated-oil-contracts.html

160. Ibid.

161. Steinbock, D., "The Rise of Petro Yuan."
162. Bulloch, D., "Why The Petro Dollar Is A Myth, And The Petro-Yuan Mere Fantasy," April 26, 2018, *Forbes*, https://www.forbes.com/sites/douglasbulloch/2018/04/2 6/the-petro-dollar-is-a-myth-the-petro-yuan-mere-fantasy/#1d83ef0b6a14
163. Ibid.

Chapter 8

1. Elliott, D. et al, "Shadow banking in China: A primer," April 1, 2015, Brookings Institution, https://www.brookings.edu/research/shadow-banking-in-china-a-primer/
2. Bloomberg, "Cracks Are Showing in China's Shadow Banking Industry," January 24, 2018, https://www.bloomberg.com/news/articles/2018-01-23/china-s-15-trillion-shadow-banking-edifice-showing-more-cracks
3. Bulloch, D., "BIS Report On China's Shadow Banking Sector Suggests A Problem That's Not Going Away," February 21, 2018, *Forbes*, https://www.forbes.com/sites/douglasbulloch/2018/02/2 1/chinas-shadow-banking-comes-into-the-light/#67a7b761c07d
4. Elliott, D. et al, "Shadow banking in China: A primer."
5. Ehlers, T. et al, " BIS Working Papers No 701 Mapping shadow banking in China: structure and dynamics," February 2018, Bank of International Settlement, https://www.bis.org/publ/work701.pdf
6. Bloomberg, "Cracks Are Showing in China's Shadow Banking Industry."
7. Ehlers, T. et al, " BIS Working Papers No 701 Mapping

shadow banking in China: structure and dynamics."

8. Elliott, D. et al, "Shadow banking in China: A primer."

9. Ehlers, T. et al, " BIS Working Papers No 701 Mapping shadow banking in China: structure and dynamics."

10. Ibid.

11. Ibid.

12. Tham, E., et al, "China's leaders fret over debts lurking in shadow banking system," December 28, 2017, Reuters, https://www.reuters.com/investigates/special-report/china-risk-shadowbanking/

13. Ibid.

14. Bulloch, D., "BIS Report On China's Shadow Banking Sector Suggests A Problem That's Not Going Away."

15. He, L., "China's shadow banking system expands to 82% of GDP: Moody's," December 13, 2016, *South China Morning Post*, http://www.scmp.com/business/companies/article/2054189/chinas-shadow-banking-system-expands-82pc-gdp-moodys

16. Ehlers, T. et al, " BIS Working Papers No 701 Mapping shadow banking in China: structure and dynamics."

17. Ibid.

18. Ibid.

19. Ibid.

20. Ibid.

21. Ibid.

22. Ibid.

23. Tan, H., "Chinese shadow banking has slowed – but that's not as good as it seems," November 19, 2017, CNBC, https://www.cnbc.com/2017/11/19/china-shadow-banking-has-slowed-chinese-debt-may-just-go-elsewhere.html

24. He, L., "China's shadow banking system expands to

82% of GDP: Moody's."

25. Tham, E., et al, "China's leaders fret over debts lurking in shadow banking system."

26. Bloomberg, "Cracks Are Showing in China's Shadow Banking Industry."

27. Ibid.

28. Ibid.

29. Ibid.

30. Tham, E., et al, "China's leaders fret over debts lurking in shadow banking system."

31. Tan, H., "Chinese shadow banking has slowed – but that's not as good as it seems."

32. Ibid.

33. Bulloch, D., "BIS Report On China's Shadow Banking Sector Suggests A Problem That's Not Going Away."

Chapter 9

1. Bloomberg, "China's Alarming Debt Pile Could Finally Stabilize This Year," April 3, 2018, https://www.bloomberg.com/news/articles/2018-04-03/china-s-alarming-debt-pile-seen-finally-stabilizing-this-year

2. Bloomberg, "Moody's cuts China's credit rating over worsening debt outlook," May 24, 2017, *South China Morning Post*, http://www.scmp.com/business/companies/article/2095451/moodys-cuts-chinas-credit-rating-over-worsening-debt-outlook

3. Borzykowski, B., "Trade war with US could be the tipping point for China's US$14 trillion debt-ridden economy," April 24, 2018, CNBC https://www.cnbc.com/2018/04/24/trade-war-with-us-

may-be-tipping-point-for-chinas-debt-ridden-economy.html

4. Ibid.

5. Bloomberg, "A US$7 Trillion Debt Pile Looms Large Over Chinese Households," April 25, 2018, https://www.bloomberg.com/news/articles/2018-04-24/the-7-trillion-debt-pile-looming-large-over-chinese-households

6. Polk, A., "Chinese Need to Learn to Save Again," February 15, 2018, Bloomberg, https://www.bloomberg.com/view/articles/2018-02-15/chinese-consumers-are-building-up-too-much-household-debt

7. Bloomberg, "A US$7 Trillion Debt Pile Looms Large Over Chinese Households."

8. Ibid.

9. Ibid.

10. Klein, M., "China's household debt problem," March 7, 2018, *Financial Times*, https://ftalphaville.ft.com/2018/03/06/2199125/chinas-household-debt-problem/

11. Tang, F., "How China's billion savers embarked on a household debt binge," August 7, 2017, *South China Morning Post*, http://www.scmp.com/news/china/economy/article/2104192/how-chinas-billion-savers-embarked-household-debt-binge

12. Klein, M., "China's household debt problem."

13. Polk, A., "Chinese Need to Learn to Save Again."

14. Yang, W., "Will China's high debt levels spark a financial crisis?" March 14, 2018, Deutsche Welle, http://www.dw.com/en/will-chinas-high-debt-levels-spark-a-financial-crisis/a-42976238

15. China Banking News, "China Posts Surge in Non-performing Real Estate Loans," April 13, 2018, http://www.chinabankingnews.com/2018/04/13/china-posts-surge-non-performing-real-estate-loans/

16. Reuters, "China commercial banks' NPL ratio 1.74% at end Dec," February 9, 2018, https://www.reuters.com/article/china-banks/china-commercial-banks-npl-ratio-174-pct-at-end-dec-regulator-idUSB9N1OT019

17. Bloomberg, "Fresh Doubts Raised on China's Bad-Loan Data," January 22, 2018, https://www.bloomberg.com/news/articles/2018-01-22/fresh-doubts-raised-on-china-s-bad-loan-data-as-fraud-uncovered

18. Xiang, N., "Beijing Report Exposes Serious Fraud In How Non-Performing Loans Are Handled In China," January 19, 2018, China Money Network, https://www.chinamoneynetwork.com/2018/01/19/beijing-report-reveals-serious-fraud-non-performing-loans-handled-china

19. Bloomberg, "China's Alarming Debt Pile Could Finally Stabilize This Year."

20. Tan, H. and M. Soong, "Don't count on Beijing to resolve fallout from any debt blowup, says expert," March 11, 2018, CNBC, https://www.cnbc.com/2018/03/11/china-debt-levels-dont-count-on-beijing-for-a-bailout.html

21. Bloomberg, "China's Xi Turns Deleveraging Sights on Local Governments, SOEs," April 3, 2018, https://www.bloomberg.com/news/articles/2018-04-03/china-s-xi-turns-deleveraging-sights-on-local-governments-soes

22. Borzykowski, B., "Trade war with US could be the

tipping point for China's US$14 trillion debt-ridden economy."

Chapter 10

1.   Esteban M. and M. Otero-Iglesias, "What are the prospects for the new Chinese-led Silk Road and Asian Infrastructure Investment Bank?" April 17, 2015, ARI 23/2015, http://www.realinstitutoelcano.org/wps/portal/rielcano_en/contenido?WCM_GLOBAL_CONTEXT=/elcano/elcano_in/zonas_in/ari23-2015-esteban-oteroiglesias-what-are-prospects-for-new-chinese-led-silk-road-and-asian-infrastructure-investment-bank

2.   Johnson, C., "President Xi Jinping's Belt and Road initiative," March 28, 2016, Center for Strategic and International Studies, https://www.csis.org/analysis/president-xi-jinping%E2%80%99s-belt-and-road-initiative

3.   Puls, T., "China's New Silk Road: The European perspective," June 4, 2015, Institut der Deutschen Wirtschaft, https://www.ies.be/files/New%20Silk%20Road%20Thomas%20Puls.pdf

4.   Szczudlik-Tatar, J., "China's New Silk Road Diplomacy," December 2013, Polish Institute of International Affairs, https://www.files.ethz.ch/isn/174833/PISM%20Policy%20Paper%20no%2034%20(82).pdf

5.   Johnson, C., "President Xi Jinping's Belt and Road initiative."

6.   Szczudlik-Tatar, J., "China's New Silk Road Diplomacy."

7. Johnson, C., "President Xi Jinping's Belt and Road initiative."

8. Ibid.

9. Reuters, "European development bank approves China's application to become shareholder," December 15, 2015, *South China Morning Post*, https://www.scmp.com/news/china/diplomacy-defence/article/1891289/european-development-bank-approves-chinas-application

10. Rolland, N., "China's New Silk Road," February 12, 2015, National Bureau for Asian Research, http://www.nbr.org/research/activity.aspx?id=531

11. Brugier, C., "China's way: the new Silk Road," May 2014, European Union Institute for Security Studies, https://www.iss.europa.eu/sites/default/files/EUISSFiles/Brief_14_New_Silk_Road.pdf

12. Rolland, N., "China's New Silk Road."

13. Esteban M. and M. Otero-Iglesias, "What are the prospects for the new Chinese-led Silk Road and Asian Infrastructure Investment Bank?"

14. Ibid.

15. Lin, C., "The New Silk Road: China's Energy Strategy in the Greater Middle East," April 2011, Washington Institute for Near East Policy, https://www.washingtoninstitute.org/policy-analysis/view/the-new-silk-road-chinas-energy-strategy-in-the-greater-middle-east

16. Esteban M. and M. Otero-Iglesias, "What are the prospects for the new Chinese-led Silk Road and Asian Infrastructure Investment Bank?"

17. Brugier, C., "China's way: the new Silk Road."

18. Szczudlik-Tatar, J., "China's New Silk Road Diplomacy."

19. International Energy Agency, "Oil and Gas Security, People's Republic of China," 2012, https://www.iea.org/publications/freepublications/publi cation/China_2012.pdf
20. Rolland, N., "China's New Silk Road."
21. Ibid.
22. Lin, C., "The New Silk Road: China's Energy Strategy in the Greater Middle East."
23. Ibid.
24. Keck, Z., "China Secretly Sold Saudi Arabia DF-21 Missiles With CIA Approval," January 31, 2014, The Diplomat, https://thediplomat.com/2014/01/china-secretly-sold-saudi-arabia-df-21-missiles-with-cia-approval/
25. Lin, C., "The New Silk Road: China's Energy Strategy in the Greater Middle East."
26. Ibid.
27. Ibid.
28. Ibid.
29. Johnson, C., "President Xi Jinping's Belt and Road initiative."
30. Esteban M. and M. Otero-Iglesias, "What are the prospects for the new Chinese-led Silk Road and Asian Infrastructure Investment Bank?"
31. Zhao, M., "China's New Silk Road Initiatives," 2015, IAI Working Papers 15, http://www.iai.it/sites/default/files/iaiwp1537.pdf
32. Johnson, C., "President Xi Jinping's Belt and Road initiative."
33. Esteban M. and M. Otero-Iglesias, "What are the prospects for the new Chinese-led Silk Road and Asian Infrastructure Investment Bank?"
34. Johnson, C., "President Xi Jinping's Belt and Road

initiative."

35. Esteban M. and M. Otero-Iglesias, "What are the prospects for the new Chinese-led Silk Road and Asian Infrastructure Investment Bank?"

36. Zimmerman, T., "The New Silk Roads: China, the US, and the Future of Central Asia," October 2015, New York University, Center on International Cooperation, https://cic.nyu.edu/sites/default/files/zimmerman_new_silk_road_final_2.pdf

37. Esteban M. and M. Otero-Iglesias, "What are the prospects for the new Chinese-led Silk Road and Asian Infrastructure Investment Bank?"

38. Ibid.

39. Ibid.

40. Asian Infrastructure Investment Bank, "Introduction: Who We Are," https://www.aiib.org/en/about-aiib/index.html

41. *The Economist*, "Why China is creating a new 'World Bank' for Asia," November 11, 2014, http://www.economist.com/blogs/economist-explains/2014/11/economist-explains-6

42. Ibid.

43. Wong, S., "China launches new AIIB development bank as power balance shifts," January 16, 2016, Reuters, http://www.reuters.com/article/us-asia-aiib-investment-idUSKCN0UU03Y

44. Panda, A. "The Asian Infrastructure Investment Bank Is Open for Business: What Now?" January 19, 2016, The Diplomat, https://thediplomat.com/2016/01/the-asian-infrastructure-investment-bank-is-open-for-business-what-now/

45. Perlezdec, J., "China Creates a World Bank of Its Own," December 4, 2015, *New York Times*,

http://www.nytimes.com/2015/12/05/business/internatio
nal/china-creates-an-asian-bank-as-the-us-stands-
aloof.html?_r=0

46. Panda, A. "The Asian Infrastructure Investment Bank Is
    Open for Business: What Now?"

47. Perlezdec, J., "China Creates a World Bank of Its Own."

48. Ibid.

49. UNCTAD, "ASEAN Investment Report 2016, Foreign
    Direct Investment and MSME Linkages,"
    http://asean.org/storage/2016/09/ASEAN-Investment-
    Report-2016.pdf

50. Abbate, F. and S. Rosina, "ASEAN-China trade growth:
    facts, factors and prospects," June 14, 2016, New
    Mandala, http://www.newmandala.org/asean-china-
    trade-growth-facts-factors-and-prospects/

51. UNCTAD, "ASEAN Investment Report 2016, Foreign
    Direct Investment and MSME Linkages."

52. Salidjanova, N. et al, "China's Economic Ties with
    ASEAN: A Country-by-Country Analysis," March 17,
    2015, US-China Economic and Security Review
    Commission,
    https://www.uscc.gov/sites/default/files/Research/China
    %27s%20Economic%20Ties%20with%20ASEAN.pdf

53. Ibid.

54. Abbate, F. and S. Rosina, "ASEAN-China trade growth:
    facts, factors and prospects."

55. Ibid.

56. Ibid.

57. UNCTAD, "ASEAN Investment Report 2016, Foreign
    Direct Investment and MSME Linkages."

58. Abbate, F. and S. Rosina, "ASEAN-China trade growth:
    facts, factors and prospects."

59. Salidjanova, N. et al, "China's Economic Ties with

ASEAN: A Country-by-Country Analysis."

60. Ibid.
61. Ibid.
62. Ibid.
63. UNCTAD, "ASEAN Investment Report 2016, Foreign Direct Investment and MSME Linkages."
64. Salidjanova, N. et al, "China's Economic Ties with ASEAN: A Country-by-Country Analysis."
65. Asia Regional Integration Center, "Free Trade Agreements," https://aric.adb.org/fta-country
66. Focus-Economics, "Singapore Economic Outlook," June 19, 2018, http://www.focus-economics.com/countries/singapore
67. Heritage Foundation, "2018 Index of Economic Freedom, Singapore," http://www.heritage.org/index/country/singapore
68. Aggarwal, N., "S'pore is China's largest investor," November 6, 2015, Business Times, http://www.businesstimes.com.sg/hub/business-china-special/spore-is-chinas-largest-investor
69. Bloomberg, "Temasek: The Model for China's Sovereign Wealth Fund?" July 31, 2008, https://www.bloomberg.com/news/articles/2008-07-30/temasek-the-model-for-chinas-sovereign-wealth-fund-businessweek-business-news-stock-market-and-financial-advice
70. Williams, A., "Singapore and China central banks renew bilateral currency swap arrangement," March 15, 2016, *Straits Times*, http://www.straitstimes.com/business/banking/singapore-and-china-central-banks-renew-bilateral-currency-swap-arrangement
71. Sino-Singapore Guangzhou Knowledge City,

"Overview," http://www.ssgkc.com/P02_01.asp

72. Chang, R., "Success of Guangzhou Knowledge City raises bar in Sino-Singapore projects: PM Lee," September 12, 2014, *Straits Times*, http://www.straitstimes.com/asia/east-asia/success-of-guangzhou-knowledge-city-raises-bar-in-sino-singapore-projects-pm-lee

73. Sino-Singapore Guangzhou Knowledge City, "Company Profile," http://www.ssgkc.com/P01_01.asp

74. World Bank, "The World Bank In Thailand," March 2018, http://www.worldbank.org/en/country/thailand/overview

75. The Global Economy, "Thailand: Trade balance, percent of GDP," http://www.theglobaleconomy.com/Thailand/Trade_balance/

76. Workman, D., "Thailand's Top Trading Partners," February 1, 2018, WTEx, http://www.worldstopexports.com/thailands-top-import-partners/

77. Bilaterals.org,"China-Thailand," May 2012, http://www.bilaterals.org/?-China-Thailand-

78. China Invests Overseas, "Chinese Investment in Thailand Gains Speed," September 2, 2016, http://www.china-invests.net/20160902/41620.aspx

79. The American Interest, "Thailand's Pivot to China Continues," February 18, 2016 http://www.the-american-interest.com/2016/02/17/thailands-pivot-to-china-continues/

80. Reuters, "Thailand approves US$1.47 billion budget to join China-led AIIB," January 26, 2016, http://www.reuters.com/article/thailand-aiib-

idUSL3N15A3O3

81. Villadiego, L., "Thailand chases Chinese money, but at what cost?" July 23, 2017, *South China Morning Post*, https://www.scmp.com/week-asia/society/article/2102934/thailand-chases-chinese-money-what-cost

82. Reuters, "Thailand pins growth hopes on big infrastructure projects, but outlays tiny so far," September 8, 2016, *South China Morning Post*, http://www.scmp.com/news/asia/southeast-asia/article/2017530/thailand-pins-growth-hopes-big-infrastructure-projects

83. Potkin, F., "Thailand bets on China-led AIIB to finance massive infrastructure needs," East By Southeast, February 16, 2016, http://www.eastbysoutheast.com/thailand-bets-on-china-led-aiib-to-finance-massive-infrastructure-needs/

84. Sriring O. and S. Staporncharnchai, "From car parts to condos, faltering Thailand lures Chinese money," Reuters, May 17, 2016, http://www.reuters.com/article/us-thailand-china-investment-idUSKCN0Y72D5

85. Xinhua, "More Chinese investment welcomed in Thailand's high-tech sector: Minister," January 22, 2016, *China Daily*, http://www.chinadaily.com.cn/business/2016-01/22/content_23206795.htm

86. Sriring O. and S. Staporncharnchai, "From car parts to condos, faltering Thailand lures Chinese money."

87. Shi J., "Chinese investors upbeat on prospects in Thailand despite uncertainty after king's death," October 18, 2016, *South China Morning Post*, http://www.scmp.com/news/china/economy/article/2028

986/chinese-remain-upbeat-investment-prospects-thailand-despite

88. Trading Economics, "Vietnam GDP per capita, 1984–2018," http://www.tradingeconomics.com/vietnam/gdp-per-capita

89. Heritage Foundation, "2018 Index of Economic Freedom, Vietnam," http://www.heritage.org/index/country/Vietnam

90. World Bank, "Vietnam/GDP per capita (current US$)," https://data.worldbank.org/indicator/NY.GDP.PCAP.CD?locations=VN

91. Heritage Foundation, "2018 Index of Economic Freedom, Vietnam."

92. Vietnam Breaking News, "Eximbank has highest NPL ratio," November 4, 2016, https://www.vietnambreakingnews.com/2016/11/eximbank-has-highest-npl-ratio/

93. Global Edge, "Vietnam: Trade Statistics," 2016, https://globaledge.msu.edu/countries/vietnam/tradestats

94. Xinhua, "China top trade partner of Vietnam: Vietnamese official," March 8, 2016, http://europe.chinadaily.com.cn/business/2016-03/08/content_23781703.htm

95. Vietnam.net, "Chinese investment into Vietnam on the sharp rise," February 10, 2017, http://english.vietnamnet.vn/fms/business/172454/chinese-investment-into-vietnam-on-the-sharp-rise.html

96. Bach D., "Top FDI source China pours over US$56 billion into Vietnam with nearly 5,000 projects," May 4, 2016, VnExpress, http://e.vnexpress.net/news/news/top-fdi-source-china-pours-over-56-billion-into-vietnam-with-nearly-5-000-projects-3397081.html

97. Ibid.
98. Vietnam.net, "Chinese investment into Vietnam on the sharp rise."
99. Bach D., "Top FDI source China pours over US$56 billion into Vietnam with nearly 5,000 projects."
100. Reuters, "China firms eye 'Made in Vietnam' windfall if Obama's TPP survives," November 6, 2016, http://www.reuters.com/article/vietnam-china-trade-idUSL4N19Y2XQ
101. World Bank, "GDP per capita (current US$)," 2017, http://data.worldbank.org/indicator/NY.GDP.PCAP.CD?locations=KH
102. Heritage Foundation, "2018 Index of Economic Freedom, Cambodia," http://www.heritage.org/index/country/Cambodia
103. GAN Business Portal, "Cambodia Corruption Report," August 2017, http://www.business-anti-corruption.com/country-profiles/cambodia
104. *The Economist*, "The giant's client: Why Cambodia has cosied up to China," January 21, 2017, http://www.economist.com/news/asia/21715010-and-why-it-worries-cambodias-neighbours-why-cambodia-has-cosied-up-china
105. UNCTAD, "ASEAN Investment Report 2016, Foreign Direct Investment and MSME Linkages."
106. Trading Economics, Cambodia Balance of Trade: 2009-2018," http://www.tradingeconomics.com/cambodia/balance-of-trade
107. Observatory of Economic Complexity, "Cambodia," 2016, http://atlas.media.mit.edu/en/profile/country/khm/
108. UNCTAD, "ASEAN Investment Report 2016, Foreign Direct Investment and MSME Linkages."

109. Ibid.

110. Ibid.

111. Salidjanova, N. et al, "China's Economic Ties with ASEAN: A Country-by-Country Analysis."

112. Kunmakara, M., "Trade With China to Grow," December 1, 2016, Khmer Times, http://www.khmertimeskh.com/news/32646/trade-with-china-to-grow/

113. Ibid.

114. Sophavy S., "Cambodia, China Sign MOU to Boost Two-way Trade," March 28, 2017, Agence Kampuchea Presse, http://www.akp.gov.kh/?p=99120,

115. Trading Economics, "Laos GDP per capita, 1984–2018," https://tradingeconomics.com/laos/gdp-per-capita

116. Heritage Foundation, "2018 Index of Economic Freedom, Laos," http://www.heritage.org/index/country/Lao

117. World Bank, "Exports of goods and services (% of GDP)," https://data.worldbank.org/indicator/NE.EXP.GNFS.ZS

118. Observatory of Economic Complexity, "Laos," 2016, http://atlas.media.mit.edu/en/profile/country/lao/

119. Corben, R., "Slowing China Economy Ripples Into Laos," July 13, 2016, Voice of America, http://www.voanews.com/a/slowing-china-economy-ripples-into-laos/3416226.html

120. Ibid.

121. Vientiane Times, "Laos, China boost trade and investment cooperation," June 21, 2016, http://www.asianews.network/content/laos-china-boost-trade-and-investment-cooperation-20338

122. Ibid.

123. Vietstock, "Lao, China banks join forces to boost trade,"

November 25, 2016,
http://en.vietstock.com.vn/2016/11/lao-china-banks-join-
forces-to-boost-trade-71-247641.htm

124. Trading Economics, "Laos GDP Annual Growth Rate,
1989–2018," https://tradingeconomics.com/laos/gdp-
growth-annual

125. Corben, R., "Slowing China Economy Ripples Into
Laos."

126. UNCTAD, "ASEAN Investment Report 2016, Foreign
Direct Investment and MSME Linkages."

127. Deutsche Welle, "Economic corridor – CPEC could turn
Pakistan into China's 'client state'," November 14, 2016,
http://www.dw.com/en/economic-corridor-cpec-could-
turn-pakistan-into-chinas-client-state/a-36384662

128. Ibid.

129. Al Jazeera, "CPEC: Pakistan and China strengthen
economic ties," November 12, 2016,
http://www.aljazeera.com/news/2016/11/cpec-pakistan-
china-strengthen-economic-ties-161112105108608.html

130. Nakhoda, A., "FTA and FDI Need to be Closely
Monitored," October 9, 2016, *Express Tribune*,
http://tribune.com.pk/story/1196165/investment-scope-
ftas-fdi-need-closely-monitored/

131. Farrukh Nawaz Kayani et al, "China-Pakistan Economic
Relations Lessons for Pakistan," Pakistan Journal of
Commerce and Social Sciences, 2013, Vol. 7(3), p. 454-
462.

132. Aneja, U., "Pakistan-China Relations Recent
Developments," June 2006, IPCS Special Report,
https://www.files.ethz.ch/isn/95438/IPCS-Special-
Report-26.pdf

133. Ibid.

134. *China Daily*, "China-Pakistan relations," November 14,

2006, http://www.chinadaily.com.cn/china/2006-11/14/content_732562.htm

135. Aneja, U., "Pakistan-China Relations Recent Developments."

136. Farrukh Nawaz Kayani et al, "China-Pakistan Economic Relations Lessons for Pakistan."

137. Aneja, U., "Pakistan-China Relations Recent Developments."

138. Farrukh Nawaz Kayani et al, "China-Pakistan Economic Relations Lessons for Pakistan."

139. Reuters, "Pakistan wants China to build it a naval base," May 21, 2011, *Dawn*, https://www.dawn.com/news/630506/pakistan-says-wants-china-to-build-naval-base

140. Mangi, F., "China's Billions Luring Once Shy Foreign Investors to Pakistan," November 7, 2016, https://www.bloomberg.com/news/articles/2016-11-07/china-s-billions-luring-once-shy-foreign-investors-to-pakistan

141. Ibid.

142. Ibid.

143. Deloitte, "How will CPEC boost Pakistan economy?" https://www2.deloitte.com/content/dam/Deloitte/pk/Documents/risk/pak-china-eco-corridor-deloittepk-noexp.pdf

144. CPEC, "About CPEC," http://cpec.gov.pk/introduction/1

145. Deloitte, "How will CPEC boost Pakistan economy?"

146. Ibid.

147. Ibid.

148. Ibid.

149. Ibid.

150. Ibid.

151. Ibid.

152. Ibid.

153. Husain, K., "IMF warns of looming CPEC bill," October 17, 2016, *Dawn*, https://www.dawn.com/news/1290523

154. *The Nation*, "Pakistan to secure US$1bn in Chinese financing for CPEC roads: official," December 28, 2016, http://nation.com.pk/national/28-Dec-2016/pakistan-to-secure-1bn-in-chinese-financing-for-cpec-roads-official

155. Raza, S., "China to finance three more road projects under CPEC," December 27, 2016, *Dawn*, http://www.dawn.com/news/1304619

156. *Pakistan Observer*, "CPEC likely to unleash potential of Islamic finance schemes," January 13, 2017, http://pakobserver.net/cpec-likely-to-unleash-potential-of-islamic-finance-schemes/

157. Ibid.

158. Ibid.

159. Maierbrugger, A., "China-Pakistan corridor set to unleash potential of Islamic finance schemes," January 10, 2017, *Gulf Times*, http://www.gulf-times.com/story/527559/China-Pakistan-corridor-set-to-unleash-potential-o

160. Ibid.

161. *Pakistan Observer*, "CPEC likely to unleash potential of Islamic finance schemes."

162. Aneja, U., "Pakistan-China Relations Recent Developments."

163. Parasha, S., "Russia throws its weight behind China-Pakistan corridor, keeps India on tenterhooks," December 19, 2016, *Times of India*, http://timesofindia.indiatimes.com/india/russia-throws-its-weight-behind-china-pakistan-corridor-keeps-india-on-tenterhooks/articleshow/56053869.cms

164. Kaura, V., "Russia's tilt towards Pakistan will be a body

blow for India's security," Daily-O, May 1, 2017,
http://www.dailyo.in/politics/isis-india-pak-ties-russia-pakistan-afghanistan-ties-cpec-china-taliban/story/1/14918.html

165. *Pakistan Today*, "Russia's joining of CPEC to enhance China, Russia and Pakistan cooperation," January 7, 2017,
https://www.pakistantoday.com.pk/2017/01/07/russias-joining-of-cpec-to-enhance-china-russia-and-pakistan-cooperation/

166. Ibid.

167. The Hindu Times, "Behind Pakistan's CPEC offer," December 28, 2016,
http://www.thehindu.com/opinion/editorial/Behind-Pakistan%E2%80%99s-CPEC-offer/article16950512.ece

168. Ibid.

169. Wolf, S., "Pakistan and Terrorism: China-Pakistan Economic Corridor as Critical Juncture?" May 11, 2016, E-International Relations, http://www.e-ir.info/2016/05/11/pakistan-and-terrorism-china-pakistan-economic-corridor-as-critical-juncture/

170. Deutsche Welle, "Economic corridor – CPEC could turn Pakistan into China's 'client state'."

171. Geo TV, "India expresses concern over UK's support to CPEC," January 14, 2017,
https://www.geo.tv/latest/127259-India-express-concern-over-UKs-support-to-CPEC

172. Ahmed, K., "Corridor Of Uncertainty," December 31, 2016, *The Indian Express*,
http://indianexpress.com/article/opinion/columns/cpec-pakistan-china-economic-corridor-4452364/

173. Deloitte, "How will CPEC boost Pakistan economy?"

174. Ibid.

175. Husain, K., "IMF warns of looming CPEC bill," October 17, 2016, *Dawn*, https://www.dawn.com/news/1290523

176. Husain, I., "The economics of CPEC," January 3, 2017, *Dawn*, http://www.dawn.com/news/1305992

177. Husain, K., "IMF warns of looming CPEC bill."

178. Rana, S. "Senior economist raises several questions regarding CPEC," January 13, 2017, *Express Tribune*, https://tribune.com.pk/story/1292975/analysis-senior-economist-raises-several-questions-regarding-cpec/

179. *Dawn*, "Chambers voice concern at China's plan to 'set up industry along CPEC route'," January 2, 2017, http://www.dawn.com/news/1305865/chambers-voice-concern-at-chinas-plan-to-set-up-industry-along-cpec-route

180. Rana, S. "Senior economist raises several questions regarding CPEC."

181. *Dawn*, "Chambers voice concern at China's plan to 'set up industry along CPEC route'."

182. Rana, S. "Senior economist raises several questions regarding CPEC."

183. *Dawn*, "Chambers voice concern at China's plan to 'set up industry along CPEC route'."

184. Ibid.

185. Rana, S. "Senior economist raises several questions regarding CPEC."

186. Husain, K., "IMF warns of looming CPEC bill."

187. Ibid.

188. Rana, S. "Senior economist raises several questions regarding CPEC."

189. Ibid.

190. Ibid.

191. Deutsche Welle, "Economic corridor – CPEC could turn Pakistan into China's 'client state'."

192. Ibid.
193. Shah, A., "China's Trouble With Pakistan's Turbulent Democracy," January 7, 2017, The Diplomat, http://thediplomat.com/2017/01/chinas-trouble-with-pakistans-turbulent-democracy/
194. Ibid.
195. Ibid.
196. Ibid.
197. Ibid.
198. Ibid.
199. Aneja, U., "Pakistan-China Relations Recent Developments."
200. Ibid.
201. Deutsche Welle, "Economic corridor – CPEC could turn Pakistan into China's 'client state'."
202. Wolf, S., "Pakistan and Terrorism: China-Pakistan Economic Corridor as Critical Juncture?"
203. Ibid.
204. Ibid.
205. Deutsche Welle, "Economic corridor – CPEC could turn Pakistan into China's 'client state'."
206. Defense News, "China Pakistan Economic Corridor: A Chinese Nightmare," June, 2016, http://defensenews-alert.blogspot.com/2016/06/china-pakistan-economic-corridor.html
207. Ibid.
208. Deutsche Welle, "Economic corridor – CPEC could turn Pakistan into China's 'client state'."
209. Wolf, S., "Pakistan and Terrorism: China-Pakistan Economic Corridor as Critical Juncture?"
210. Ahmed, K., "Corridor Of Uncertainty."
211. Shah, A., "China's Trouble With Pakistan's Turbulent Democracy."

212. Shakil, F., "Pakistan seeks bailout from China and Saudis, rather than the IMF," April 4, 2018, Asia Times, http://www.atimes.com/article/pakistan-seeks-bailout-china-saudis-rather-imf/?

213. Ibid.

214. "Beijing's 'Belt and Road Initiative' will benefit the world," February 12, 2018, *South China Morning Post*, http://www.scmp.com/comment/insight-opinion/article/2132943/beijings-belt-and-road-initiative-will-benefit-world

215. Hillman, J., "China's Belt and Road Initiative: Five Years Later," January 25, 2018, Center for Strategic and International Studies, https://www.csis.org/analysis/chinas-belt-and-road-initiative-five-years-later-0

216. Gabuev, A., "Belt and Road to Where?" December 11, 2017, Global Affairs, http://eng.globalaffairs.ru/book/Belt-and-Road-to-Where-19214

217. Heide, D. et al, "EU ambassadors band together against Silk Road," April 17, 2018, Handelsblatt, https://global.handelsblatt.com/politics/eu-ambassadors-beijing-china-silk-road-912258

218. Ibid.

219. Ibid.

220. Ibid.

221. He H., "Is China's belt and road infrastructure development plan about to run out of money?" April, 14, 2018, *South China Morning Press*, http://www.scmp.com/news/china/economy/article/2141739/chinas-belt-and-road-infrastructure-development-plan-about-run

222. Ibid.

Chapter 11

1. Bank of International Settlement, "Statistical Analysis of the U.S. Trade with China for Calendar Year 2015," 2016, https://www.bis.doc.gov/index.php/forms-documents/technology-evaluation/ote-data-portal/country-analysis/1513-2015-statistical-analysis-of-us-trade-with-china-pdf/file

2. Reckard, E, and J. Makinen, "Chinese investments in U.S. businesses are accelerating," May 20, 2015, *Los Angeles Times*, http://www.latimes.com/business/la-fi-chinese-us-investment-20150520-story.html

3. Garcia-Herrero, A. et al, "China's outbound foreign direct investment: How much goes where after round-tripping and offshoring?" June 2015, BBVA Research, https://www.bbvaresearch.com/wp-content/uploads/2015/06/15_17_Working-Paper_ODI.pdf

4. Chazen Global Insights, "Is China Buying America?" March 30, 2015, https://www8.gsb.columbia.edu/articles/chazen-global-insights/china-buying-america

5. Reckard, E, and J. Makinen, "Chinese investments in U.S. businesses are accelerating."

6. Gao, C. and T. Hanemann, "Chinese FDI in the United States: 3Q 2015 Update," November 12, 2015, Rhodium Group, https://rhg.com/research/chinese-fdi-in-the-united-states-3q-2015-update/

7. Reckard, E, and J. Makinen, "Chinese investments in U.S. businesses are accelerating."

8. Mullen, J., "China is no longer the biggest foreign holder of US debt," December 16, 2016, CNN Money, http://money.cnn.com/2016/12/16/investing/china-japan-

us-debt-treasuries/

9. Trading Economics, "United States Gross Federal Debt to GDP 1940–2018," https://tradingeconomics.com/united-states/government-debt-to-gdp

10. Trading Economics, "Japan Government Debt to GDP 1980–2017," https://tradingeconomics.com/japan/government-debt-to-gdp and: Trading Economics, "Germany Government Debt to GDP 1995–2017," https://tradingeconomics.com/germany/government-debt-to-gdp

11. Trading Economics, "China Government Debt to GDP 1995–2018," https://tradingeconomics.com/china/government-debt-to-gdp

12. Floyd, D., "China's Debt Reaches 237% of GDP," April 25, 2016, Investopedia, http://www.investopedia.com/articles/markets/042516/chinas-debt-reaches-237-gdp.asp

13. Ibid.

14. Amadeo, K., "Why Is America's Trade Deficit With China So High?" The Balance, June 14, 2018, https://www.thebalance.com/u-s-china-trade-deficit-causes-effects-and-solutions-3306277

15. Rennison, J., "China reclaims title as biggest foreign holder of US debt," August 16, 2017, Financial Times, https://www.ft.com/content/4804064e-3baf-3de2-8179-22689750bd9d?mhq5j=e5

16. Payscale.com, "Factory Worker Salary (United States)" viewed February 24, 2017, http://www.payscale.com/research/US/Job=Factory_Worker/Hourly_Rate and: Thayer Consulting, "How (and

how much) do factory workers get paid in China?" May 5, 2016, http://www.thayer-consulting.com/blog/2016/05/04/how-and-how-much-do-factory-workers-get-paid-in-china/

17. World Bank, "GDP per capita (current US$)" viewed on February 24, 2017, http://data.worldbank.org/indicator/NY.GDP.PCAP.CD
18. Ibid.
19. Ibid.
20. Trading Economics, "China Foreign Exchange Reserves 1980–2018," http://www.tradingeconomics.com/china/foreign-exchange-reserves
21. Egan, M., "China is dumping US debt."
22. Trading Economics, "China Foreign Exchange Reserves, 1980–2018."
23. Palmer, D., "Defying Trump, Treasury says China not a currency manipulator," October 14, 2016, Politico, http://www.politico.com/story/2016/10/treasury-china-not-currency-manipulator-trade-229812
24. Worstall, T., "Proof That China Is A Currency Manipulator As Donald Trump Says – So Subsidise Imports From China," December 2, 2016, *Forbes*, https://www.forbes.com/sites/timworstall/2016/12/02/proof-that-china-is-a-currency-manipulator-as-donald-trump-says-so-subsidise-imports-from-china/#741666cb43fe
25. Reckard, E, and J. Makinen, "Chinese investments in U.S. businesses are accelerating."
26. *The Economist*, "China's 'going out' strategy," July 21, 2009, http://www.economist.com/blogs/freeexchange/2009/07/chinas_going_out_strategy

27. US Department of Commerce, "US Commerce Department Releases New Report on Foreign Direct Investment Trends," June 20, 2016, https://www.commerce.gov/news/press-releases/2016/06/us-commerce-department-releases-new-report-foreign-direct-investment

28. Gopal, P. and J. Gittelsohn, John, "Chinese Lead Foreign US Home Purchases for First Time," June 17, 2015, Bloomberg, http://www.bloomberg.com/news/articles/2015-06-17/chinese-top-list-of-foreign-buyers-of-u-s-homes and: Reckard, E, and J. Makinen, "Chinese investments in U.S. businesses are accelerating."

29. Zhang, S. and M. Miller, "China's Wanda buys Ironman Triathlon owner for US$650 million," August 27, 2015, Reuters, http://www.reuters.com/article/us-world-triathlon-m-a-dalian-wanda-idUSKCN0QW04X20150827 and

30. Gao, C. and T. Hanemann, "Chinese FDI in the United States: 3Q 2015 Update" and: Gao, C. and T. Hanemann, "China's Global Outbound M&A in 2014," January 5, 2015, Rhodium Group, http://rhg.com/notes/chinas-global-outbound-ma-2014-recap

31. Baker, L., "Dalian Wanda clinches deal for Legendary Entertainment," January 6, 2016, Reuters, https://www.reuters.com/article/us-legendaryentertainment-m-a-dalianwand-idUSKBN0UJ01B20160106

32. Reckard, E, and J. Makinen, "Chinese investments in U.S. businesses are accelerating," and: Osawa, J. "Tencent Acquires Full Control of US-Based Riot Games," December 17, 2015, *Wall Street Journal*, https://www.wsj.com/articles/tencent-acquires-full-

control-of-u-s-based-riot-games-1450342769

33. Sun, C. "Top 10 M&A deals between China and US in 2015," September 18, 2015, *China Daily*, http://www.chinadaily.com.cn/world/2015xivisitus/2015 -09/18/content_21912918.htm

34. D'Onfro, J., "Chinese Giant Alibaba Might Be Trying To Kill Amazon With Its New American Online Store," February 12, 2014, *Business Insider*, http://www.businessinsider.com/alibaba-opens-us-ecommerce-site-2014-2

35. Young, P., "China is buying US assets. So what?" September 17, 2015, Dialogue, http://dialoguereview.com/china-buying-us-assets/

36. Hanemann, T., "Made by China – in America?" Rhodium Group, http://rhg.com/notes/made-by-china-in-america

37. Akan, E, "Chinese Companies Just Love US Assets," October 13, 2015, *Epoch Times* http://www.theepochtimes.com/n3/1876844-chinese-companies-just-love-u-s-assets/

38. Ibid.

39. Ibid.

40. Gao, C. and T. Hanemann, "Chinese FDI in the United States: 3Q 2015 Update" and: Gao, C. and T. Hanemann, "China's Global Outbound M&A in 2014."

41. Ibid.

42. Searcey, D. and K. Bradsher, "Chinese Cash Floods US Real Estate Market," November 28, 2015, *New York Times*, https://www.nytimes.com/2015/11/29/business/internati onal/chinese-cash-floods-us-real-estate-market.html

43. Engels, T., "What's Behind The Surge Of Chinese Real Estate Investment in the USA?" Realtrends.com.

345

44. Searcey, D. and K. Bradsher, "Chinese Cash Floods US Real Estate Market."

45. Ibid.

46. Ibid.

47. Rothman, A., "What next? A China housing crash?" August 11, 2015, *Financial Times*, http://www.ft.com/intl/cms/s/0/8d3c2752-3b54-11e5-bbd1-b37bc06f590c.html#axzz3wGSMa34W

48. Searcey, D. and K. Bradsher, "Chinese Cash Floods US Real Estate Market."

49. Ibid.

50. Badkar, M., "China Bought US$22 Billion Worth Of US Homes Over A Recent 12-Month Span," July 15, 2014, *Business Insider*, https://www.businessinsider.in/China-Bought-22-Billion-Worth-Of-US-Homes-Over-A-Recent-12-Month-Span/articleshow/38396504.cms

51. Searcey, D. and K. Bradsher, "Chinese Cash Floods US Real Estate Market."

52. Dickinson, S., "China Real Estate Laws, Part 1," May 1, 2007, China Law Blog, https://www.chinalawblog.com/2007/05/china_real_estate_laws_part_i.html

53. Velt, T., "What's Behind The Surge Of Chinese Real Estate Investment In The USA?" April 22, 2015, Realtrends.com

54. *New York Times* video at https://www.nytimes.com/2015/11/29/business/international/chinese-cash-floods-us-real-estate-market.html

55. Lopez, L., "China Is In The Midst Of A Triple Bubble," July 9, 2015, *Business Insider*, http://www.businessinsider.com/china-is-in-the-midst-of-a-triple-bubble-2015-7

56. Zhang, M., "From Public to Private: The Newly Enacted

Chinese Property Law and the Protection of Property Rights in China," *Berkeley Business Law Journal* Vol. 5 (2) (2008).

57. Stahl, L., "China's real estate bubble," August 3, 2014, CBS News, https://www.cbsnews.com/news/china-real-estate-bubble-lesley-stahl-60-minutes/

58. Lopez, L., "China Is In The Midst Of A Triple Bubble."

59. Hewitt, D., "Capital Flight From China: Why Investors Are Taking Their Money Elsewhere," November 9, 2015, *International Business Times*, http://www.ibtimes.com/capital-flight-china-why-investors-are-taking-their-money-elsewhere-2174989

60. Thompson, M. and C. Riley, "World Markets Plunge As China Stocks Crash," August 24, 2015, CNN Money, http://money.cnn.com/2015/08/23/investing/world-stock-markets/index.html

61. Ibid.

62. Long, H., "China's Economy Is In Trouble. How Bad Is It?" August 21, 2015, CNN Money, http://money.cnn.com/2015/08/21/news/economy/china-economy-slowdown/index.html

63. Hoffmann, A. et al, "How Investor Perceptions Drive Actual Trading And Risk-Taking Behavior | CFA Institute Publications," July 2015, CFA Institute, https://www.cfainstitute.org/en/research/cfa-digest/2015/07/how-investor-perceptions-drive-actual-trading-and-risk-taking-behavior-digest-summary

64. Long, H., "China's Economy Is In Trouble. How Bad Is It?" and Hewitt, D., "Capital Flight From China: Why Investors Are Taking Their Money Elsewhere."

65. Shen, L., "The Chinese Super-Rich Are About To Flood The US Real-Estate Market," August 29, 2015, *Business Insider*, http://www.businessinsider.com/the-chinese-

super-rich-are-about-to-flood-the-us-real-estate-market-2015-8

66. Hewitt, D., "Capital Flight From China: Why Investors Are Taking Their Money Elsewhere."

67. Institute of International Education, Inc., "Open Doors 2014 Report," https://www.iie.org/Why-IIE/Announcements/2014-11-17-Open-Doors-Data

68. Shen, L., "The Chinese Super-Rich Are About To Flood The US Real-Estate Market."

69. Satow, J., "Want A Green Card? Invest In Real Estate," May 15, 2015, *New York Times*, https://www.nytimes.com/2015/05/17/realestate/want-a-green-card-invest-in-real-estate.html

70. Lu Huang, K., "How Do Rich Chinese Elude Foreign Exchange Laws To Move Their Money Abroad? Take Your Pick Of Ways," July 11, 2014, *South China Morning Post*, http://www.scmp.com/business/banking-finance/article/1551510/how-elude-chinese-foreign-exchange-laws-take-your-pick-ways

71. *New York Times* video at https://www.nytimes.com/2015/11/29/business/international/chinese-cash-floods-us-real-estate-market.html

72. Hewitt, D., "Capital Flight From China: Why Investors Are Taking Their Money Elsewhere."

73. *New York Times* video at https://www.nytimes.com/2015/11/29/business/international/chinese-cash-floods-us-real-estate-market.html

74. Velt, T., "What's Behind The Surge Of Chinese Real Estate Investment In The USA?"

75. Wee, H., "The rise of 'Made by China' in America," February 6, 2015, CNBC, http://www.cnbc.com/2015/02/05/the-rise-of-made-by-china-in-america.html

76. Hanemann, T., "Made by China – in America?"

77. Robertson, J. "Beef, big bucks and buy-ups: are Chinese investors changing the face of Australia?" August 6, 2015, *The Guardian*, http://www.theguardian.com/australia-news/2015/aug/06/beef-big-bucks-and-buy-ups-are-chinese-investors-changing-the-face-of-australia

78. Rebala, P., and H. Beech, "See Where China Is Spending Billions on American Businesses," September 28, 2015, *Time*, http://time.com/4050517/china-investment-map/

79. Akan, E, "Chinese Companies Just Love US Assets."

80. *The Economist*, "We are the champions."

81. Graham, J., "Economists warn of possible trade war with China," November 10, 2016, *The Boston Globe*, http://www.bostonherald.com/business/business_markets/2016/11/economists_warn_of_possible_trade_war_with_china

82. Nie, W., "Why America Would Lose a Trade War With China," December 22, 2016, *Fortune*, http://fortune.com/2016/12/22/donald-trump-china-trade-war/

83. Ibid.

84. Office of the United States Trade Representative, 2017 Special 301 Report, https://ustr.gov/sites/default/files/301/2017%20Special%20301%20Report%20FINAL.PDF

85. Schuman, M., "Who Wins a Trade War? China," November 11, 2016, Bloomberg, https://www.bloomberg.com/view/articles/2016-11-11/china-might-welcome-trade-war-with-u-s

86. Gillespie, P., "President Trump can levy tariffs without Congress," January 23, 2017, CNN Money, http://money.cnn.com/2017/01/23/news/economy/trump

-tariff-power/

87. McKirdy, E. and K. Hunt, "Trump commits to 'One China' policy in phone call with Xi," February 10, 2017, CNN, http://www.cnn.com/2017/02/09/politics/trump-xi-phone-call/

88. McManus, B., "Tillerson, Wang in 'Highest-level US-China meet under Trump'", February 17, 2017, AFP, https://www.yahoo.com/news/tillerson-wang-highest-level-us-china-meet-under-094625387.html

89. Ross, E., "Donald Trump Awarded New Trademarks in China Which Could represent Further Conflicts of Interest," June 14, 2017, *Newsweek*, http://www.newsweek.com/donald-trump-awarded-seven-new-trademarks-china-which-could-present-further-625347

90. Barkin, N. and E. Piper, "In Davos, Xi makes case for Chinese leadership role," January 17, 2017, Reuters, https://www.reuters.com/article/us-davos-meeting-china-idUSKBN15118V

91. Bloomberg, "China's Spending $500 Billion to Reshape the World in Its Image," May 12, 2017, https://www.bloomberg.com/news/articles/2017-05-11/xi-s-500-billion-push-to-reshape-the-world-in-china-s-image

92. Campbell, C., "Xi Jinping Becomes an Unlikely Advocate of Free Trade at Davos," January 17, 2017, *Time*, http://time.com/4635963/xi-jinping-china-davos-world-economic-forum-trade-donald-trump/ and: L. Zhou, "US has failed to spread benefits of globalisation, Jack Ma tells Davos," January 19, 2017, *South China Morning Post*, http://www.scmp.com/news/china/diplomacy-defence/article/2063305/watch-alibabas-jack-ma-live-

world-economic-forum-davos

93. Barkin, N. and E. Piper, "In Davos, Xi makes case for Chinese leadership role."

94. World Bank, "Exports of goods and services (% of GDP)" https://data.worldbank.org/indicator/NE.EXP.GNFS.ZS

95. Statista.com, "China: Share of exports in gross domestic product (GDP) from 2007 to 2017," https://www.statista.com/statistics/256591/share-of-chinas-exports-in-gross-domestic-product/

96. BBC, "US and China sign trade agreement," May 12, 2017, http://www.bbc.com/news/business-39894119

97. Ibid.

98. Yoon, E., "Here's who wins with the new US-China trade deals," May 12, 2017, CNBC, http://www.cnbc.com/2017/05/12/heres-who-wins-with-the-new-us-china-trade-deals.html

99. Soergel, A., "Trump Team Announces China Trade Progress," May 12, 2017, *US News and World Report*, https://www.usnews.com/news/slideshows/china-trade-deals-retail-rebounds-5-things-to-know-about-the-economy

100. Yoon, E., "Here's who wins with the new US-China trade deals."

101. BBC, "US and China sign trade agreement."

102. Yoon, E., "Here's who wins with the new US-China trade deals."

103. BBC, "US and China sign trade agreement."

104. Ibid.

105. Fox Business News, interview with Secretary of Commerce Wilbur Ross, May 12, 2017, https://www.youtube.com/watch?v=BxhQiAuPDaY

106. Ibid.

107. McGuire, F., "Kudlow: China Deal Is 'Huge' Accomplishment for Trump," News Max, May 13, 2017, http://www.newsmax.com/Finance/StreetTalk/kudlow-trump-china-huge/2017/05/13/id/789930/

108. Fox Business News, "Is the China trade deal a good move with the America?" May 12, 2017, https://www.youtube.com/watch?v=oGRBNIO6B4M

109. Soergel, A., "Trump Team Announces China Trade Progress."

110. Fox Business News, "Rep. Sherman on U.S.-China trade deal: Trump betrayed working families," May 12, 2017, https://www.youtube.com/watch?v=mWfdtkzAlXI

111. Ibid.

112. Ibid.

113. Ibid.

114. Yoon, E., "Here's who wins with the new US-China trade deals."

115. Fox Business News, "Trade deal a good first step in US relations with China?" May 12, 2017, https://www.youtube.com/watch?v=r5czWygOhKA

116. Ibid.

117. Ibid.

118. Wroughton, L. and J. Mason, "Trump orders probe of China's intellectual property practices," August 15, 2017, Reuters, https://www.reuters.com/article/us-usa-trump-trade-china/trump-orders-probe-of-chinas-intellectual-property-practices-idUSKCN1AU23N

119. Cornell Law School Legal Information Institute, "19 U.S. Code § 2411 - Actions by United States Trade Representative," https://www.law.cornell.edu/uscode/text/19/2411

120. Neeley, J., "Trump Administration Moves Forward on Case That Could Affect All Chinese Imports," August

15, 2017, *Technology, Manufacturing, and Transportation Insider*,
http://www.tmtindustryinsider.com/2017/08/trump-administration-moves-forward-on-case-that-could-affect-all-chinese-imports/

121. Hong Kong Trade Development Council, "USTR Launches Section 301 Probe Against Mainland China," September 1, 2017,
http://hkmb.hktdc.com/en/1X0ABCS8/hktdc-research/USTR-Launches-Section-301-Probe-Against-Mainland-China

122. Gao, C., "China 'Strongly Dissatisfied' with US Trade Investigation," August 22, 2017, *The Diplomat*,
http://thediplomat.com/2017/08/china-strongly-dissatisfied-with-us-trade-investigation/

123. Ibid.

124. Ibid.

125. Ministry of Commerce of the People's Republic of China, Spokesperson's comments on the 301 Investigation of the US against China, August 23, 2017

126. Ibid.

127. Kiracofe, C., "Trouble Brewing? Washington hawks must not be allowed to disrupt China-U.S. relations," September 7, 2017, *Beijing Review*,
http://www.bjreview.com/Opinion/201709/t20170904_80 0103796.html

128. Huang, Z., "Two little-used trade weapons Trump might employ against China," August 3, 2017, Quartz,
https://qz.com/1045448/section-301-and-the-ieeepa-two-trade-weapons-trump-might-employ-against-chinese-ip-theft/

129. Graceffo, A., "US-China Trade Relations in the wake of the US Section 301 IP Investigation," November 9, 2017,

Foreign Policy Journal,
https://www.foreignpolicyjournal.com/2017/11/09/us-
china-trade-relations-in-the-wake-of-the-us-section-301-
ip-investigation/

130. Fuller, C., "China investigation should scrutinize Special
Economic Zones," September 13, 2017, AEIdeas,
http://www.aei.org/publication/china-investigation-
should-scrutinize-special-economic-zones

131. Wang L., "US using Section 301 probe as a weapon,"
September 5, 2017, *China Daily*,
http://europe.chinadaily.com.cn/opinion/2017-
09/05/content_31575393.htm

132. Office of the United States Trade Representative, 2017
Special 301 Report

133. Neeley, J., "Trump Administration Moves Forward on
Case That Could Affect All Chinese Imports."

134. Veroneau, J. and C. Gibson, "Trump moves on
aluminum under Section 232; Steel investigation
update," April 28, 2017, Global Policy Watch,
https://www.globalpolicywatch.com/2017/04/trump-
moves-on-aluminum-under-section-232-steel-
investigation-update/

135. Hsu, S., "Rising US Protectionism May Hurt China's
Economy And Begin A Trade War," September 12, 2017,
Forbes,
https://www.forbes.com/sites/sarahsu/2017/09/12/rising-
u-s-protectionism-may-hurt-chinas-economy-and-begin-
a-trade-war/#647618491a32

136. Huang, Z., "Two little-used trade weapons Trump
might employ against China."

137. Lopez, L., "The US fired the first shot in a trade war
with China," August 18, 2017, *Business Insider*,
http://www.businessinsider.com/us-begins-section-301-

investigation-2017-8

138. Worstall, T., "Here Comes The Trade War - US To Investigate IP, China Won't Sit By," August 19, 2017, *Forbes*, https://www.forbes.com/sites/timworstall/2017/08/19/here-comes-the-trade-war-us-to-investigate-ip-china-wont-sit-by/#64f3d376b02c

139. Lopez, L., "The US fired the first shot in a trade war with China."

140. Ibid.

141. Xinhua, "China strengthens protection of intellectual property rights," January 17, 2017, The State Council, PRC, http://english.gov.cn/news/top_news/2017/01/17/content_281475544047740.htm

142. IAM, "A controversial Chinese tech transfer regulation could become the focus of the Trump 301 probe," September 17, 2017, http://www.iam-media.com/Blog/Detail.aspx?g=ade1075d-f054-4ef8-842a-e695981eb248

143. Ibid.

144. Lopez, L., "The US fired the first shot in a trade war with China."

145. Wang L., "US using Section 301 probe as a weapon."

146. Gao, C., "China 'Strongly Dissatisfied' with US Trade Investigation."

147. Sun W., "Anti-dumping probe into US rubber not countermove to Section 301 investigation: Ministry of Commerce," September 1, 2017, *People's Daily*, http://en.people.cn/n3/2017/0901/c90000-9263246.html

148. Hong Kong Trade Development Council, "USTR Launches Section 301 Probe Against Mainland China."

149. Huang, Z., "Two little-used trade weapons Trump

might employ against China."

150. Swanson, A., "China and the US are both going for trade's nuclear option," July 19, 2017, *Washington Post*, https://www.washingtonpost.com/news/wonk/wp/2017/07/19/china-and-the-u-s-are-both-going-for-trades-nuclear-option/?utm_term=.dc5d09b9cd6b

151. Ibid.

152. US-China Economic and Security Review Commission, Economic and Trade Bulletin, September 2017, https://www.uscc.gov/trade-bulletin/september-2017-trade-bulletin

153. Appelbaum, B., "Experts Warn of Backlash in Donald Trump's China Trade Policies," May 2, 2016, *New York Times*, https://www.nytimes.com/2016/05/03/us/politics/donald-trump-trade-policy-china.html

154. US-China Economic and Security Review Commission, Economic and Trade Bulletin, September 2017

155. Angel, M. and D. Lawder, "Despite delay, US expected to impose steel tariffs," August 15, 2015, Reuters, https://www.reuters.com/article/us-usa-steel-tariffs/despite-delay-u-s-expected-to-impose-steel-tariffs-idUSKCN1AV10R

156. Krukowska, E. et al, "EU Tilts to China in Climate Fight Amid Signs of Trump Softening," September 18, 2017, Bloomberg, https://www.bloomberg.com/news/articles/2017-09-18/eu-tilts-to-china-in-climate-fight-after-trump-exits-paris-deal

157. Kirschbaum, E., "In the age of Trump, China seen as important global partner for Germany's next chancellor," September 17, 2017, *South China Morning Post*,

http://www.scmp.com/news/world/europe/article/21115
64/age-trump-china-seen-important-global-partner-
germanys-next

158. Jennings, R., "Threats From America Will Move A Wary
Pakistan Even Closer To China," September 18, 2017,
Forbes,
https://www.forbes.com/sites/ralphjennings/2017/09/18/
china-will-capitalize-on-americas-economic-threat-
against-pakistan/#56d366737df6

159. *US News and World Report*, "Panama's President Says
Switching China Ties Not 'Checkbook Diplomacy'",
September 18, 2017, Reuters,
https://www.usnews.com/news/world/articles/2017-09-
18/panamas-president-says-switching-china-ties-not-
checkbook-diplomacy

160. Ghoshal, D., "Argentina-China Nuclear Cooperation: Is
China's Influence In South America Concern For United
States?," September 19, 2017, Eurasia Review,
http://www.eurasiareview.com/17092017-argentina-
china-nuclear-cooperation-is-chinas-influence-in-south-
america-concern-for-united-states-analysis/

161. Business Standard, "Australia, China seek to boost
economic ties," September 16, 2017, Bloomberg,
http://www.business-
standard.com/article/international/australia-china-seek-
to-boost-economic-ties-117091600894_1.html

162. Global Research, "US Sanctions Continue to Backfire:
China Opens US$10 Billion Credit Line for Iran,"
September 17, 2017, https://www.globalresearch.ca/us-
sanctions-continue-to-backfire-china-opens-10-billion-
credit-line-for-iran/5609356

163. *Daily Express*, "World War 3: China and Russia begin
naval drills near North Korea," September 18, 2017,

http://www.express.co.uk/news/world/855528/World-War-3-North-Korea-naval-drill-China-Russia-nuclear-war

164. Ebeling, P., "President Trump Challenges China and Globalization," September 15, 2017, Live Trading News, http://www.livetradingnews.com/president-trump-challenges-china-globalization-54865.html#.WcE0IcgjHIU

165. O'Sullivan, M., "US Energy Boom Can Bring China Into the Global Order," September 15, 2017, Bloomberg, https://www.bloomberg.com/view/articles/2017-09-15/u-s-energy-boom-can-bring-china-into-the-global-order

166. Ibid.

167. Chandran, N. and A. Drury, "China government advisor warns on Trump: When countries close their doors, they 'will be harmed'," September 19, 2017, CNBC, https://www.cnbc.com/2017/09/18/fu-chengyu-warns-on-trump-singapore-summit.html

168. Ibid.

169. Business Day, "Analysis: Trump's Lattice rejection is bad news for other Chinese investment," September 18, 2017, https://www.businesslive.co.za/bd/world/americas/2017-09-18-analysis-trumps-lattice-rejection-is-bad-news-for-other-chinese-investment/

170. US Department of Treasury, "Committee on Foreign Investment in the United States," September 18, 2017, https://www.treasury.gov/resource-center/international/Pages/Committee-on-Foreign-Investment-in-US.aspx

171. Business Day, "Analysis: Trump's Lattice rejection is bad news for other Chinese investment."

172. Ibid.

173. *New York Times* Editorial Board, "The China Puzzle," September 16, 2017, https://www.nytimes.com/2017/09/16/opinion/sunday/the-china-puzzle.html

174. Mayeda, A., "Trump's Top Trade Negotiator Calls China 'Unprecedented' Threat," September 18, 2017, Bloomberg, https://www.bloomberg.com/news/articles/2017-09-18/trump-s-top-trade-negotiator-calls-china-an-unprecedented-threat

175. *New York Times* Editorial Board, "The China Puzzle."

176. Mayeda, A., "Trump's Top Trade Negotiator Calls China 'Unprecedented' Threat."

177. Farley, R., "Intellectual Property and the Coming US-China Trade War," August 24, 2017, *The Diplomat*, http://thediplomat.com/2017/08/intellectual-property-and-the-coming-us-china-trade-war/

178. Swanson, A., "Trump edges closer to a trade war with China, thanks to aluminum foil," August 9, 2017, *Washington Post*, https://www.washingtonpost.com/news/wonk/wp/2017/08/09/trump-edges-closer-to-a-trade-war-with-china-thanks-to-aluminum-foil/?utm_term=.5232e6e0cae6

179. Reuters, "China's Zhongwang, Aleris extend merger deadline amid US probe," September 16, 2017, http://www.reuters.com/article/us-aluminum-china/chinas-zhongwang-aleris-extend-merger-deadline-amid-u-s-probe-idUSKCN1BR043

180. *New York Times* Editorial Board, "The China Puzzle."

181. *Shanghai Daily*, "Xi notes 'great importance' of Trump's China visit," September 19, 2017. http://www.shanghaidaily.com/nation/Xi-notes-great-importance-of-Trumps-China-visit/shdaily.shtml

182. Phillips, T. and J. McCurry, "US and China agree to 'maximise pressure' on North Korea," September 19, 2017, *The Guardian*, https://www.theguardian.com/world/2017/sep/19/us-and-china-agree-to-maximise-pressure-on-north-korea

183. Garamone, J., "US, Chinese Military Leaders Sign Agreement to Increase Communication," August 15, 2017, US Department of Defense, https://www.defense.gov/News/Article/Article/1278684/us-chinese-military-leaders-sign-agreement-to-increase-communication/

184. Yan, S., "A grain deal may signal the US-China relationship isn't as bad as it seems," July 21, 2017, CNBC, https://www.cnbc.com/2017/07/21/a-grain-deal-may-signal-the-u-s-china-relationship-isnt-as-bad-as-it-seems.html

185. Bloomberg, "Amid Donald Trump's trade war threats, China weighs helping Wall Street, Tesla," September 21, 2017, *Straits Times*, http://www.straitstimes.com/asia/east-asia/amid-donald-trumps-trade-war-threats-china-weighs-helping-wall-street-tesla

186. Bloomberg, "China Hits Back at Trump Tariffs as Trade War Finally Arrives," March 23, 2018, Bloomberg, https://www.msn.com/en-us/money/markets/trump-orders-tariffs-on-dollar50-billion-worth-of-chinese-goods/ar-BBKzqsH?ocid=spartanntp

187. Boffey, D., "Trump reveals US$60bn of fresh tariffs on China as EU wins reprieve," March 23, 2018, *The Guardian*, https://www.theguardian.com/world/2018/mar/22/eu-expects-escape-trump-steel-aluminium-tariffs-talks

188. BBC, "Trump announces tariffs on US$60bn in Chinese

imports," March 22, 2018,
https://www.bbc.com/news/business-43494001

189. Bloomberg, "China Hits Back at Trump Tariffs as Trade War Finally Arrives."

190. Ibid.

191. Ibid.

192. Ibid.

193. BBC, "Trump announces tariffs on US$60bn in Chinese imports."

194. Lauter, D. and J. Kaimant, "Trump's China tariffs get bipartisan support, reflecting widespread US disillusionment with Beijing," March 22, 2018, *Los Angeles Times*, http://www.latimes.com/politics/la-na-pol-trump-china-tariffs-20180322-story.html

195. BBC, "Trump announces tariffs on US$60bn in Chinese imports."

196. Boffey, D., "Trump reveals US$60bn of fresh tariffs on China as EU wins reprieve."

197. Ibid.

198. Bloomberg, "China Hits Back at Trump Tariffs as Trade War Finally Arrives."

199. Monaghan, A. and M. Farrer, "US trade war: Dow recovers in early trading after China signals tariff retaliation," March 23, 2018, *The Guardian*, https://www.theguardian.com/business/live/2018/mar/23/us-tariffs-shares-plummet-china-signals-retaliation-live

200. MSNBC, "President Donald Trump Slaps China With Nearly US$50 Billion In New Tariffs," March 22, 2018, https://www.youtube.com/watch?v=6fKdrzX1Y7Y

201. Bloomberg, "China Hits Back at Trump Tariffs as Trade War Finally Arrives."

202. Isidore, C., "Major retailers to Trump: New China tariffs

will hurt American shoppers," March 19, 2018. CNN Money, http://money.cnn.com/2018/03/19/news/economy/trump-business-groups-oppose-china-tariffs/index.html

203. Crichton, D., "Tech industry comes out swinging against potential Trump tariffs," March 20, 2018, Tech Crunch, https://techcrunch.com/2018/03/19/tech-industry-opposes-trump-tariffs/

204. *Wall Street Journal* Editorial Board, "The Trump Tariff Layoffs Begin," March 16, 2018, https://www.wsj.com/articles/the-trump-tariff-layoffs-begin-1521241456

205. Lauter, D. and J. Kaimant, "Trump's China tariffs get bipartisan support, reflecting widespread US disillusionment with Beijing."

206. Cox, J., "Larry Kudlow, new chief economic advisor to Trump, says China 'has earned a tough response'," March 13, 2018, CNBC, https://www.cnbc.com/2018/03/14/larry-kudlow-new-chief-economic-advisor-to-trump-says-china-has-earned-a-tough-response.html

207. Lauter, D. and J. Kaimant, "Trump's China tariffs get bipartisan support, reflecting widespread US disillusionment with Beijing."

208. Boffey, D., "Trump reveals US$60bn of fresh tariffs on China as EU wins reprieve."

209. Manchester, J., "Steel manufacturers air TV ad pushing Trump to restrict steel imports, February 27, 2018, *The Hill*, http://thehill.com/blogs/blog-briefing-room/news/375768-steel-manufacturers-call-on-trump-to-keep-promise-to-restrict

210. Lynch, D., "US Commerce Dept recommends Donald Trump raises tariffs on steel and aluminium," February

18, 2018, *New Zealand Herald*,
http://www.nzherald.co.nz/business/news/article.cfm?c_
id=3&objectid=11997051

211. BBC, "Trump announces tariffs on US$60bn in Chinese imports."

212. Lauter, D. and J. Kaimant, "Trump's China tariffs get bipartisan support, reflecting widespread US disillusionment with Beijing."

213. Ibid.

214. Bloomberg, "China Hits Back at Trump Tariffs as Trade War Finally Arrives."

215. BBC, "Trump announces tariffs on US$60bn in Chinese imports."

216. Collins, R. et al, "Wilbur Ross to China: Import More US Gas to Cut Trade Gap," March 23, 2018, Bloomberg, https://www.bloomberg.com/news/articles/2018-03-22/wilbur-ross-to-china-boost-u-s-gas-imports-to-please-trump

217. Office of the United States Trade Representative, "The People's Republic of China: US-China Trade Facts," https://ustr.gov/countries-regions/china-mongolia-taiwan/peoples-republic-china

218. Iyengar, R., "US-China trade battle: Catch up here," April 8, 2018, CNN Money, http://money.cnn.com/2018/04/08/news/economy/trump-china-us-tariffs-trade-timeline/index.html?iid=EL

219. Associated Press, "China files trade complaint against US over steel tariffs," April 10, 2018, USA Today, https://www.usatoday.com/story/money/business/2018/04/10/china-files-trade-complaint-against-u-s-over-steel-tariffs/501926002/

220. Iyengar, R., "US-China trade battle: Catch up here."

221. Mullen, J., "China's Xi Jinping says tariffs on car imports

will be cut this year," April 10, 2018, CNN Money, http://money.cnn.com/2018/04/09/news/economy/china-xi-jinping-economy-trade/index.html

222. CBS, "China making concessions in trade standoff with Trump?" April 10, 2018, https://www.cbsnews.com/news/china-xi-jinping-auto-tariffs-intellectual-property-fears-trade-war-donald-trump/

223. Associated Press, "China files trade complaint against US over steel tariffs."

224. Watts, G., "President Xi charts out his promised land in idyllic Hainan," April 10, 2018, Asia Times, http://www.atimes.com/article/president-xi-charts-promised-land-idyllic-hainan/?utm_source=The+Daily+Report&utm_campaign=5b6dfb3b85-EMAIL_CAMPAIGN_2018_04_10&utm_medium=email&utm_term=0_1f8bca137f-5b6dfb3b85-31520157

225. Ibid.

226. Ibid.

227. Ibid.

228. Mullen, J., "China's Xi Jinping says tariffs on car imports will be cut this year."

229. *USA Today* (video), "The Truth About US-China Car Trade," April 10, 2018, https://www.usatoday.com/story/money/business/2018/04/10/china-files-trade-complaint-against-u-s-over-steel-tariffs/501926002/

230. Fernholz, T., "If US trade with China is so unfair, why is GM the best-selling car there?" April 3, 2018, Quartz, https://qz.com/938648/if-us-trade-with-china-is-so-unfair-why-is-gm-the-best-selling-car-there/

231. Watts, G., "President Xi charts out his promised land in

idyllic Hainan."

232. Stevenson, A., "Xi Jinping Promotes Openness at a
China Forum Rife With Restrictions," April 11, 2018,
New York Times,
https://www.nytimes.com/2018/04/11/business/xi-
jinping-china-trade-boao.html

233. Ralph, P., "It looks like China just blinked in its trade
battle with Trump," April 2018, *Business Insider*,
http://www.businessinsider.com/trump-china-trade-
war-dow-stocks-jump-2018-4

234. Mullen, J., "China's Xi Jinping says tariffs on car imports
will be cut this year."

235. Watts, G., "President Xi charts out his promised land in
idyllic Hainan."

236. Ibid.

237. Stevenson, A., "Xi Jinping Promotes Openness at a
China Forum Rife With Restrictions."

238. Broadman, H., "The Coalition-Based Trade Strategy
Trump Should Pursue Toward China," April 9, 2018,
Forbes,
https://www.forbes.com/sites/harrybroadman/2018/04/0
9/trump-should-build-a-coalition-to-deny-chinas-
graduation-to-a-wto-market-economy/#2069c570acaa

239. Moore, S., "The US can't back down against China,"
April 10, 2018, CNN,
https://www.cnn.com/2018/04/10/opinions/trump-china-
tariffs-opinion-moore/index.html

240. Broadman, H., "The Coalition-Based Trade Strategy
Trump Should Pursue Toward China."

241. Emmott, B., "Xi's strong hand against Trump," April 16,
2018, Asia Times, http://www.atimes.com/xis-strong-
hand-
trump/?utm_source=The+Daily+Report&utm_campaign

=67ca6009c3-
EMAIL_CAMPAIGN_2018_04_16&utm_medium=email
&utm_term=0_1f8bca137f-67ca6009c3-31520157
242. CBS, "China making concessions in trade standoff with Trump?"
243. Moore, S., "Trump's trade wins are a big plus for US workers," April 1, 2018, *New York Post*, https://nypost.com/2018/04/01/trumps-trade-wins-are-a-big-plus-for-us-workers/
244. CBS, "China making concessions in trade standoff with Trump?"
245. Ibid.
246. Gillespie, P. et al, " How American cars are really sold in China," April 10, 2018, CNN Money, http://money.cnn.com/2018/04/10/news/economy/china-cars-tariffs/index.html
247. Bloomberg, "China Adds Flesh to Bones of Plan for Big Bang Financial Opening," April 11, 2018, https://www.bloomberg.com/news/articles/2018-04-11/pboc-s-yi-pledges-more-steps-to-further-open-china-s-economy
248. Watts, G., "'Big Bang' with Chinese characters? Beijing opens up sectors," April 11, 2018, Asia Times, http://www.atimes.com/article/big-bang-chinese-characters-beijing-opens-sectors/?utm_source=The+Daily+Report&utm_campaign=dc45ffd138-EMAIL_CAMPAIGN_2018_04_11&utm_medium=email&utm_term=0_1f8bca137f-dc45ffd138-31520157
249. Stevenson, A., "Xi Jinping Promotes Openness at a China Forum Rife With Restrictions."
250. Mullen, J., "China's Xi Jinping says tariffs on car imports will be cut this year."

251. Pramuk, J., "Trump says he's 'very thankful' for Chinese President Xi's remarks on trade," April 10, 2018, CNBC, https://www.cnbc.com/2018/04/10/trump-says-hes-very-thankful-for-chinese-president-xis-remarks-on-trade.html

252. Stevenson, A., "Xi Jinping Promotes Openness at a China Forum Rife With Restrictions."

253. Scott, C., "With Xi's speech, markets once again declare trade war averted," April 11, 2018, Asia Times, http://www.atimes.com/article/xis-speech-markets-declare-trade-war-averted/?utm_source=The+Daily+Report&utm_campaign=dc45ffd138-EMAIL_CAMPAIGN_2018_04_11&utm_medium=email&utm_term=0_1f8bca137f-dc45ffd138-31520157

254. Moore, S., "Trump's trade wins are a big plus for US workers."

255. Wright, G., "4 charts show why Trump's tariffs will hurt everyone – not just China," March 29, 2018, The Conversation, https://theconversation.com/4-charts-show-why-trumps-tariffs-will-hurt-everyone-not-just-china-93899

256. Bloomberg, "China's Cutting Taxes for the Industries Trump Wants to Punish," March 29, 2018, Industry Week, http://www.industryweek.com/economy/chinas-cutting-taxes-industries-trump-wants-punish

257. Zhai, K., "China Talks Stalled Over Trump's Demands on High-Tech Industries, Source Says," April 10, 2018, Bloomberg, https://www.bloomberg.com/news/articles/2018-04-10/u-s-china-talks-said-to-have-stalled-over-high-tech-industry

258. Bloomberg, "China's Cutting Taxes for the Industries

Trump Wants to Punish."

259. Zhai, K., "China Talks Stalled Over Trump's Demands on High-Tech Industries, Source Says."

260. Asia Times and Reuters, "Top Democrat backs Trump bid to realign dealings with Beijing," April 1, 2018, Asia Times, http://www.atimes.com/article/top-democrat-backs-trump-bid-realign-dealings-beijing/?utm_source=The+Daily+Report&utm_campaign=1af0a9d641-EMAIL_CAMPAIGN_2018_04_02&utm_medium=email&utm_term=0_1f8bca137f-1af0a9d641-31520157

261. Rogin, J., "America is hanging up on China's telecom industry," April 1, 2018, *Washington Post*, https://www.washingtonpost.com/opinions/global-opinions/america-is-hanging-up-on-chinas-telecom-industry/2018/04/01/2a746710-35b1-11e8-8fd2-49fe3c675a89_story.html?utm_term=.16ca0cf131a0

262. Tom Cotton Official Website, "Cotton and Rubio Introduce Legislation to Prohibit US Government Use of Chinese Telecommunications Companies," February 7, 2018, https://www.cotton.senate.gov/?p=press_release&id=887

263. Rogin, J., "America is hanging up on China's telecom industry."

264. Ibid.

265. Ibid.

266. Ibid.

267. Ibid.

268. Moore, S., "The US can't back down against China."

269. Ibid.

270. Stumo, M., "China treats US like a colony — luckily, Trump is fighting back," April 10, 2018, *The Hill*, http://thehill.com/opinion/finance/382280-china-treats-

us-like-a-colony-luckily-trump-is-fighting-back

271. Lovelace, B., "Trump economic advisor Larry Kudlow bashes China for 'decades of misdeeds' on trade," April 9, 2018, CNBC, https://www.cnbc.com/2018/04/09/larry-kudlow-says-trump-is-warning-china-with-tariffs-youre-no-longer-a-developing-nation-act-like-it.html

272. Ibid.

273. Zhai, K., "China Talks Stalled Over Trump's Demands on High-Tech Industries, Source Says."

274. *USA Today* (video), "Trump Top Advisor Downplays Trade War With China," April 10, 2018, https://www.usatoday.com/story/money/business/2018/04/10/china-files-trade-complaint-against-u-s-over-steel-tariffs/501926002/

275. *USA Today* (video), "US Treasury Secretary Mnuchin Says He Does Not Expect a Trade War," April 10, 2018, https://www.usatoday.com/story/money/business/2018/04/10/china-files-trade-complaint-against-u-s-over-steel-tariffs/501926002/

276. Lovelace, B., "Trump economic advisor Larry Kudlow bashes China for 'decades of misdeeds' on trade."

277. 滕泰、张海冰, 2018, 实施"软价值战略"应对中美贸易摩擦[J], 《清华金融评论》2018年5月刊

278. Ibid.

279. 刘红霞、于佳欣、高攀、张辛欣、申铖, (2018, May) 中美经贸关系健康发展符合两国人民利益——透视中美华盛顿经贸磋商成果传递的积极信号, http://www.xinhuanet.com/world/2018-05/22/c_1122871522.htm

280. Ibid.

281. 白明, (2018, April) 中美两张500亿美元加征关税清单 谁的更有冲击力? http://finance.ifeng.com/a/20180410/16065281_0.shtml

282. Ibid.

283. Ibid.

284. Ibid.

285. Ibid.

286. 严瑜, (2018, May) 中美都对"零和游戏"说不！. 《人民日报海外版》
,http://wemedia.ifeng.com/61646004/wemedia.shtml

287. Ibid.

288. Ibid.

289. Ibid.

290. Ibid.

291. Daiss, T., "Trump's Tariffs Can't Deter Chinese LNG Investment," Oil Price, March 30, 2018,
https://oilprice.com/Energy/Natural-Gas/Trumps-Tariffs-Cant-Deter-Chinese-LNG-Investment.html

292. Emmott, B., "Xi's strong hand against Trump."

A Short Course on the Chinese Economy

By Dr. Antonio Graceffo

Originally written as a short course for foreign university students visiting China, this book is a must-read for anyone trying to make sense of the world's second largest economy.

In 1949, when the People's Republic of China was established, it was one of the poorest countries on Earth. China remained poor until 1978, when Deng Xiaoping started to transform the country's economic system to what has been called Market Socialism or Socialism with Chinese characteristics. Through a system of five-year plans, successive Chinese leaders have continued the liberalization of the Chinese economy, first through the opening of free trade areas, then the protection of private property and private enterprise, as well as the admission of entrepreneurs into the Communist Party. China's transformation continues under the current leadership of President Xi Jinping whose 13th Five-Year Plan and Belt and Road Initiative seek to forever change the global economic order.

Read *A Short Course on the Chinese Economy*, by Dr. Antonio Graceffo, Available in Kindle and paperback from Amazon

The Wrestler's Dissertation: Chinese and Western Wrestling

By Dr. Antonio Graceffo

Pankration, gladiators, Mongolia, Shaolin kung fu, catch wrestling, the Olympics, wushu, pro wrestling, sanda, and MMA...

The Wrestler's Dissertation traces the history and evolution of Western wrestling, from Ancient Greece, to catch wrestling champion Frank Gotch, and on to Gorgeous George, Hulkamania, and UFC champion Daniel Cormier. During the same period, on the other side of the world, China was transforming itself from a loose collection of warring kingdoms to a modern nation state. Behind the Great Wall, Chinese *shuai jiao* wrestling was growing out of countless regional and ethnic wrestling styles from Mongolia, Manchuria, and Korea. Shaolin Temple was also incorporating Chinese wrestling techniques into wushu forms and, eventually, sanda (kickboxing). In the last twenty years, Chinese wrestling has collided with Western wrestling in the Olympics, MMA, and now pro wrestling. This book explores the similarities and differences between Western and Chinese wrestling from cultural, historical, and technical standpoints—and seeks to understand why Western wrestling is so much more aggressive, competitive, and violent.

In 2013, martial arts author and traveler Antonio Graceffo was awarded a PhD scholarship to Shanghai University of Sport (SUS). His major was Chinese wushu and his dissertation title was "A Cross-Cultural Comparison of Chinese and Western Wrestling." The entire three-year course was taught in Chinese, during which time, Antonio conducted both academic and field research, training with the wrestling team, learning Chinese traditional *shuai jiao* wrestling, as well as Greco-Roman and freestyle wrestling. At SUS, he cross-trained in Chinese sanda and Japanese judo. He also trained freestyle in Cambodia, sanda in Vietnam, catch wrestling in Singapore, and professional wrestling in New York. After graduating in 2016, he set about translating his dissertation into English. In Antonio's own words: "A standard PhD dissertation is a dry, academic affair with all of the life sucked out of it." This book, however, is not the actual dissertation; it is an English-language version brimful with fascinating facts and asides.

Read more in **The Wrestler's Dissertation** by Dr. Antonio Graceffo, available in paperback and Kindle from Amazon.

Printed in Great Britain
by Amazon